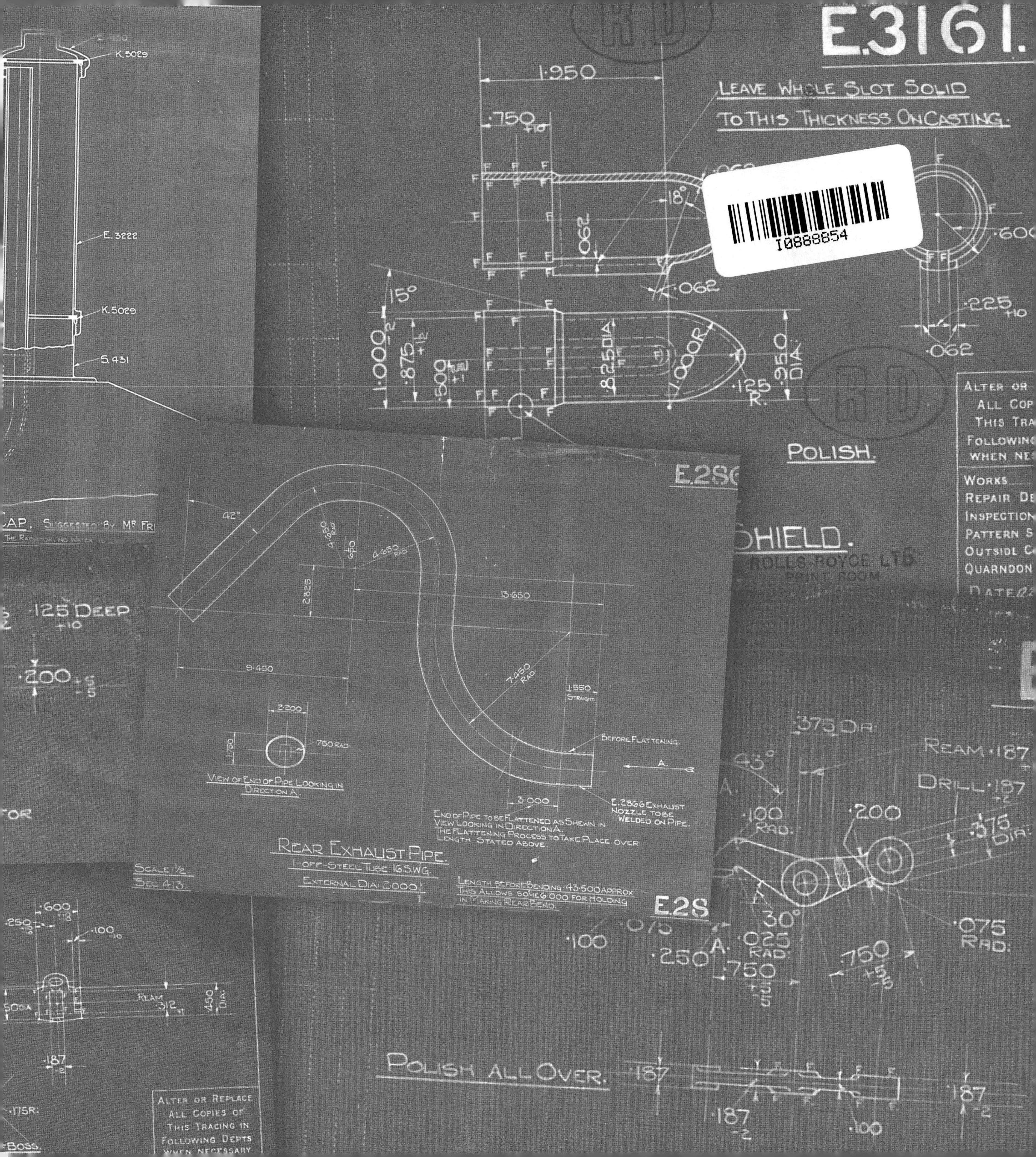

E.3161.
Leave Whole Slot Solid
To This Thickness On Casting.
Polish.
Shield.
Rolls-Royce Ltd
Print Room
Alter or
All Cop
This Tra
Following
When Ne
Works
Repair De
Inspection
Pattern S
Outside C
Quarndon
Cap. Suggested By Mr Fri
125 Deep
E.2S6
Rear Exhaust Pipe.
1-off-Steel Tube 16 S.W.G.
External Dia: 2·000.
Scale ½.
Sec 413.
View of End of Pipe Looking in Direction A.
Before Flattening.
E.2866 Exhaust Nozzle to be Welded on Pipe.
End of Pipe to be Flattened as Shewn in View Looking in Direction A. The Flattening Process to Take Place over Length Stated Above.
Length before Bending 43·500 Approx. This Allows Some 6·000 for Holding in Making Rear Bend.
E2S
Ream ·187
Drill ·187
Polish All Over.
Alter or Replace
All Copies of
This Tracing in
Following Depts
When Necessary

Mr Radley Drives To Vienna

John Kennedy

Mr Radley Drives To Vienna

A Rolls-Royce Silver Ghost Crossing the Alps

1913 & 2013

HIRMER

CONTENTS

FOREWORD

As a lover of motor cars and fine motoring experiences, naturally focused on Rolls-Royce, it was with great expectations that I travelled to Northern Italy to join the Alpine Centenary Rally. To meet John Kennedy and to know that the car he was driving – the famous Radley car – was the only surviving original Works Special Alpine model was extraordinary in itself. To be invited by John to join him for the Stelvio Pass drive day was something that I could not refuse.

Thursday 20 June 2013 turned out to be the most exceptional day's motoring that I have ever experienced. Ascending the dramatic Stelvio Pass, being caught in a thunderstorm of note, driving into a small village and sitting out the afternoon deluge in a local pub, before finally arriving at the shores of the beautiful Lake Garda at sunset were all experiences that I will never forget. To cap it all we were joined for the evening by almost 100 Rolls-Royce Silver Ghosts, the largest number ever to be assembled in one place. The event marked 100 years, almost to the day that the original 1913 Alpenfahrt Rally would have been preparing to set off from Vienna.

Amongst all the emotions that this experience created, two things are cemented in my mind: driving in a wonderfully original and smoothly powerful 100 year old Rolls-Royce, and the exceptional company I enjoyed for the day – was I with Mr Radley, or John Kennedy? The two seemed almost indistinguishable when John got behind the wheel of his motor car.

I have enjoyed reliving that day through the pages of this book, and can only wish John Kennedy, and the Radley car, many more motoring miles together.

Bon Voyage, my dear friends.

Richard Carter
Director of Global Communications
Rolls-Royce Motor Cars
Goodwood
March 2015

SAME CAR, SAME LOCATIONS - 100 YEARS APART

Vienna 1913 – the heart of Europe, capital of the Austro-Hungarian Empire, centre of the Artistic World, home to Hitler and Tito, refuge of Stalin and Trotsky, home of Sigmund Freud and Gustav Klimt.

Unbeknownst to its visitors and inhabitants, this was to be the last golden year of the Austro-Hungarian Empire.

The ageing Emperor, Franz Josef, ruling since 1848, would soon be dead. His apparent successor, Franz Ferdinand would die in little more than a year, in circumstances which would cause profound and permanent changes not only to the Empire and the rest of Europe, but throughout the world.

But this was still 1913, and the party was still in full swing, even though the portents of doom were there for those who chose to see them.

This was also the rising age of the automobile, whose rapid advances saw it grow from a delicate and precarious toy, to a modern and reliable means of transport in little more than a decade. This advance was frequently the result of motor competitions, originally run as social events where the cars were almost exclusively owned by the nobility of Europe.

As these events were of minimal value to the car producers, a number of more extensive competitions were organised, and from 1911 onwards, the most important and demanding of these events was the Austrian Alpenfahrt or Alpine Contest.

Most of the European manufacturers participated, their cars often driven by the engineers or owners of the companies, although private vehicle owners also competed, for the sporting enjoyment of the challenge.

One such man was James Radley, pioneer aviator and general adventurer, who entered a new Rolls-Royce in the 1912 event. The car was probably the best car taking part, but due to lack of knowledge of some of the extreme roads and steep mountain passes used, his car was equipped with high gearing and proved unable to climb the steep Katschberg Pass on the very first day without stopping.

He withdrew from the contest, causing consternation to Rolls-Royce who were in the process of opening a major depot in Vienna to serve the growing market for their cars.

Thus Rolls-Royce entered a three car team in the event planned for June 1913 and James Radley again entered a car. All four cars were new and had extensive enhancements based on exhaustive testing in the Alps in the autumn of 1912.

The Rolls-Royce team cars went out to Austria in late April and tested on most of the mountain passes when the snow had melted sufficiently for the task.

The new car for James Radley was delivered in March 1913 to his Huntingdon works where he built the coachwork. He set out for Austria in May 1913 with Rolls-Royce man Tubby Ward as his mechanic and two other passengers, one of whom was his friend Reginald Hooton Hope, an amateur photographer who recorded the journey to Vienna.

Remarkably, both the car and Hope's photo album survived, making it possible to recreate the journey with the same car and repeat the photographs in the identical locations exactly 100 years later, in May & June 2013.

This book is the result of this unique set of circumstances.

Mr Radley Drives To Vienna

Photographs from 1913 & 2013

BROWN'S HOTEL

London, England

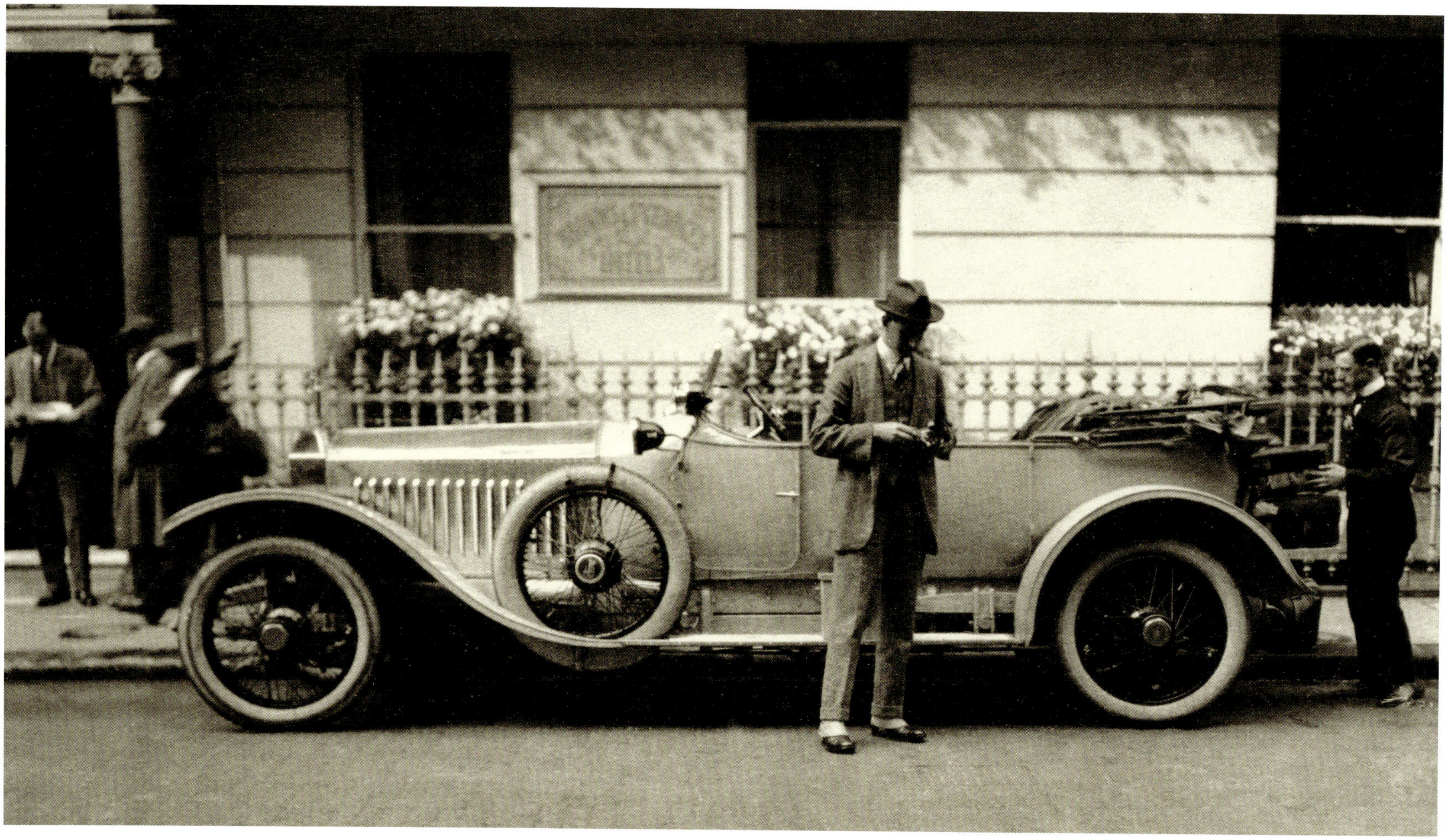

1913

Radley's car outside Brown's Hotel, in 1 Albemarle Street, London W1.
This elegant hotel was used by Radley as his London address.
Photo taken as the party set out for Vienna in May 1913.

BROWN'S HOTEL

London, England

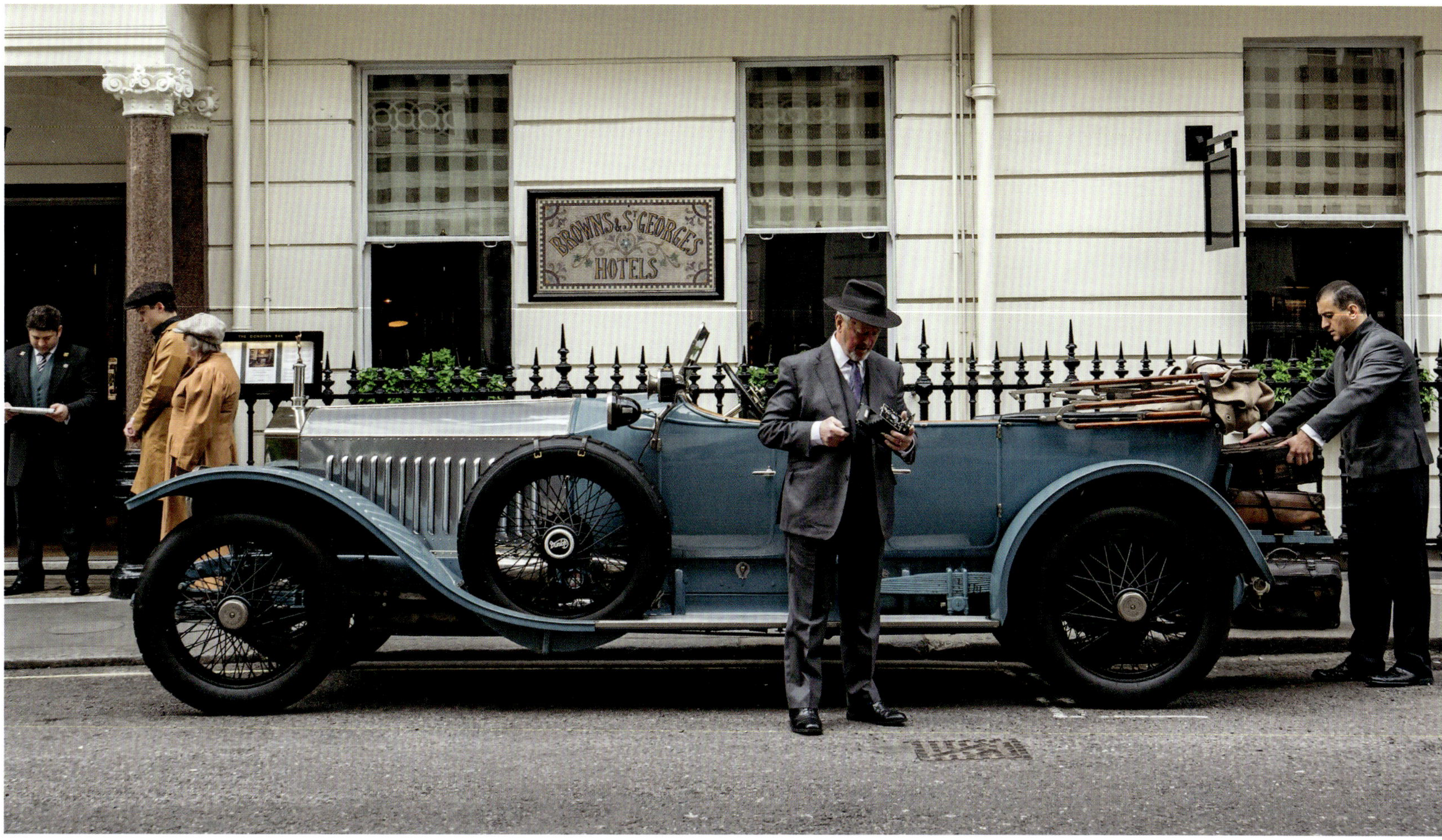

2013

Brown's Hotel remains little changed to this day, with the wrought iron railings still in place. Even the mosaic sign behind the car reading 'Browns & St Georges Hotels' is still there.

ALBERMARLE STREET

London, England

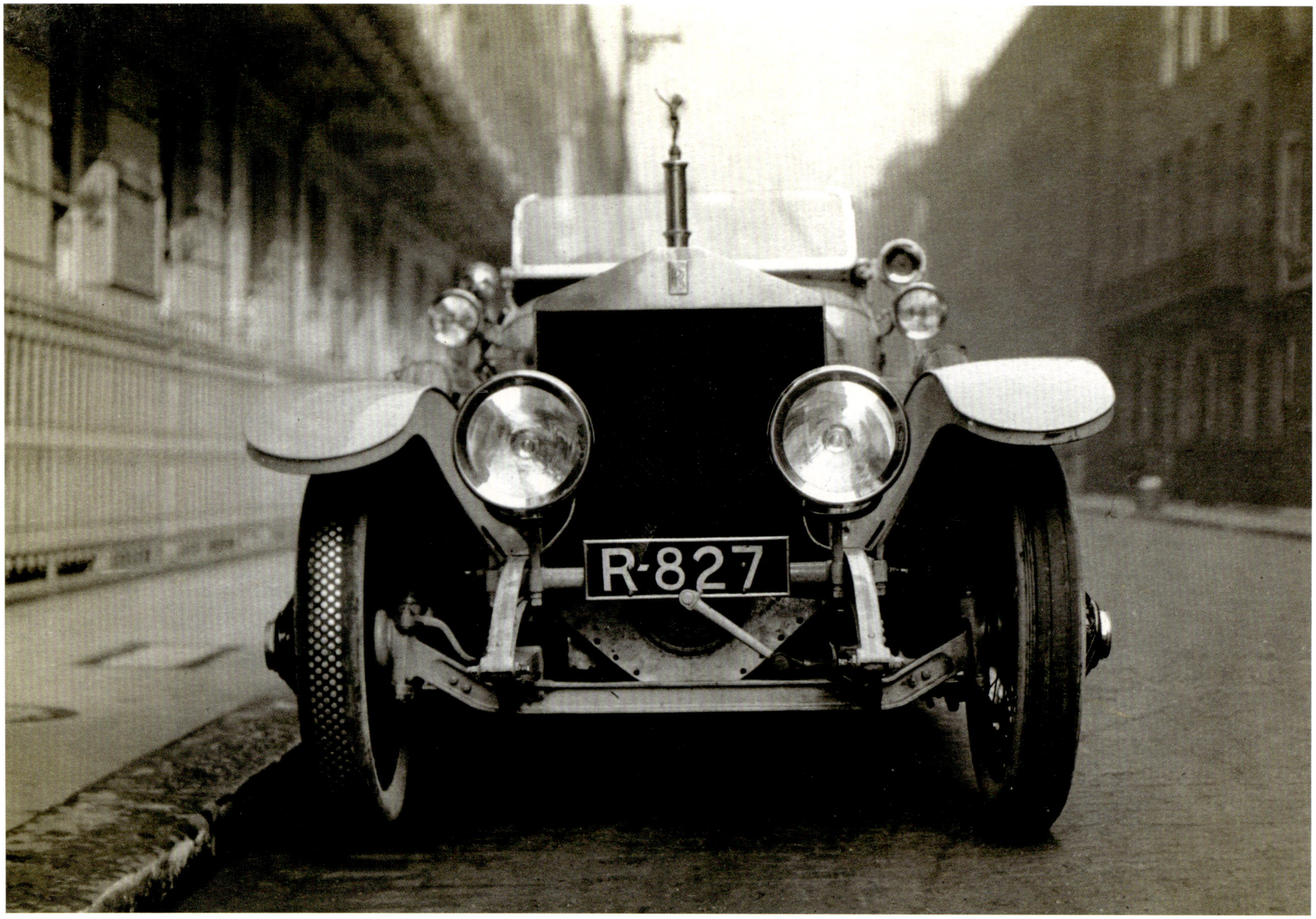

1913

The Radley car parked in the same location at Brown's Hotel in London as the picture on the previous page.

ALBERMARLE STREET

London, England

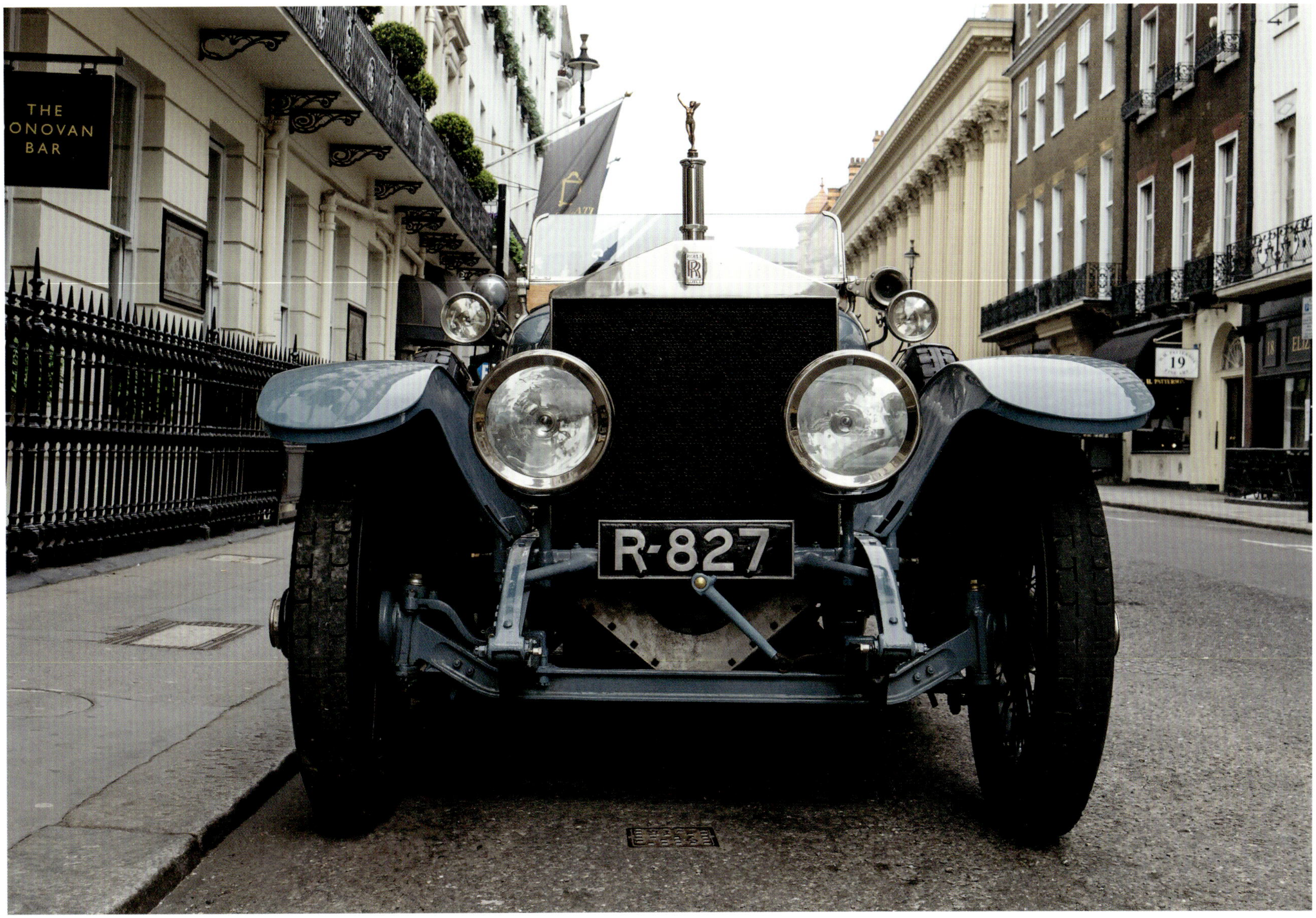

2013

The view stays the same.
Even the manhole covers are still there.

CHANNEL CROSSING

Folkestone, England

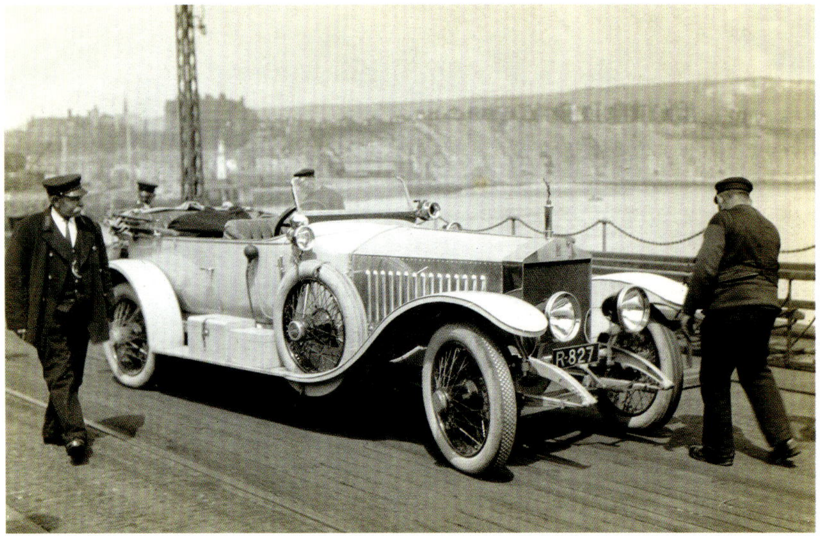

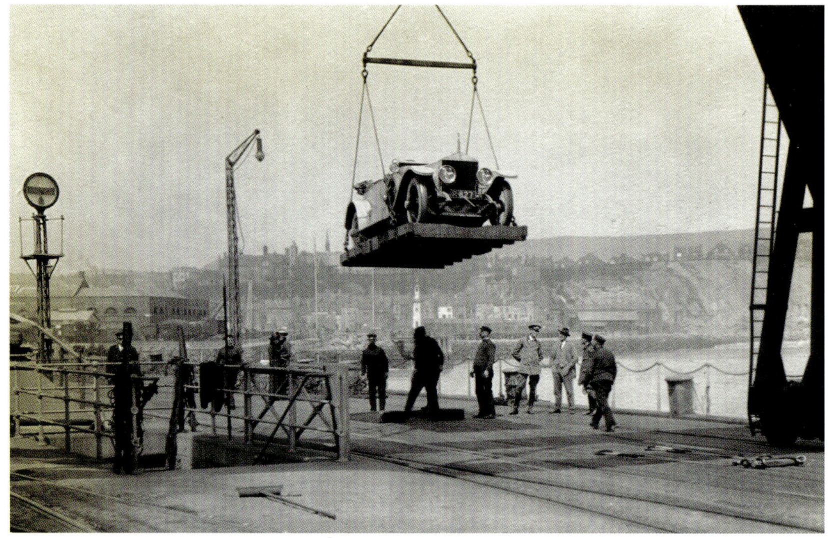
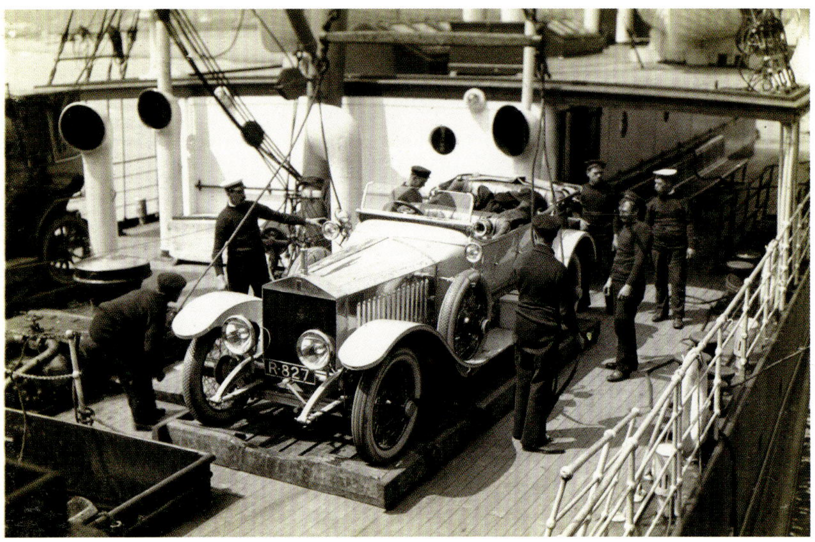

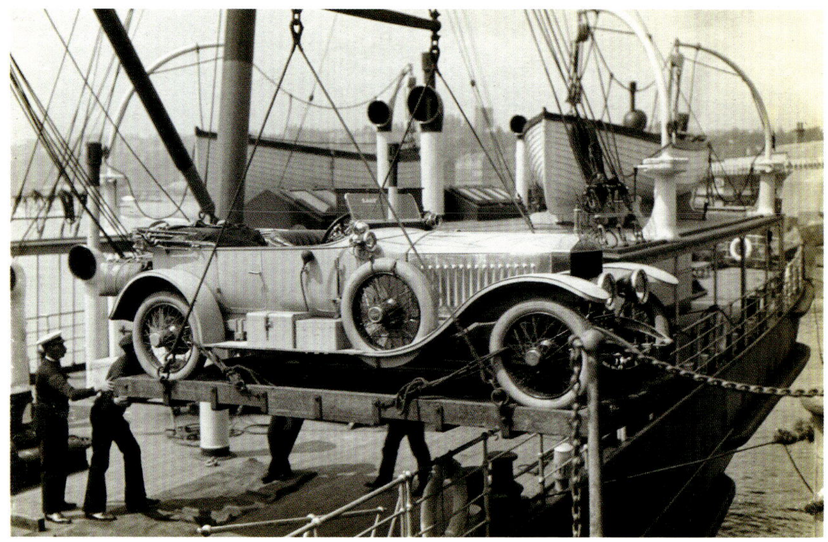

1913

On the wharf at Folkestone loading onto the ferry for Boulogne
in late afternoon, presumably on the same day as leaving London.

CHANNEL CROSSING

Eurotunnel

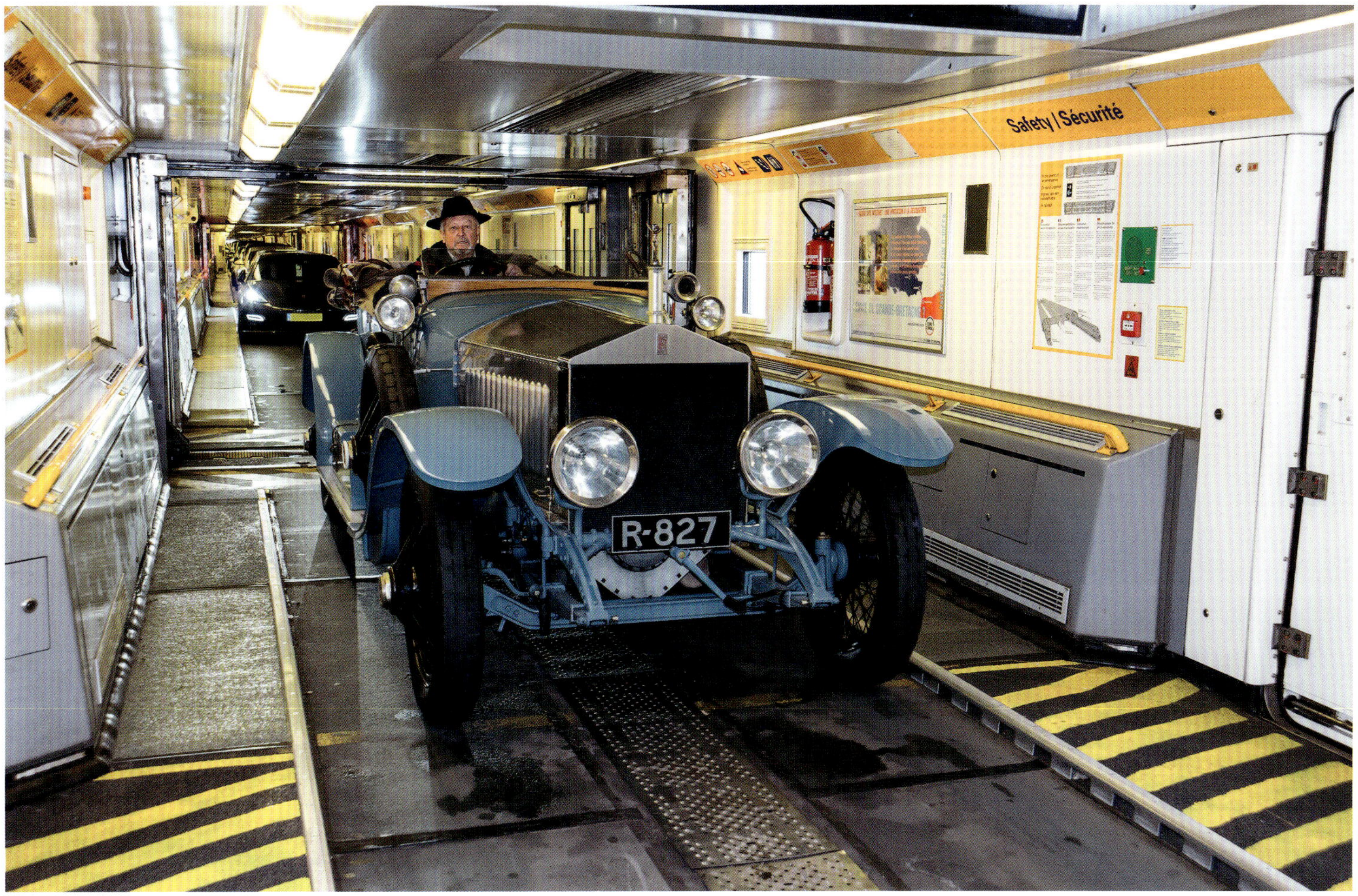

2013

Neither Folkestone nor Boulogne are used for channel ferry crossings any longer. The nearby Eurotunnel now provides much of the channel crossing capacity.

PARIS BOAT TRAIN

Boulogne, France

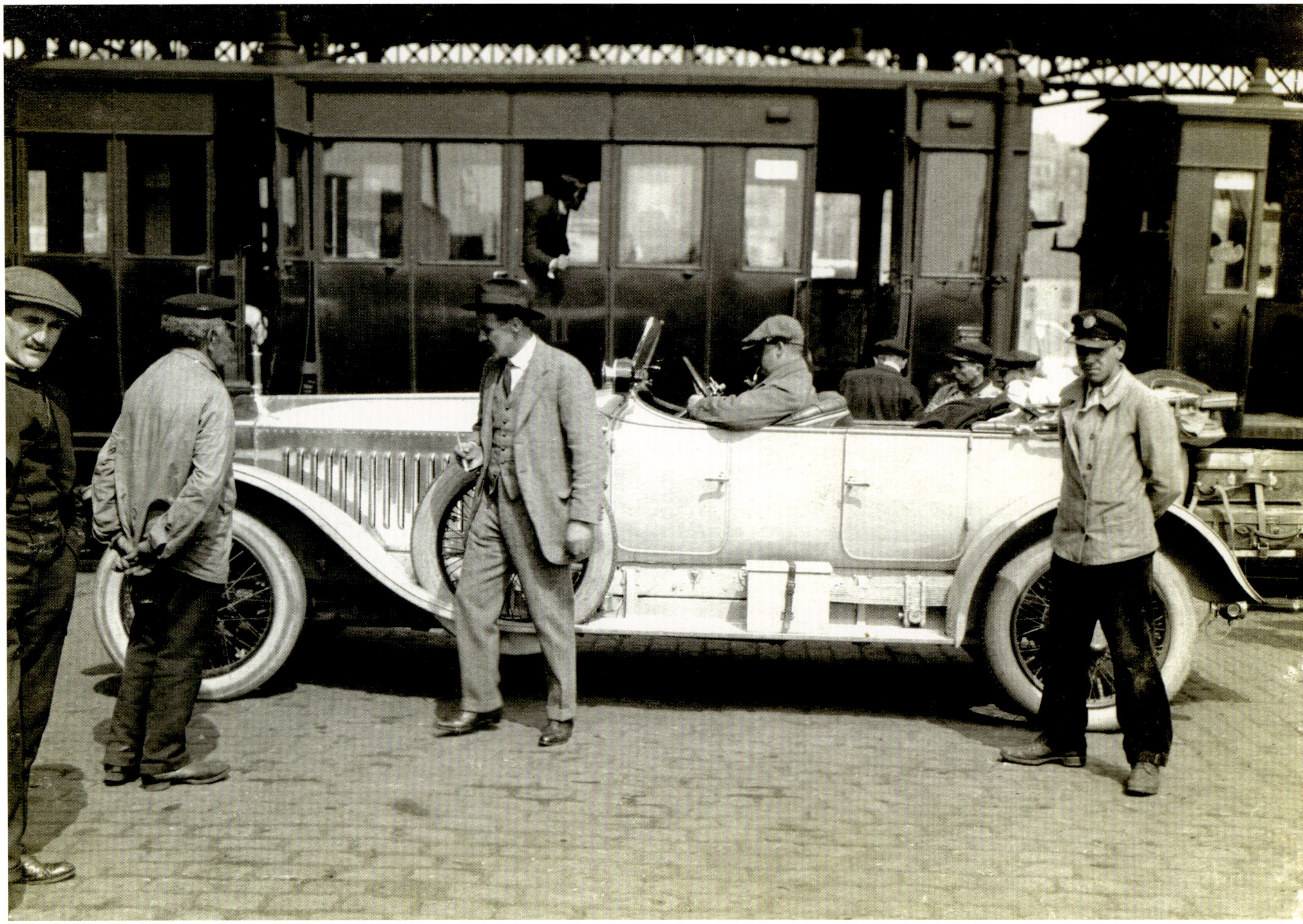

1913

Radley in front of his car with train carriages
of the Boulogne to Paris boat train immediately behind.

SOMME TOURIST TRAIN

Noyelles, France

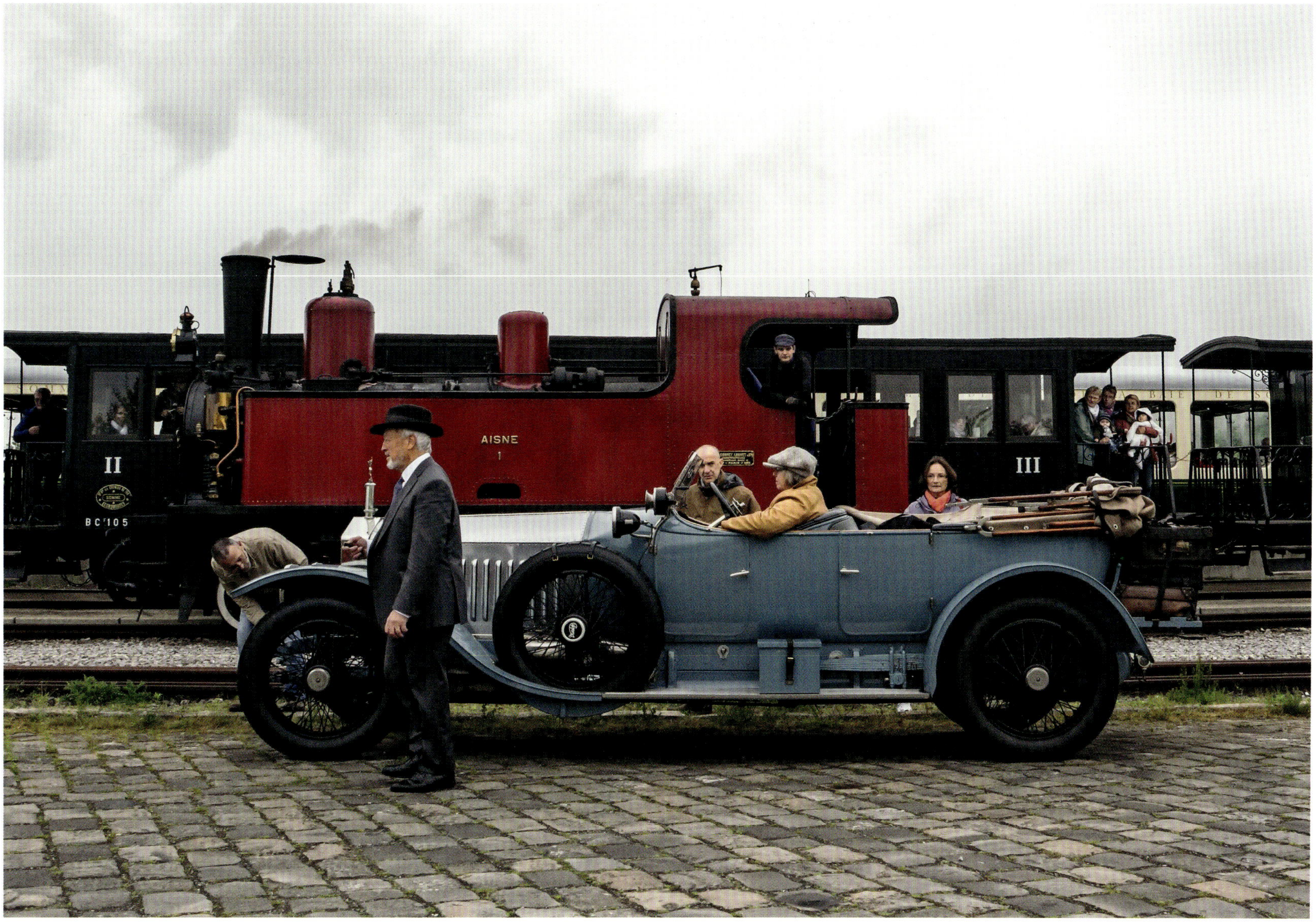

2013

The boat train has ceased to exist since the introduction of the direct rail service through the Channel Tunnel in 1993. The scenic railway alongside the Bay of the Somme includes early steam locomotives and carriages even older than those in the 1913 picture.

CHÂTEAU LA ROCHEPOT

France

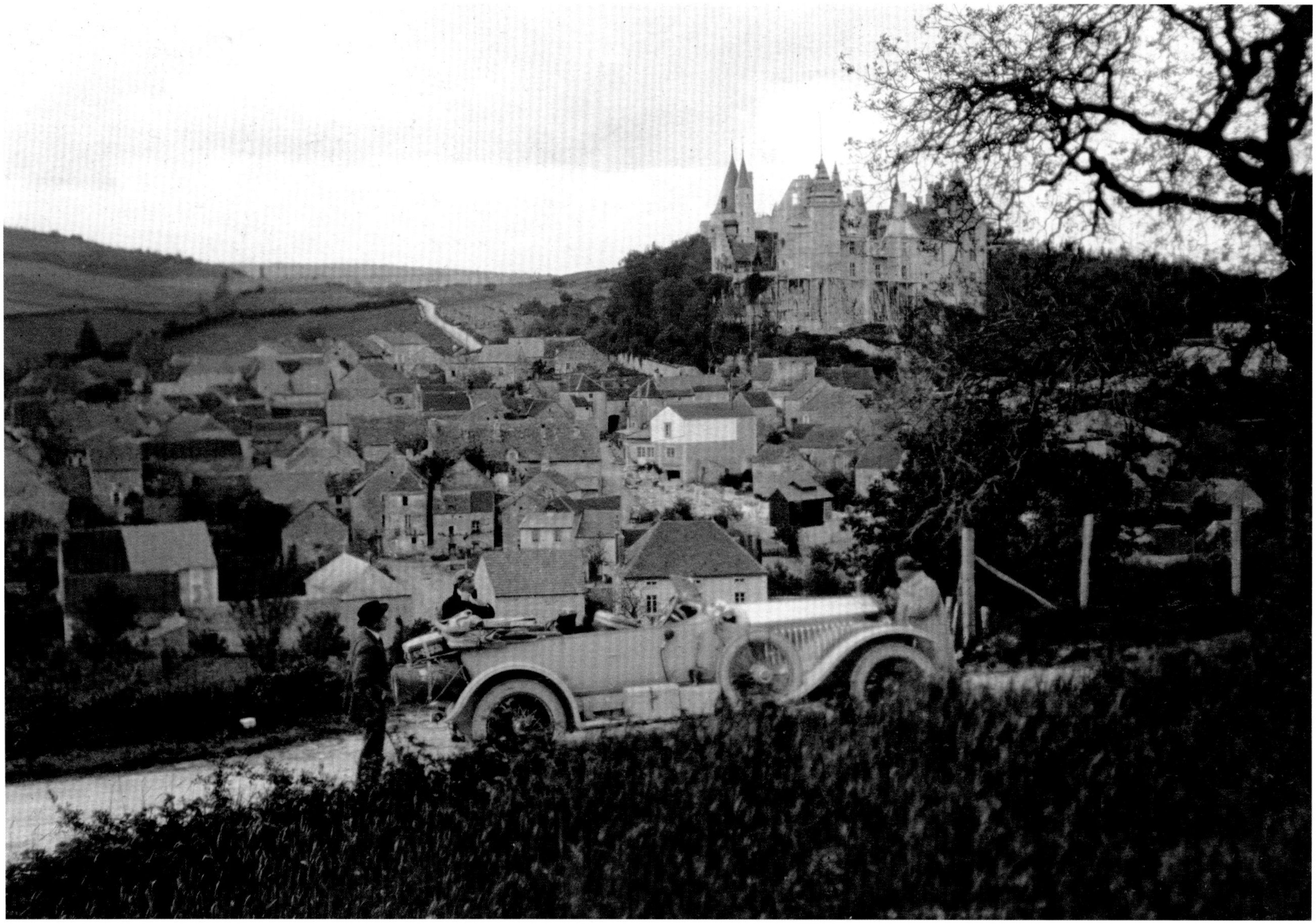

1913

View of the car on the old N6 near Beaune with the small village of la Rochepot behind.
The 13th c. château on the hilltop was refurbished in the 15th c. by a crusading knight Régnier Pot.
The château sits on its ridge that now bears his name.

CHÂTEAU LA ROCHEPOT

France

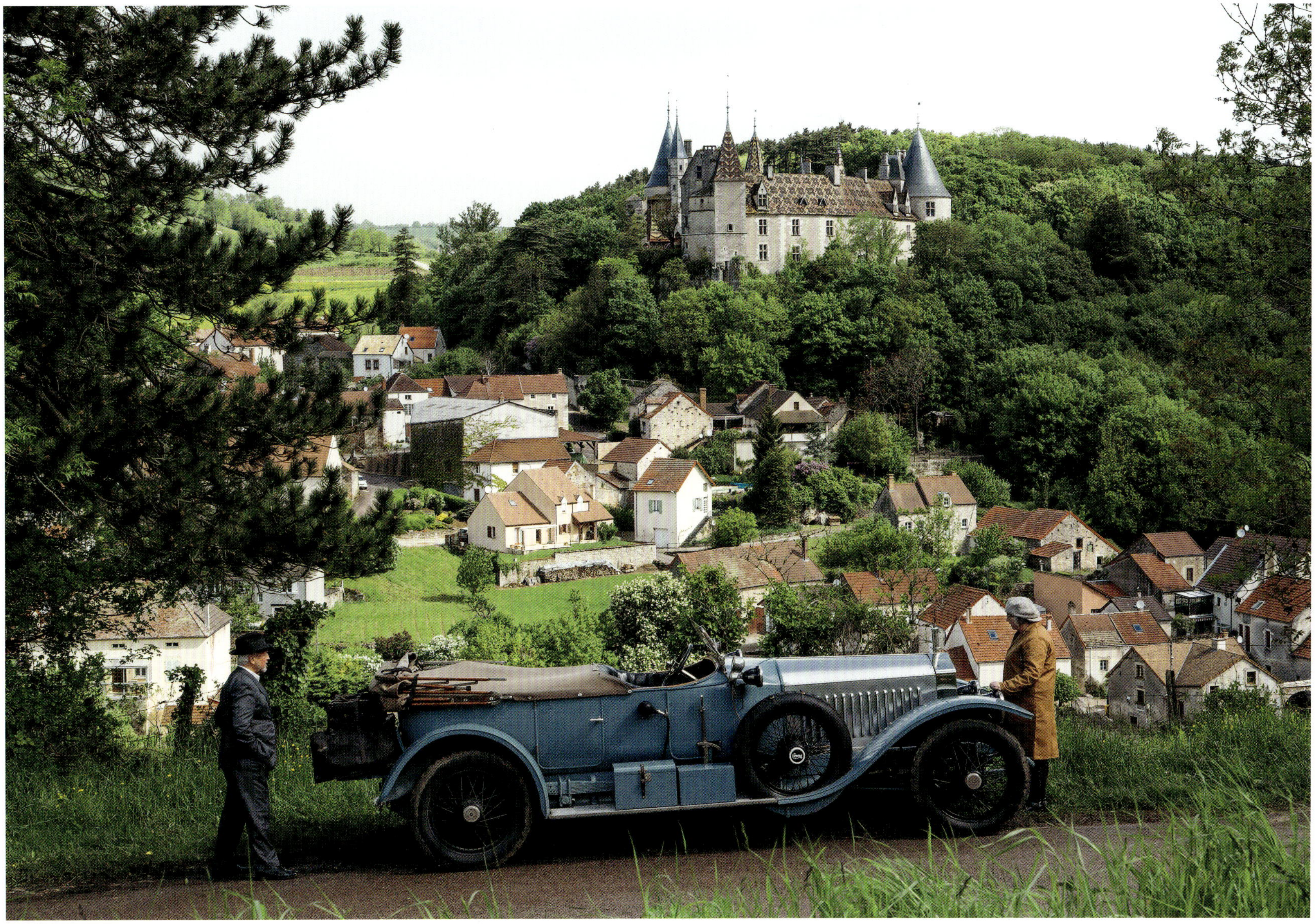

2013

The glistening Burgundian tiled roof now on the château was added after the 1913 photograph was taken. In a state of ruin after the Revolution, it was restored by Sadi Carnot, son of a former President of France. The car is parked on a quiet local road, as the modern N6 is now a newer road to the west.

ROADSIDE CHECKS

France

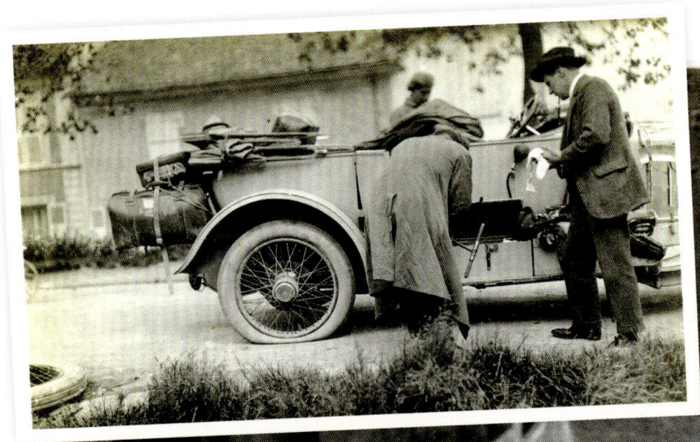

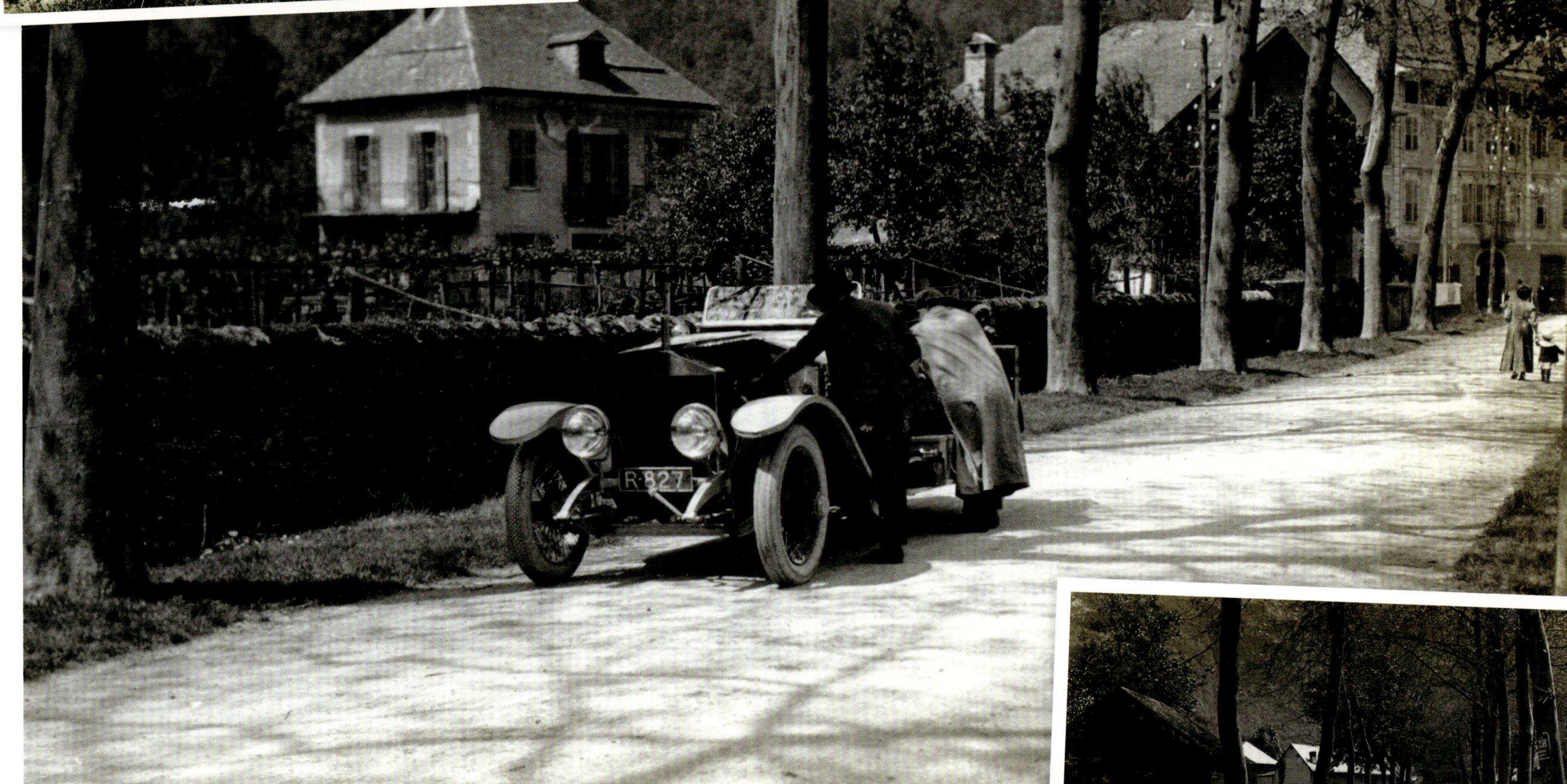

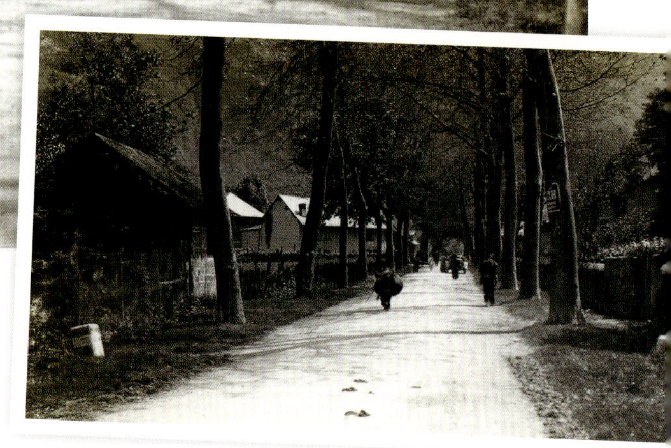

1913

Roadside halt in France, probably on the N6 in the Côte-d'Or area. Radley examines near side of engine.
Inset upper: Fixing a puncture. Radley and Ward in front of tool box. The same location as the next photo.
Inset lower: Radley car in distance in tree lined road in France. Same location for all three photographs.

ROADSIDE CHECKS

France

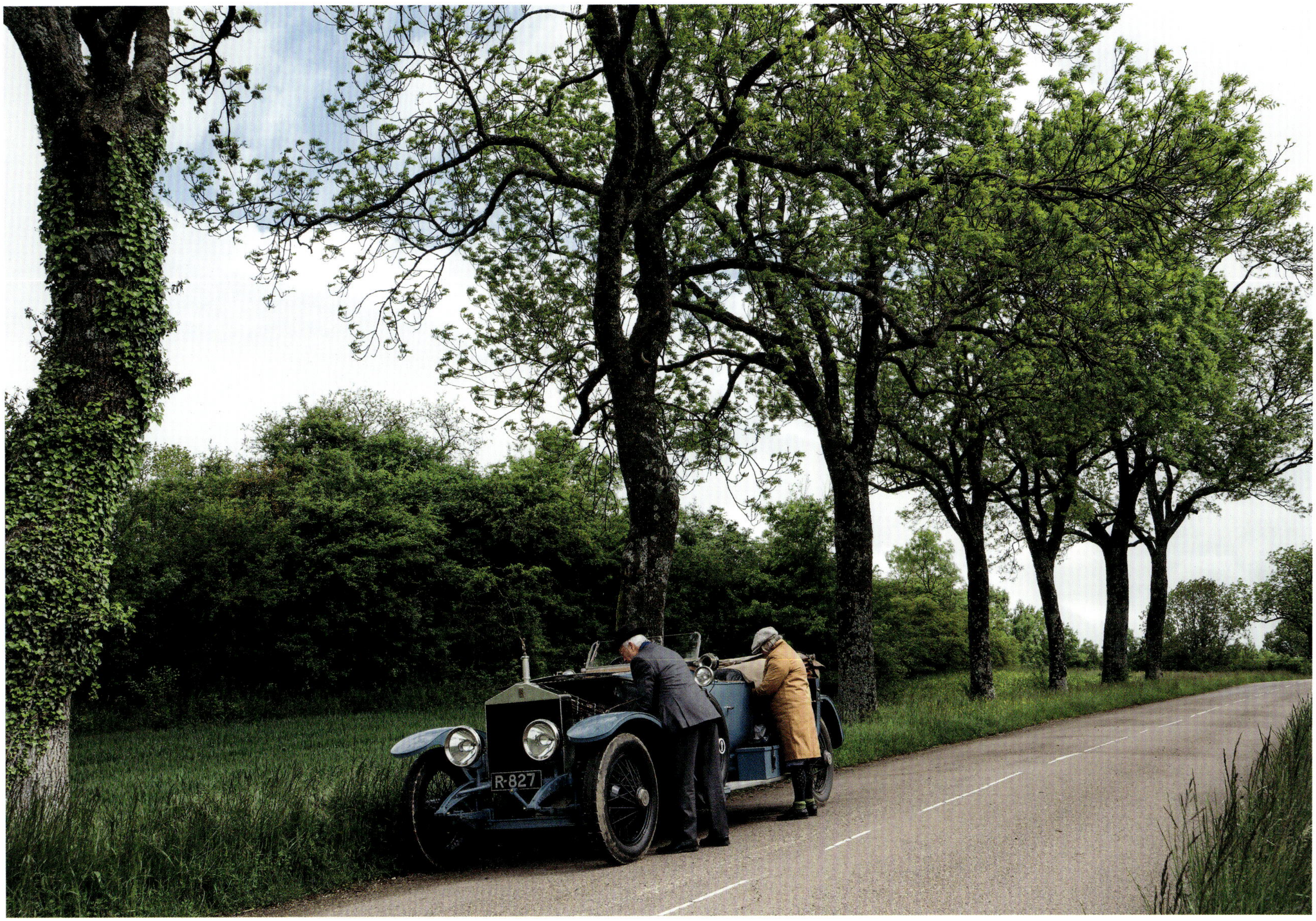

2013

The tree lined roads of 100 years ago have often been removed for safety or for road widening but they still exist along pieces of the old Routes Nationales, where the road has been realigned as in this picture. Perhaps the lack of horses and horseshoe nails meant that there were no punctures in 2013.

ROADSIDE HALT

France

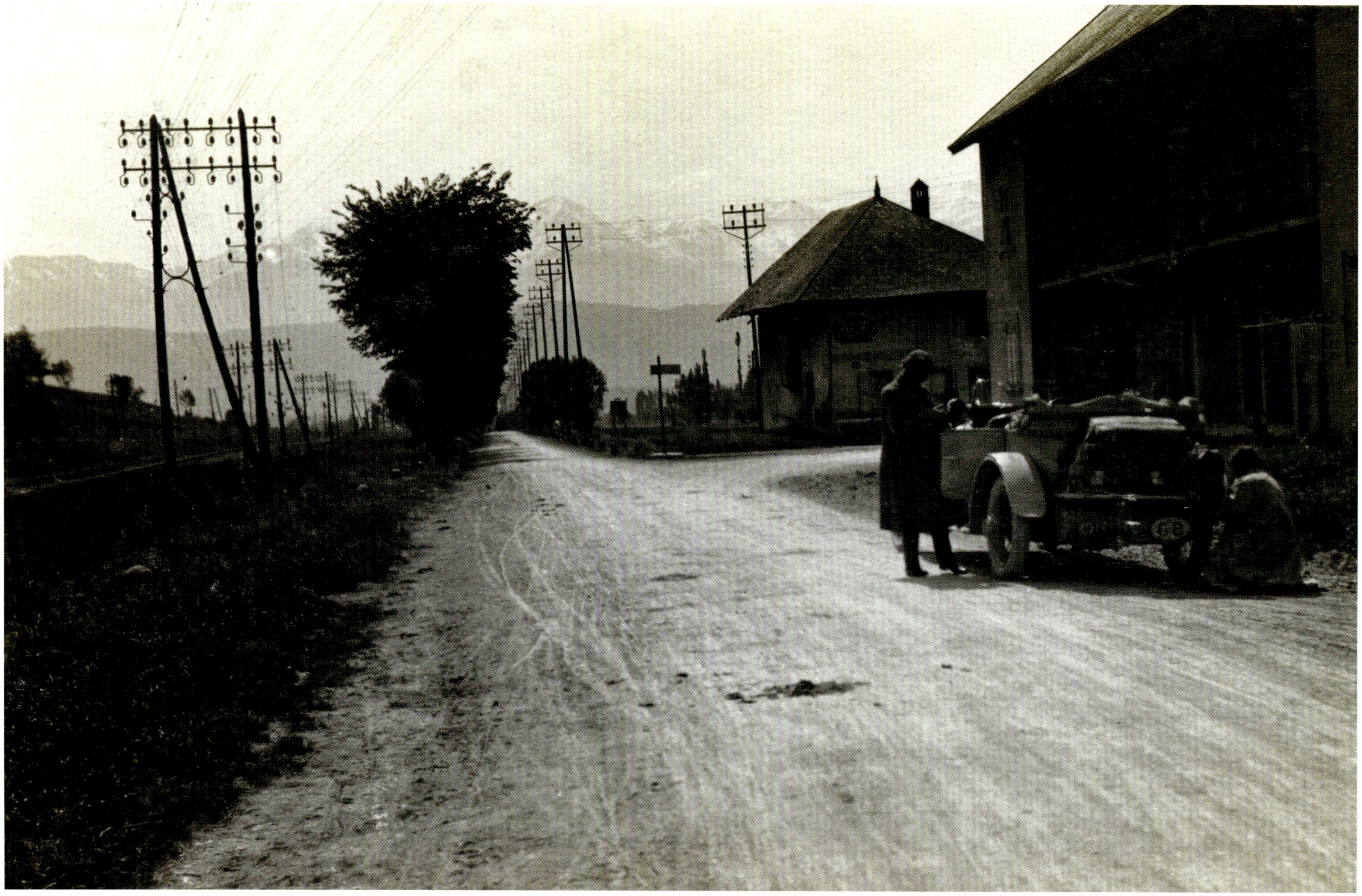

1913

The car stopped on a straight with the railway on left and high mountains ahead.
Passenger appears to be checking the luggage or rear wheel; the road sign reads 'Chapareillan'.
The sign on the building at the road junction reads 'Hotel Tissot'.
The location is the old junction of the N6 and N90 just before reaching Montmélian.

ROADSIDE HALT

France

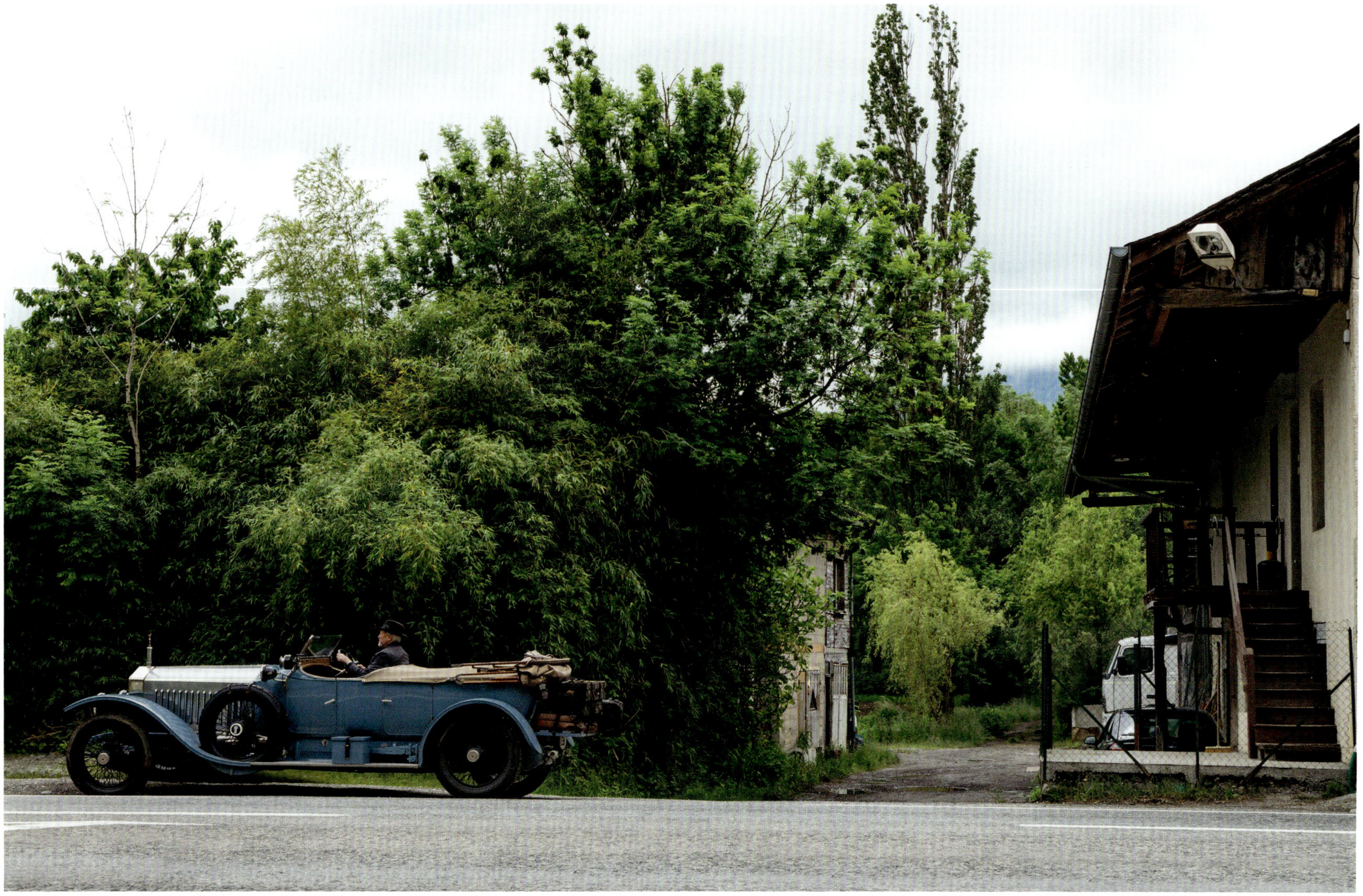

2013

The junction is now totally altered; a new A41 autoroute cuts off the old side road which is now only an access lane to a few houses. It has been replaced by new roundabout some 200 metres west of the old junction. The N6 has since been renumbered D1006 and remains a busy road; the N90 is the D1090.

AIGUEBELLE

France

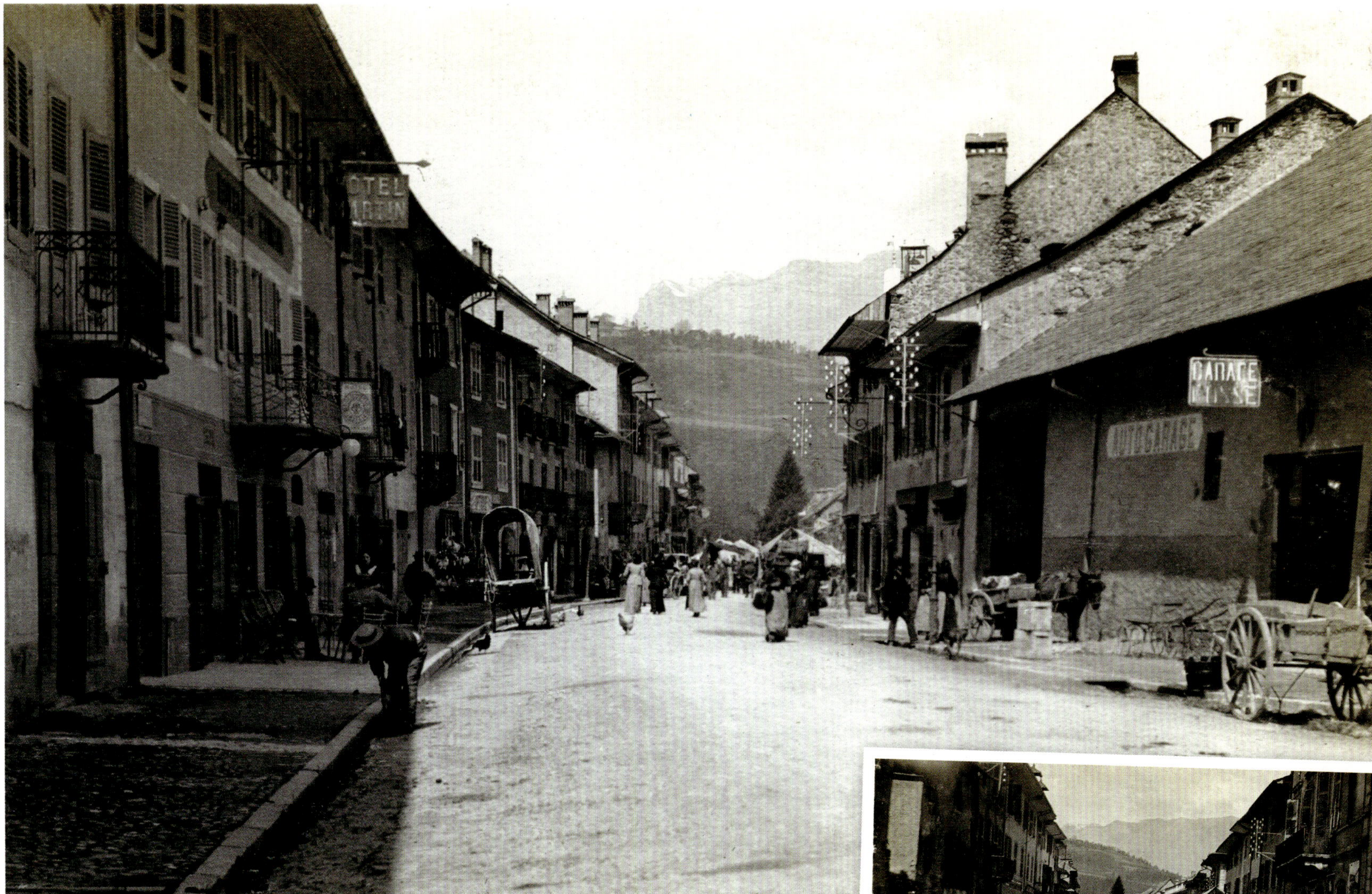

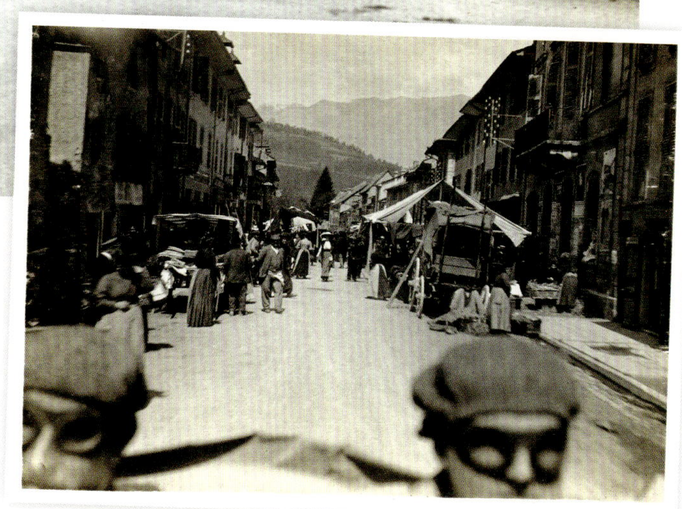

1913

Street scene in Aiguebelle on route N6, 60 km before start of Col du Mont Cenis road.
Right: View of market in the main street taken by the front seat passenger 100 metres earlier than the main photo shows the two rear passengers wearing motoring goggles and caps.

AIGUEBELLE

France

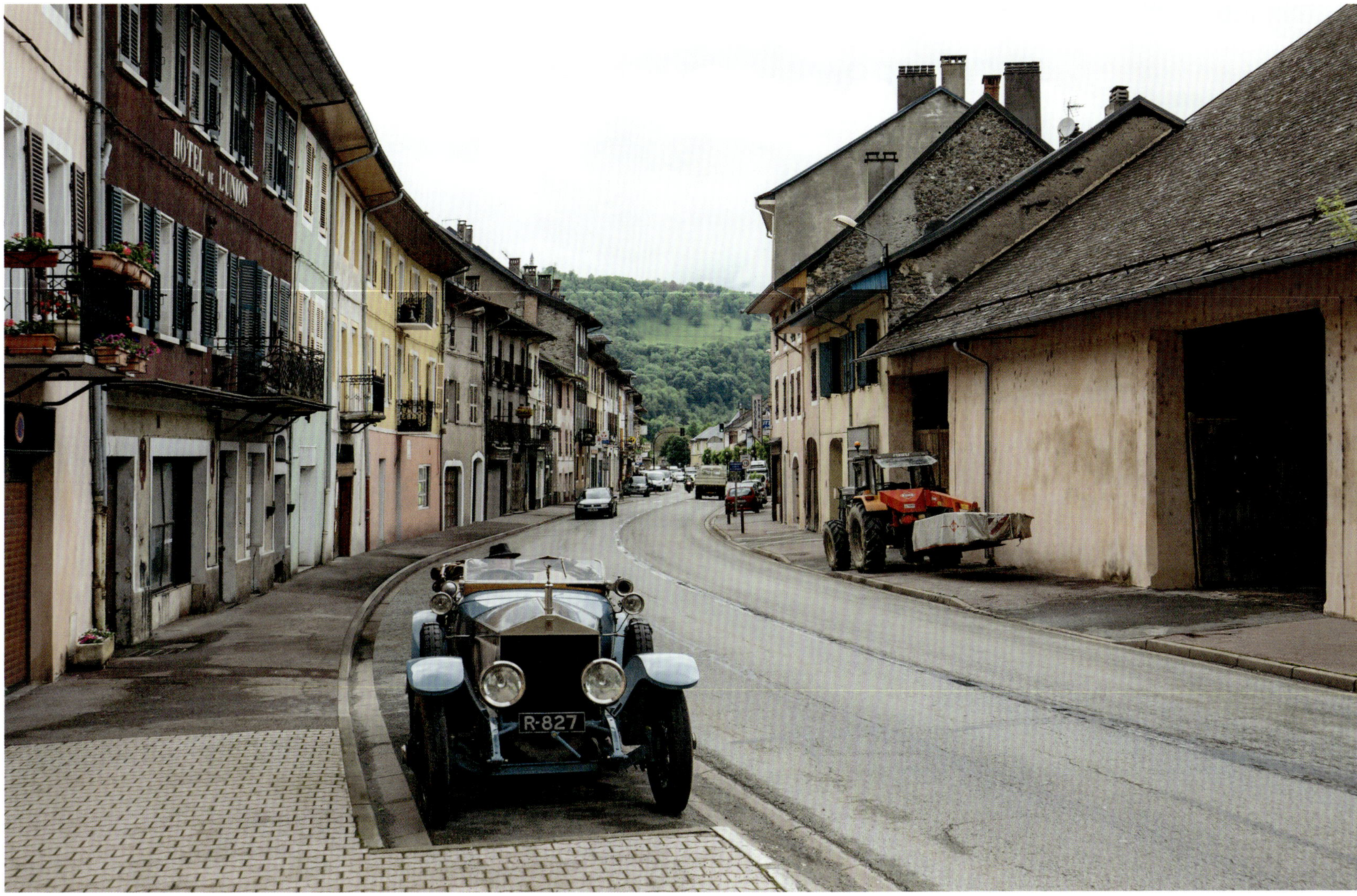

2013

The farm carts are replaced by a tractor; the barn has one door extended in height for modern farm machinery. One building on the right has been extended in height; the buildings on the left are unchanged since 1913.

LANSLEBOURG-MONT-CENIS

France

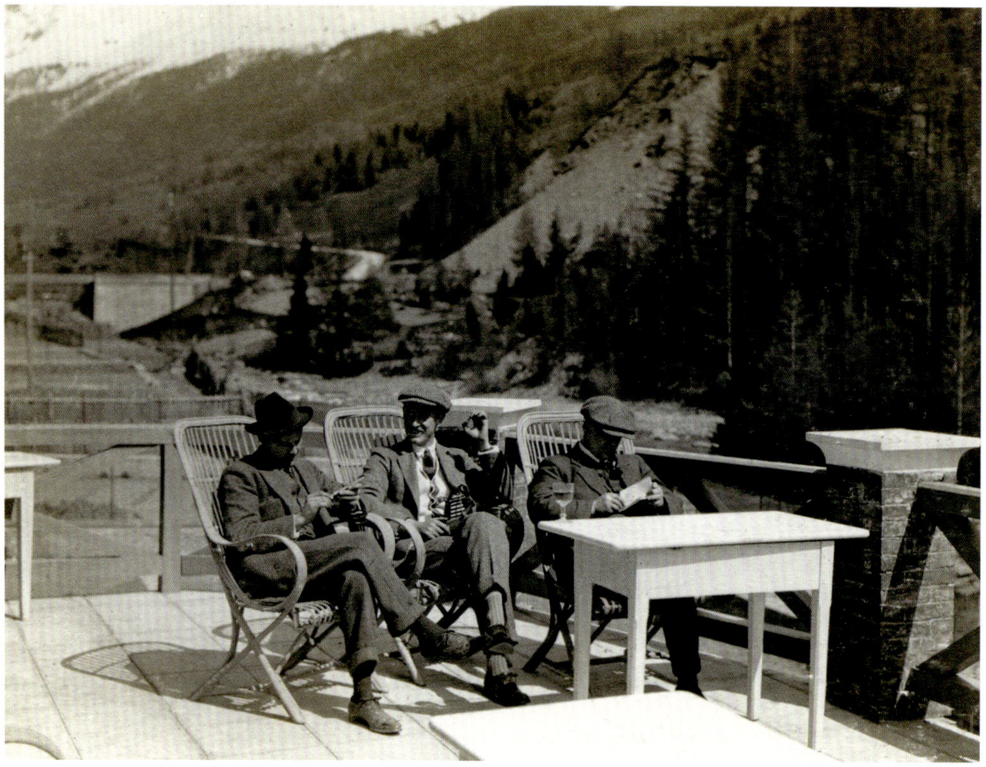

1913

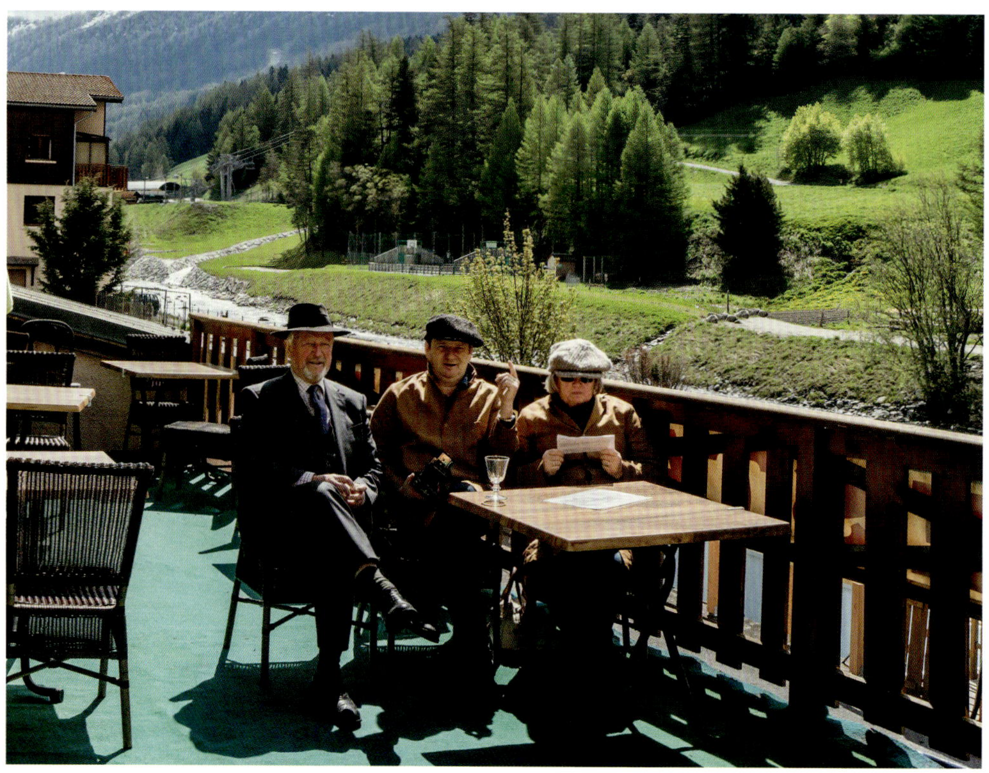

2013

L'ARC, LANSLEBOURG-MONT-CENIS

France

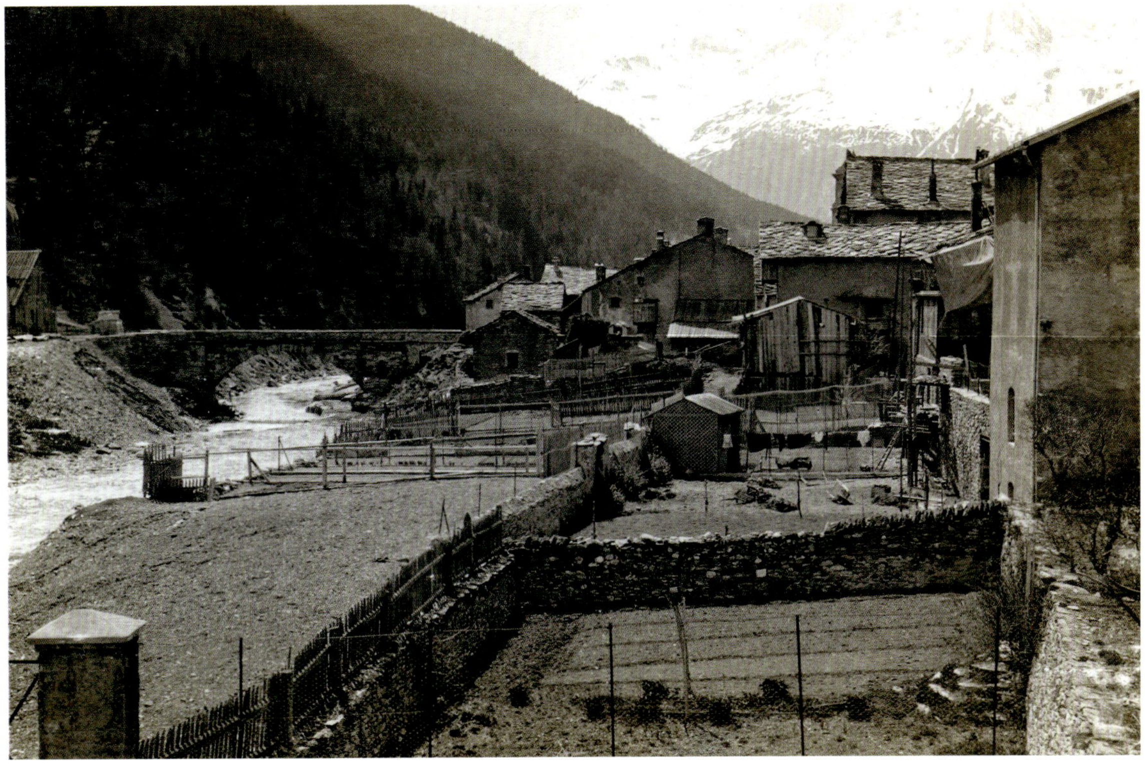

1913

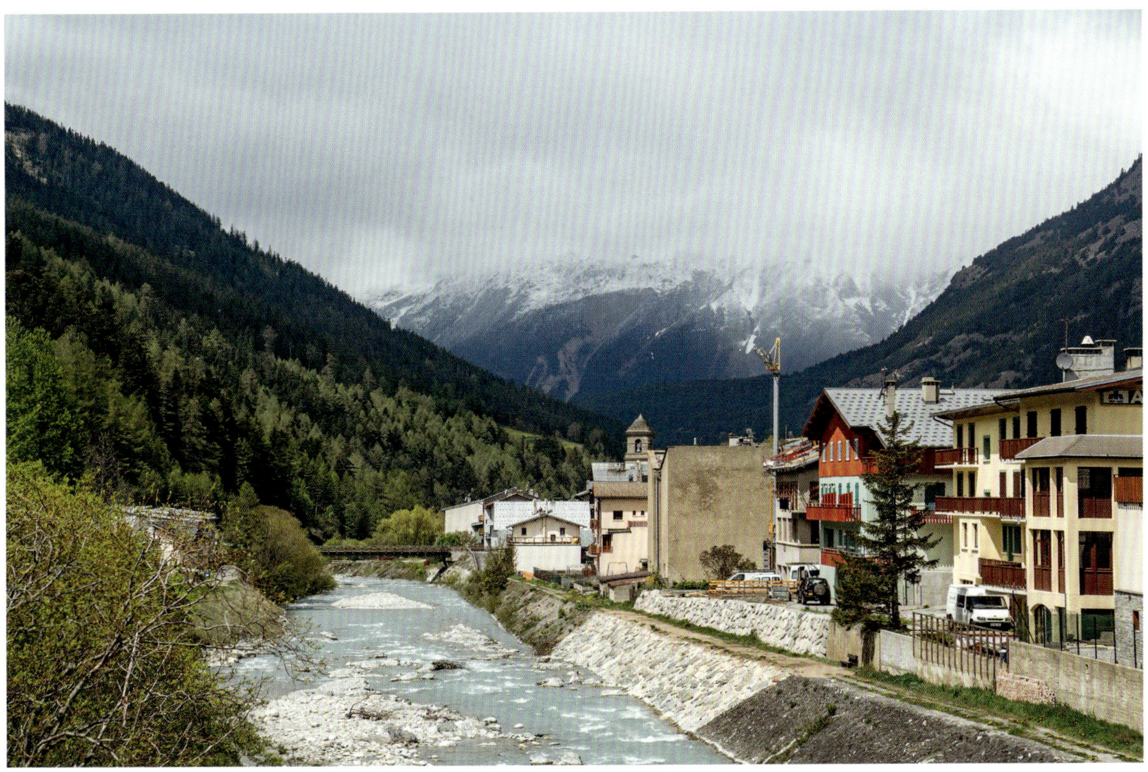

2013

LANSLEBOURG-MONT-CENIS

France

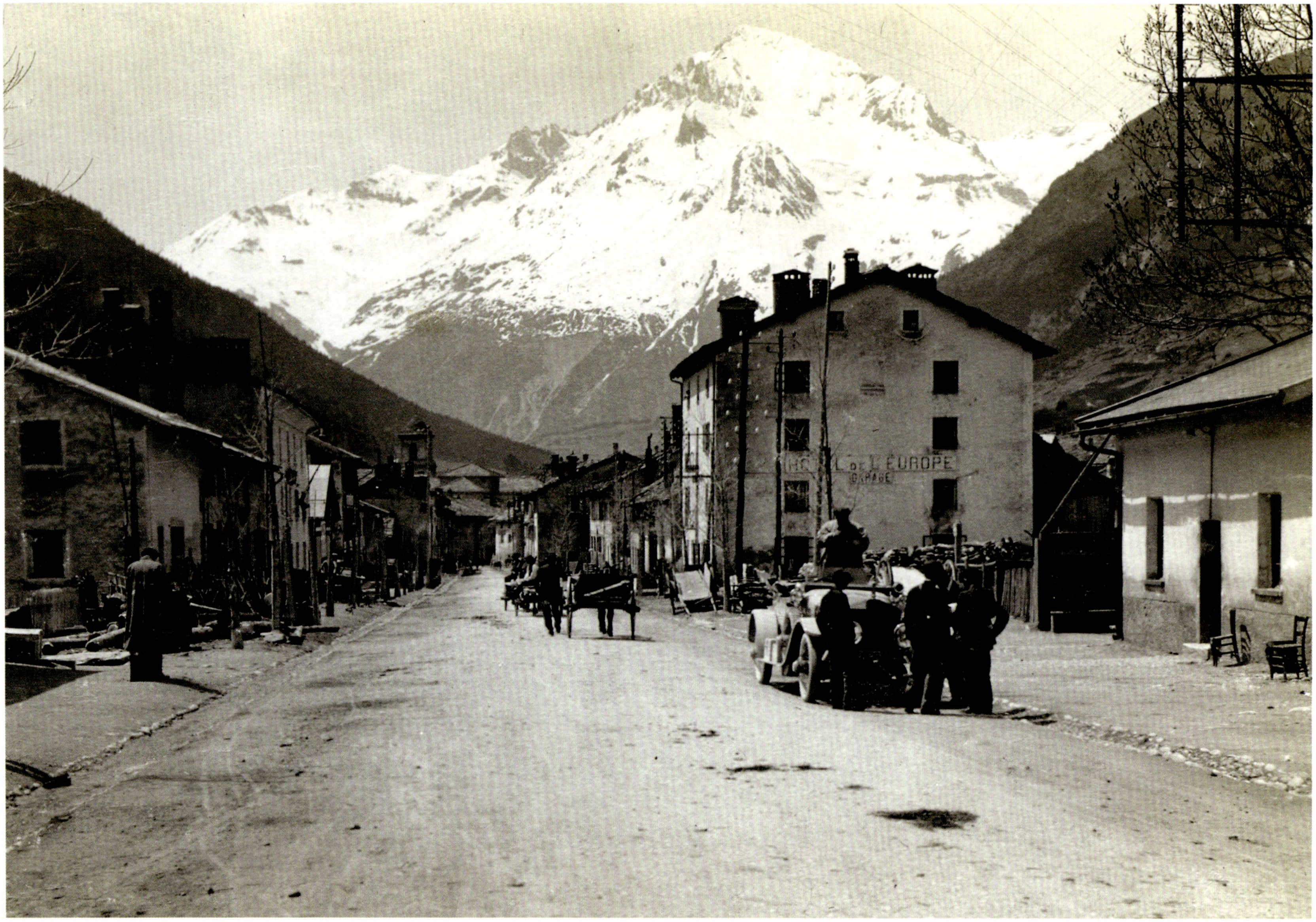

1913

Village scene in the mountains with officials looking at the car. This picture shows the car nearly head on; the man on the left of this picture is preparing to take the picture on the following page.

LANSLEBOURG-MONT-CENIS

France

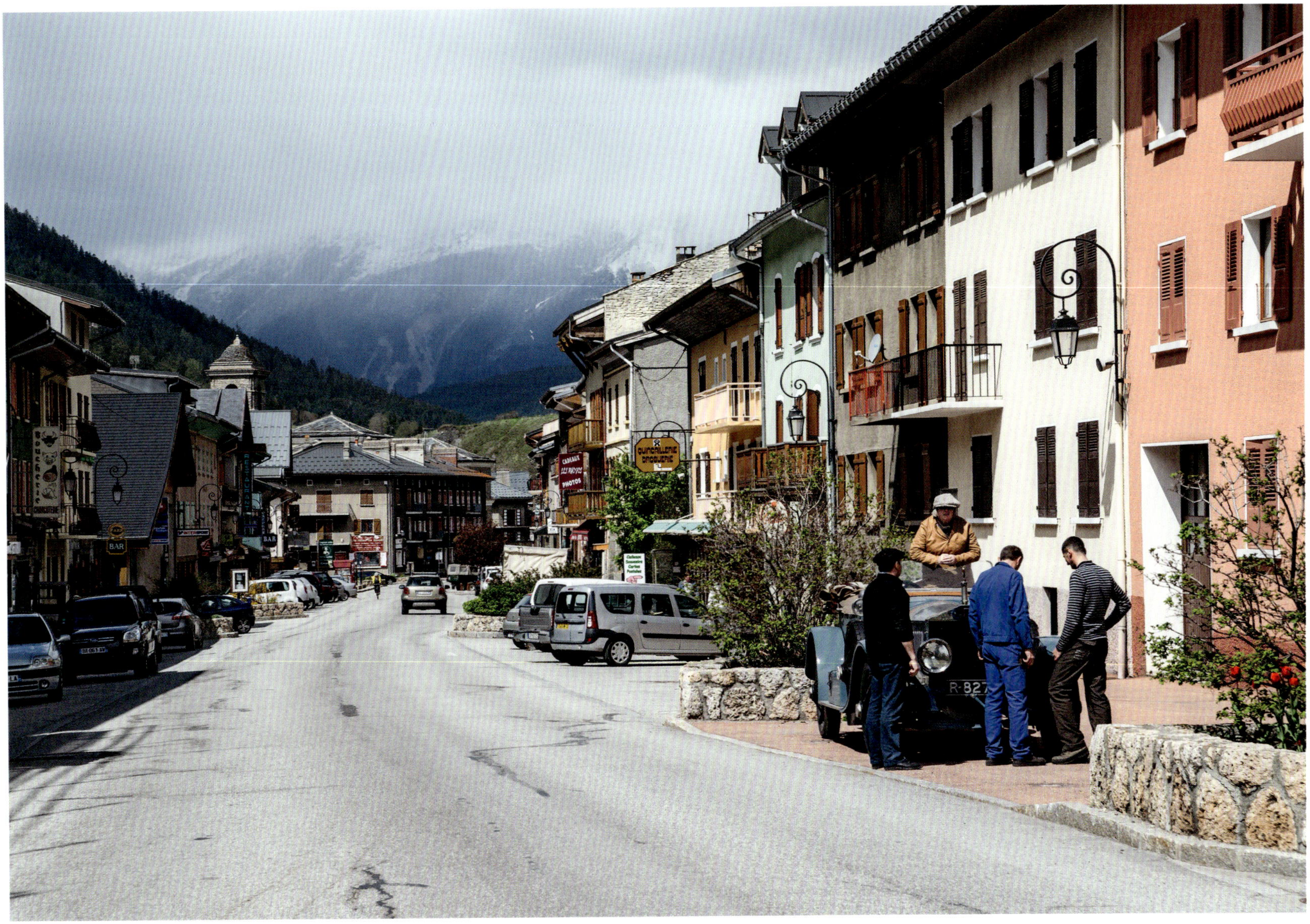

2013

No border officials but local mechanics leave their workshop to investigate the car.
The mountain village of Lanslebourg was totally devastated during the war in 1944.
The church is the only building existing in 1913 which can still be seen from this location.

LANSLEBOURG-MONT-CENIS

France

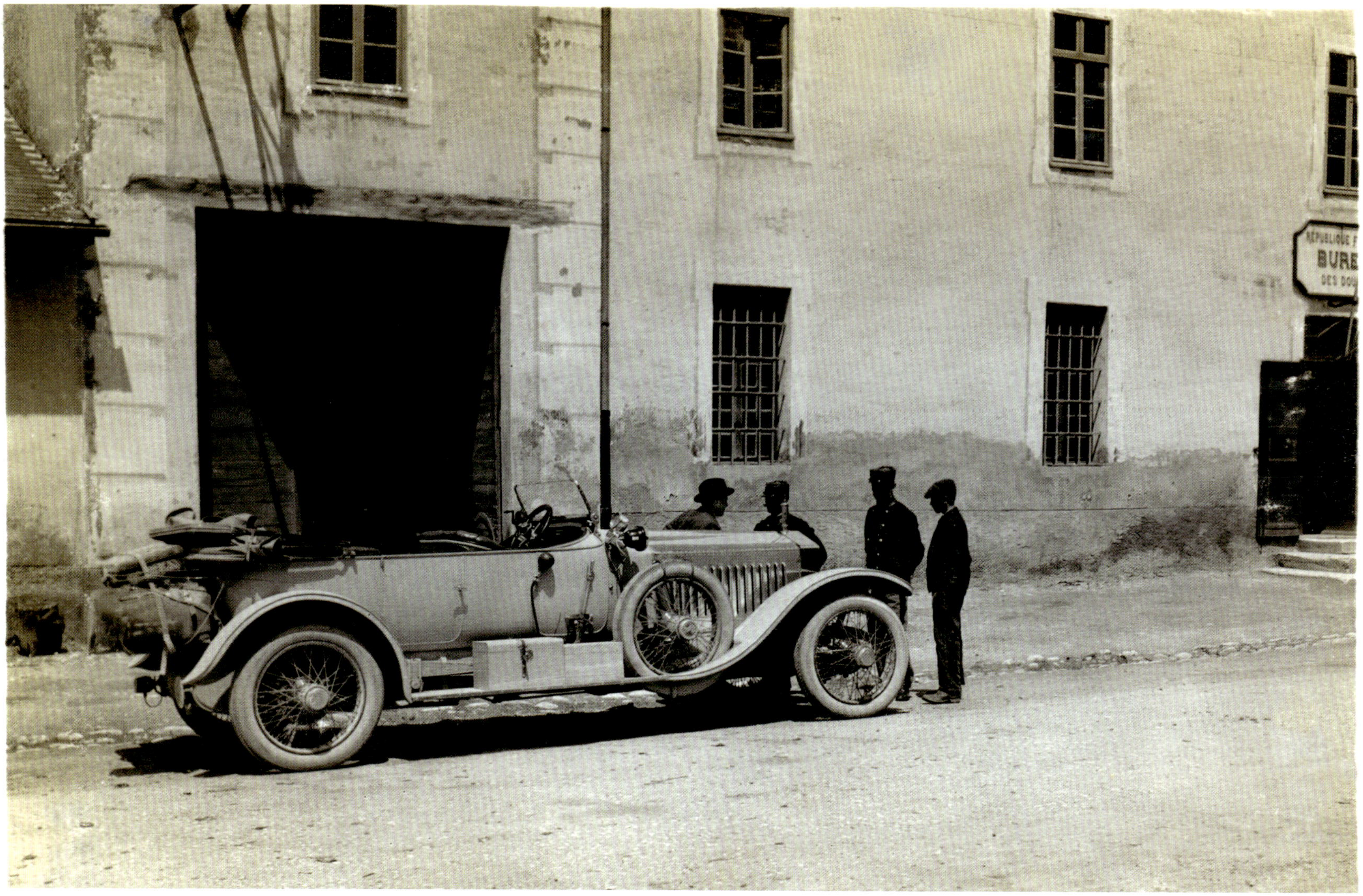

1913

Radley leans on his car and talks to two customs officials whilst a local looks on.
The car is parked in the same position as on the previous page but is viewed from the off side.

LANSLEBOURG-MONT-CENIS

France

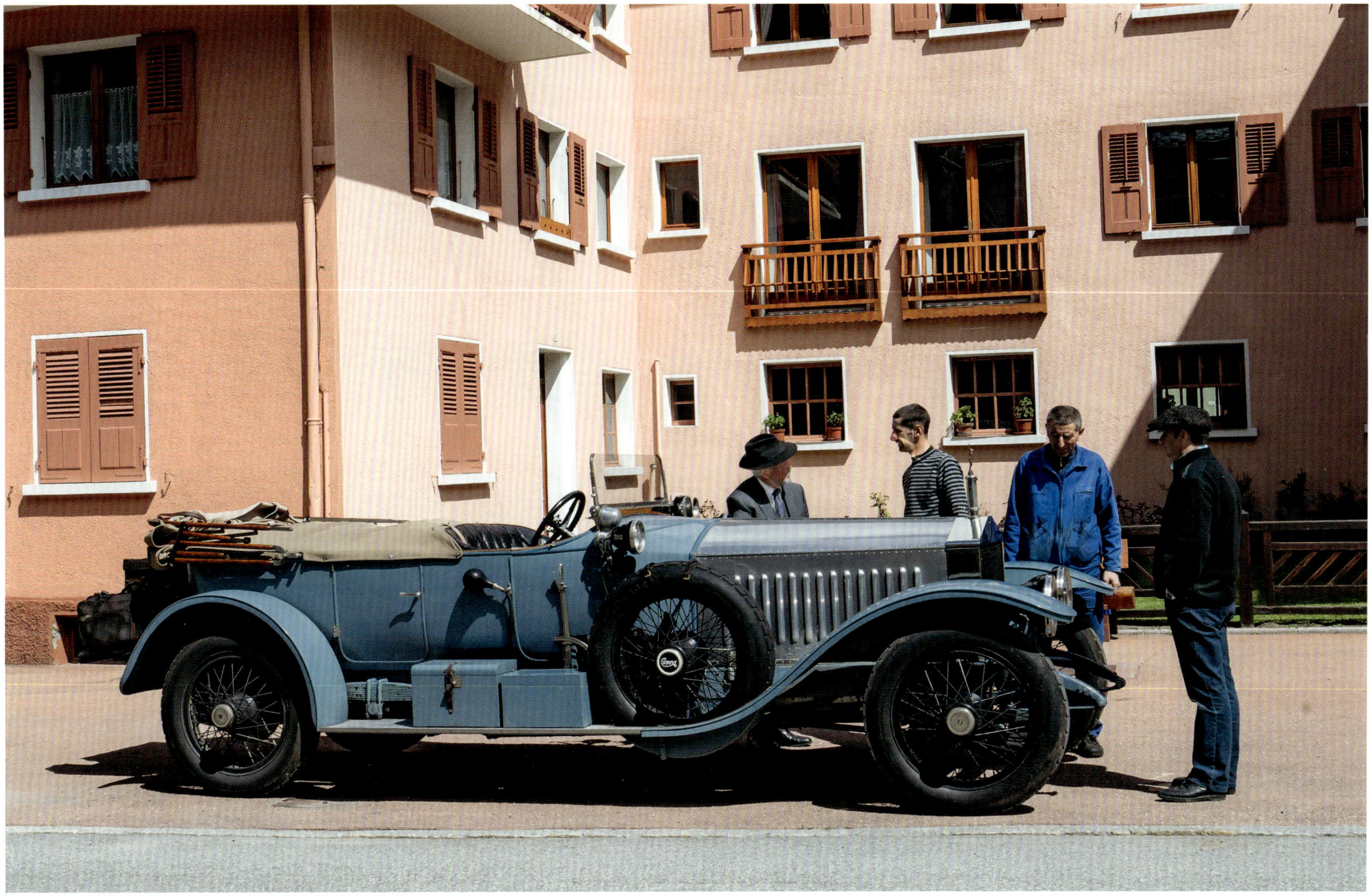

2013

Same location, this time with local mechanics taking a keen interest in the car.

MONT CENIS

France

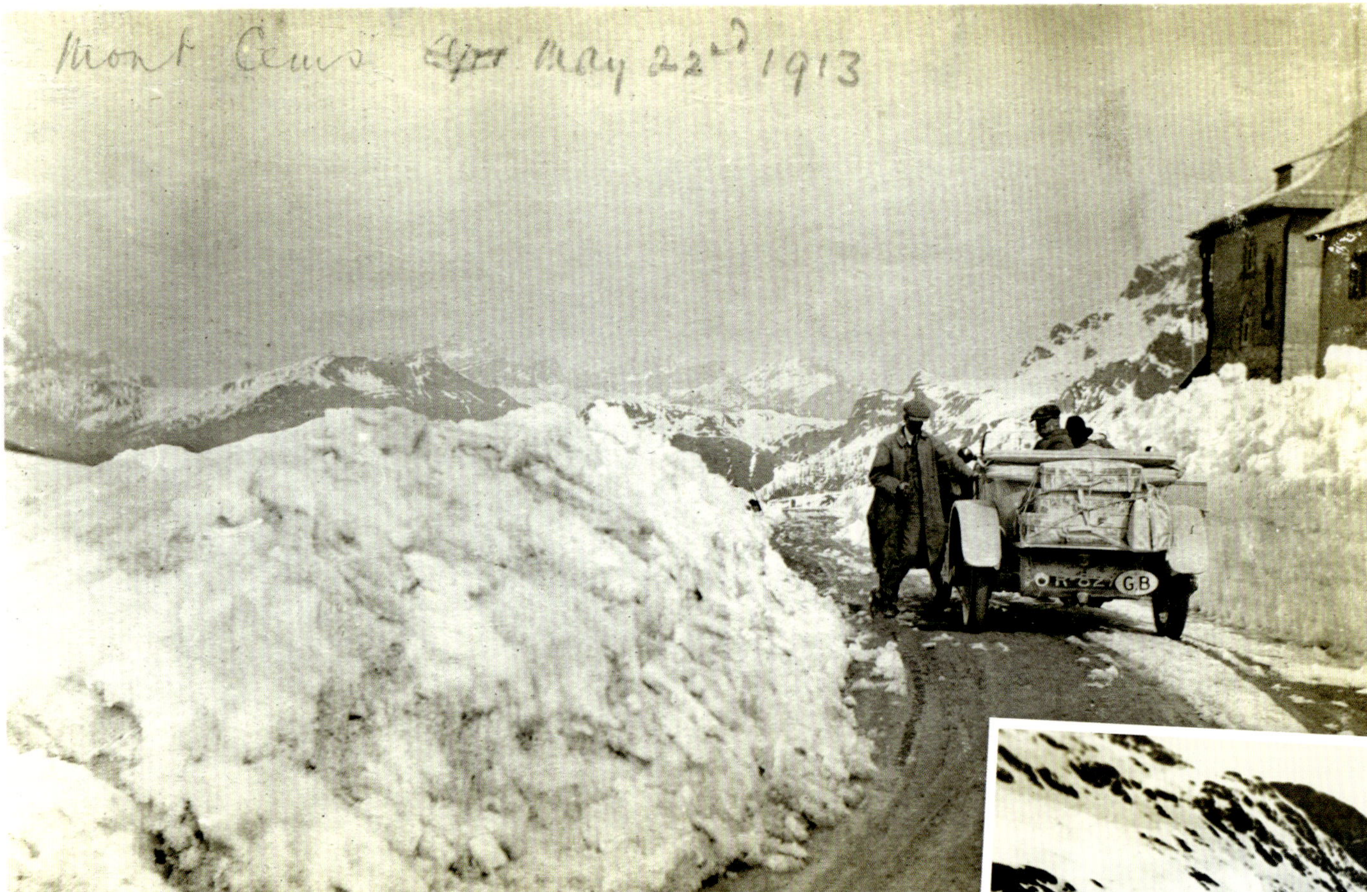

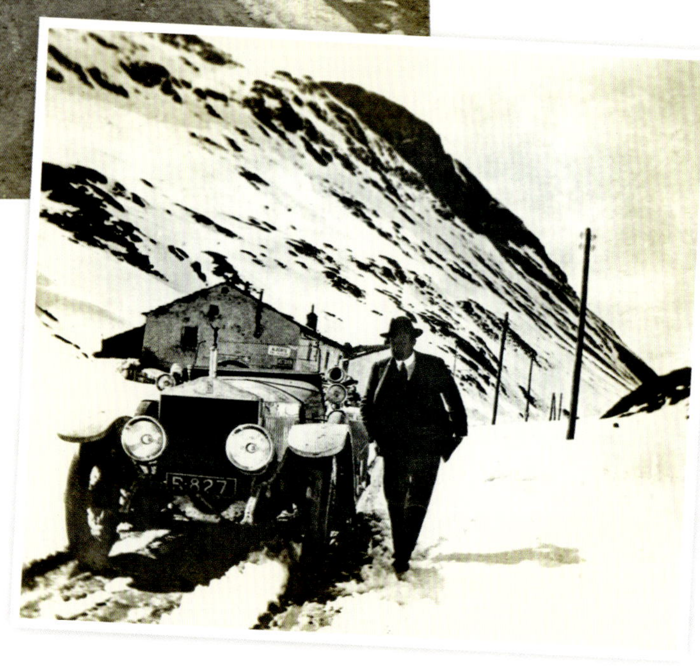

1913

The only picture from the original album with its own date and caption.
Inset: A picture not from the Radley-Hope album which had been wrongly captioned as the Pordoi Pass.
Only after the picture opposite was made, did the real location for this picture become evident.

MONT CENIS

France

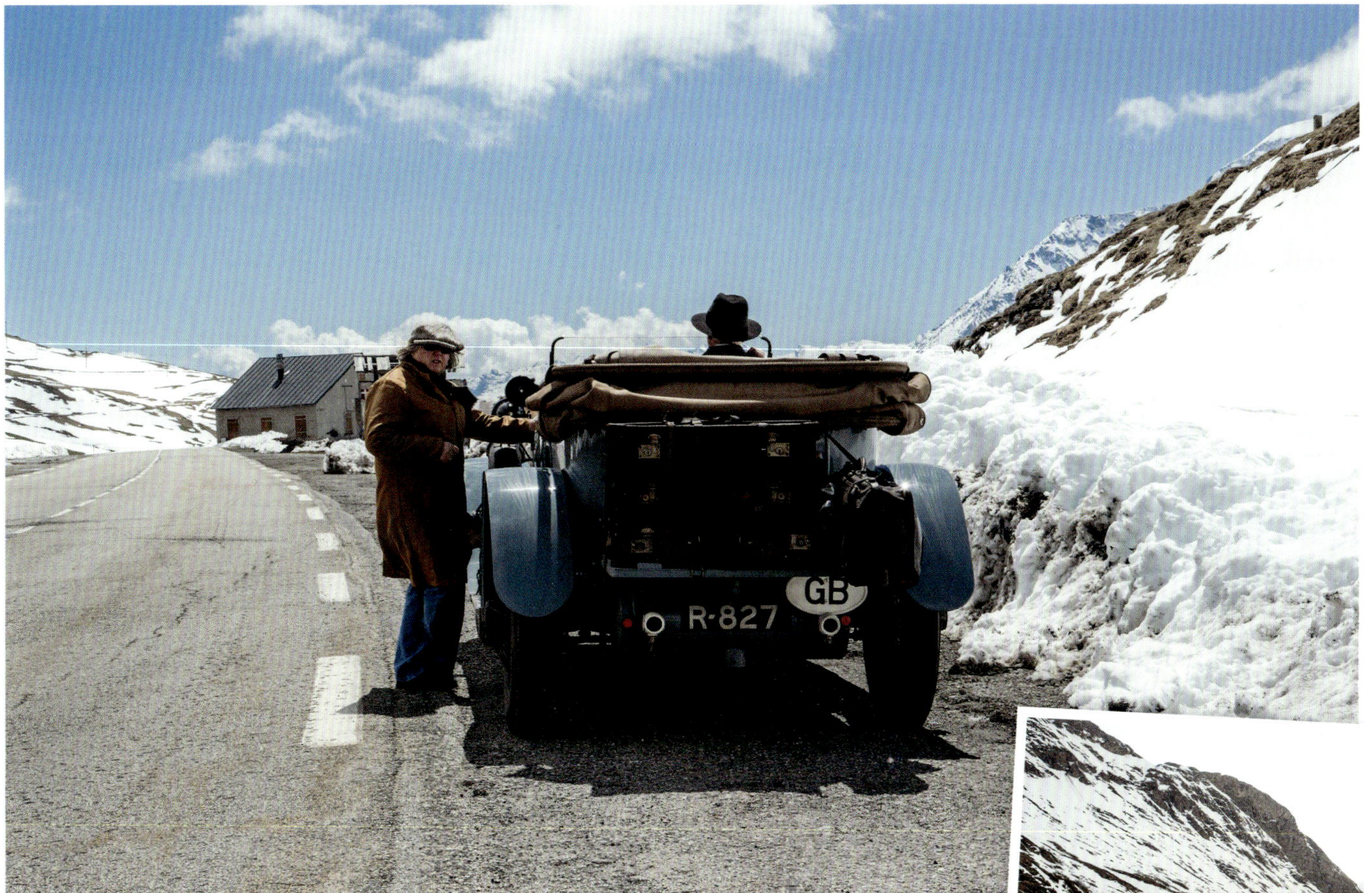

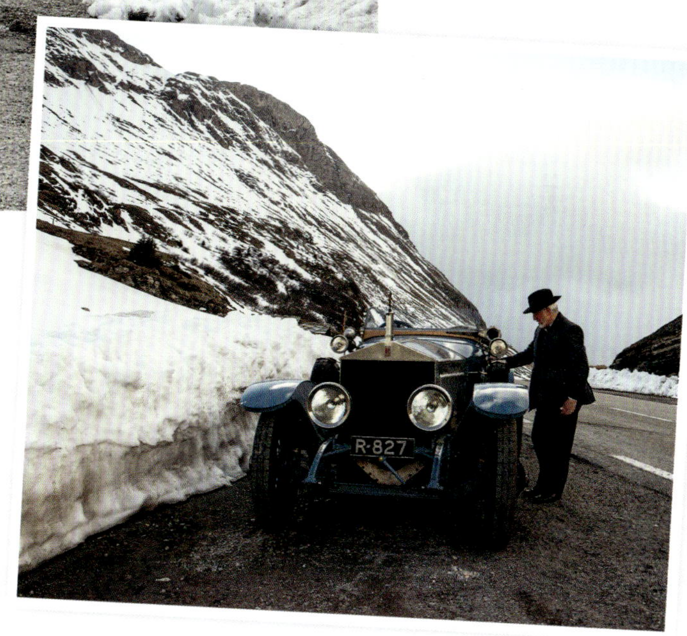

2013

100 years on and the summit (2084 m) has snow banks after the coldest winter for many years.
Inset: A picture taken on the precise centenary of Radley reaching the Mont Cenis Pass.
This became the evidence for the location of the similar picture on the opposite page.

BRESCIA

Italy

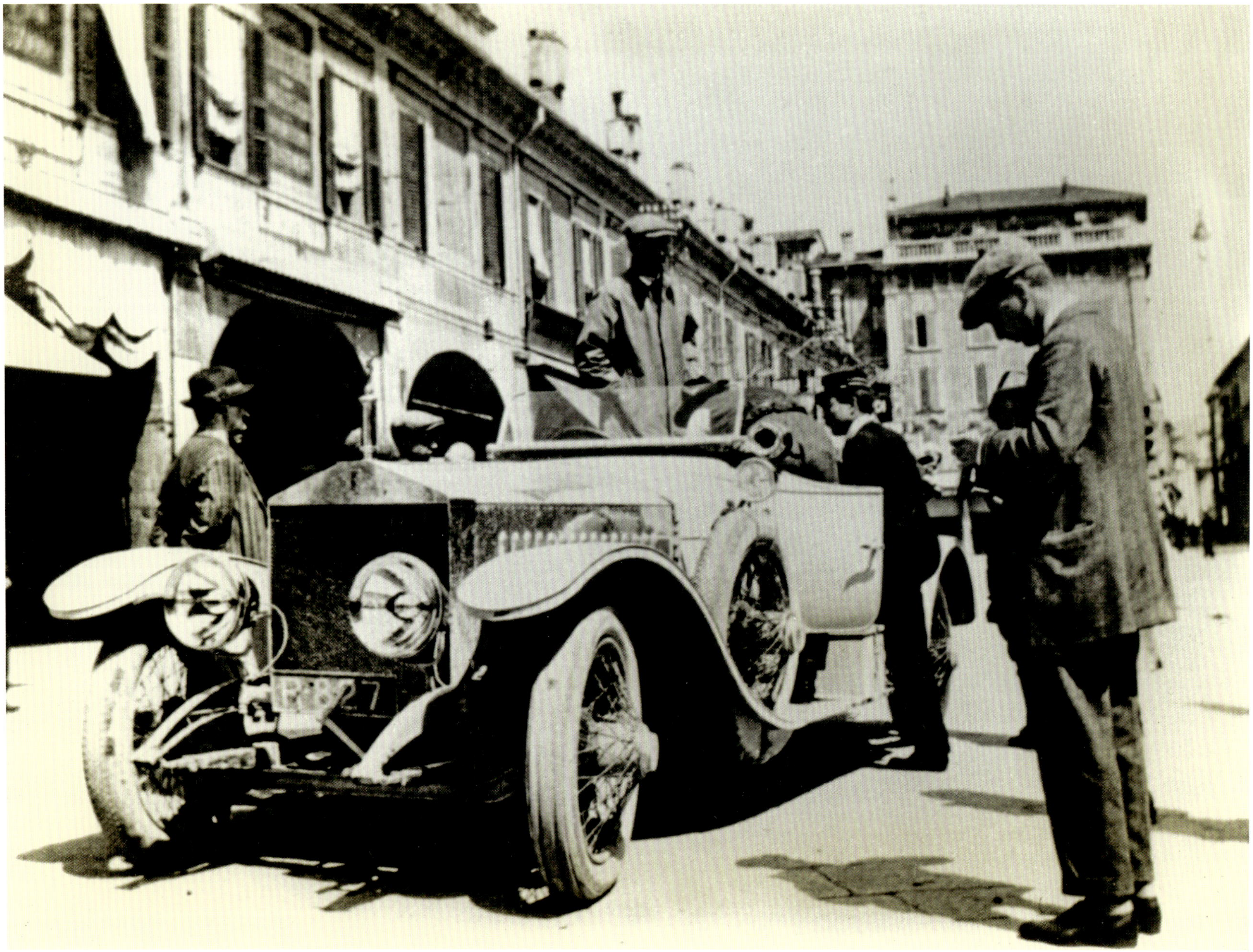

1913

Radley takes a lunchtime break in Corso Zanardelli.

BRESCIA

Italy

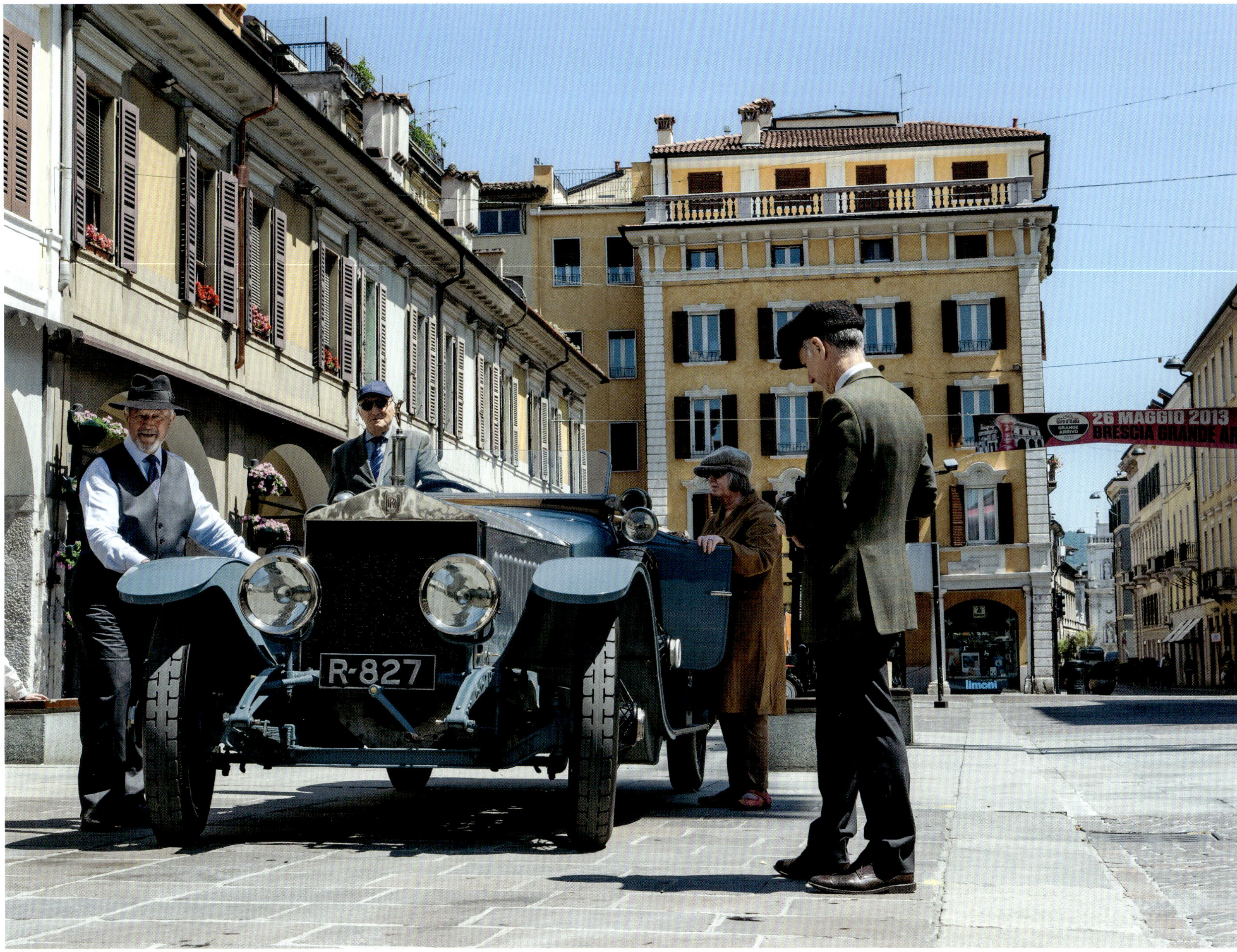

2013

A hundred years on and the buildings in Corso Zanardelli remain unaltered.

LAGO D'IDRO

Italy

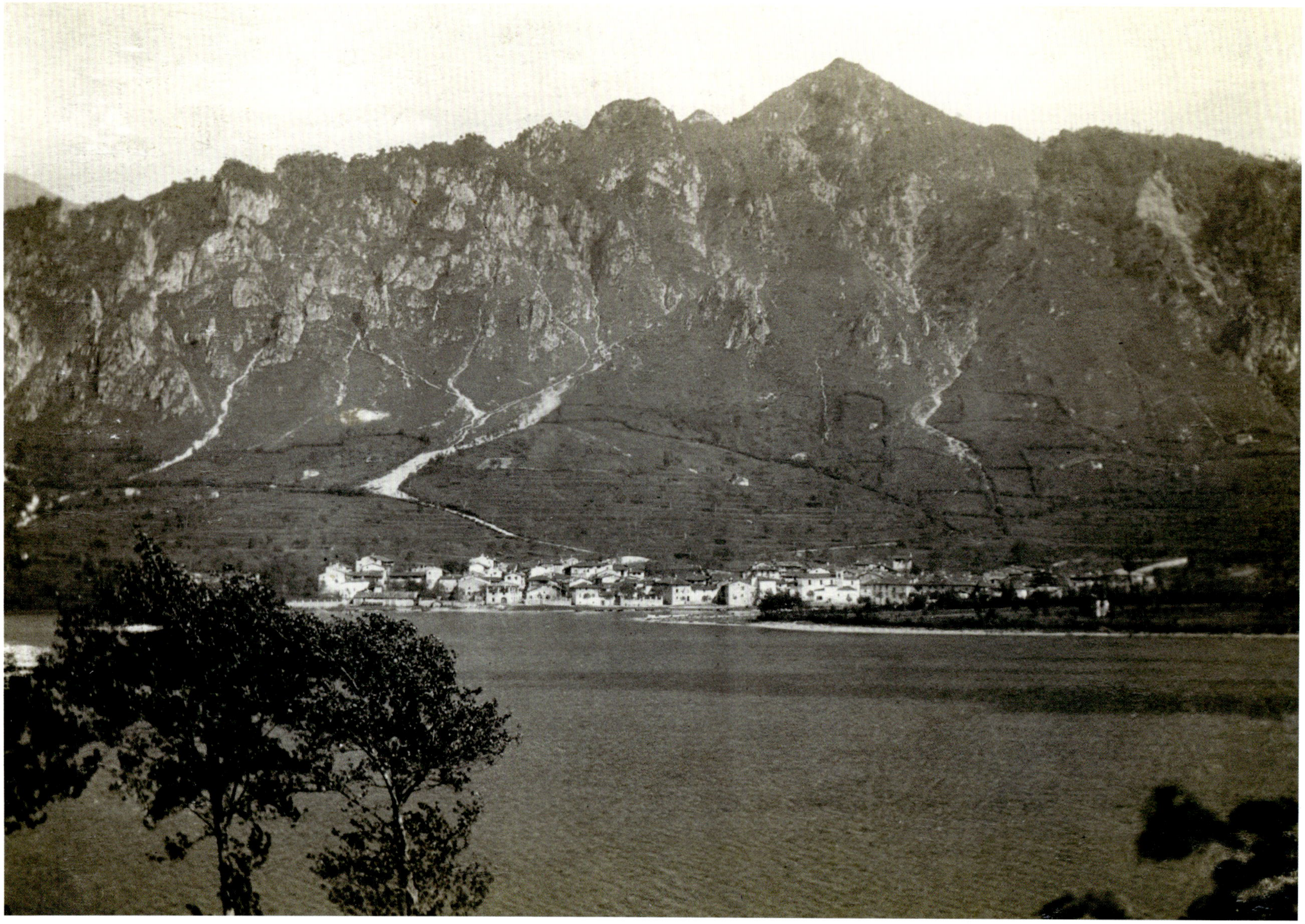

1913

View from the old main road between Brescia & Riva,
looking across Lago d'Idro to the villages of Crone, Idro & Lemprato.

LAGO D'IDRO

Italy

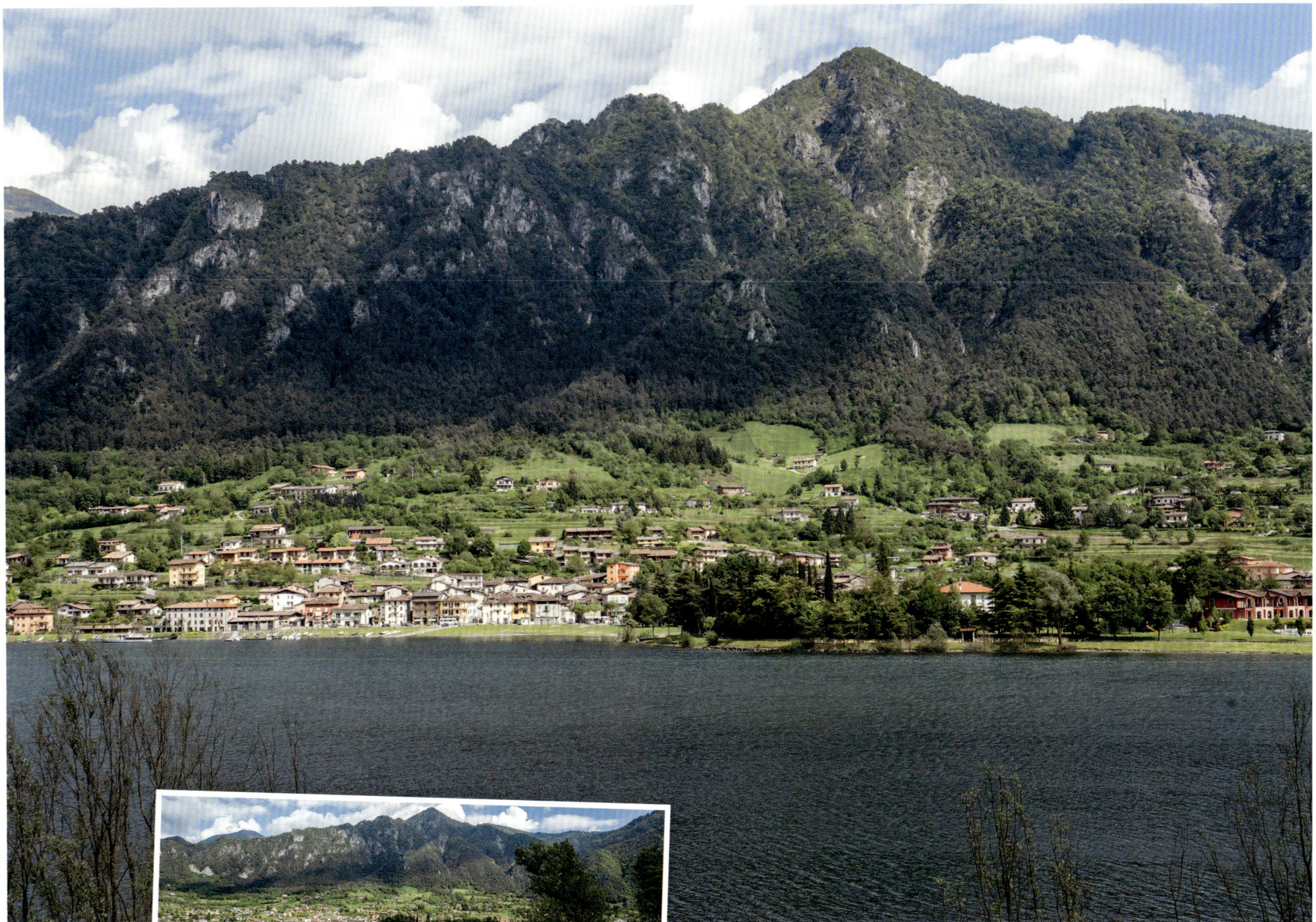

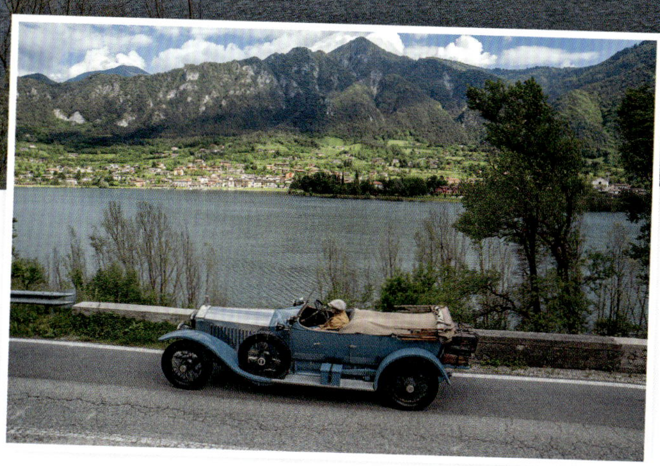

2013

More trees, more houses, the view from the road is otherwise still the same.

LAGO D'IDRO

Italy

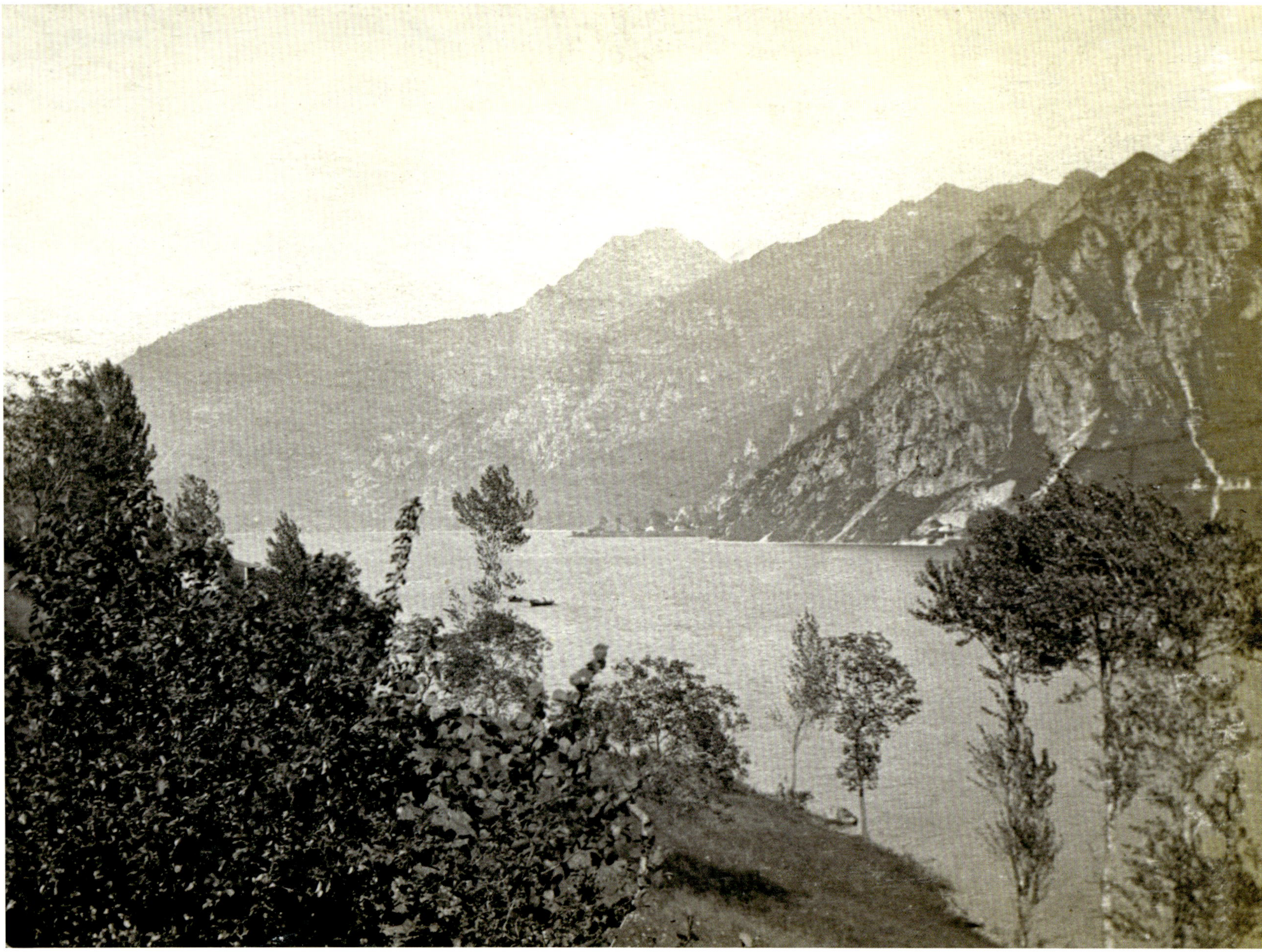

1913

View of Lago d'Idro looking north east, from a point close to where the previous photo was taken.

LAGO D'IDRO

Italy

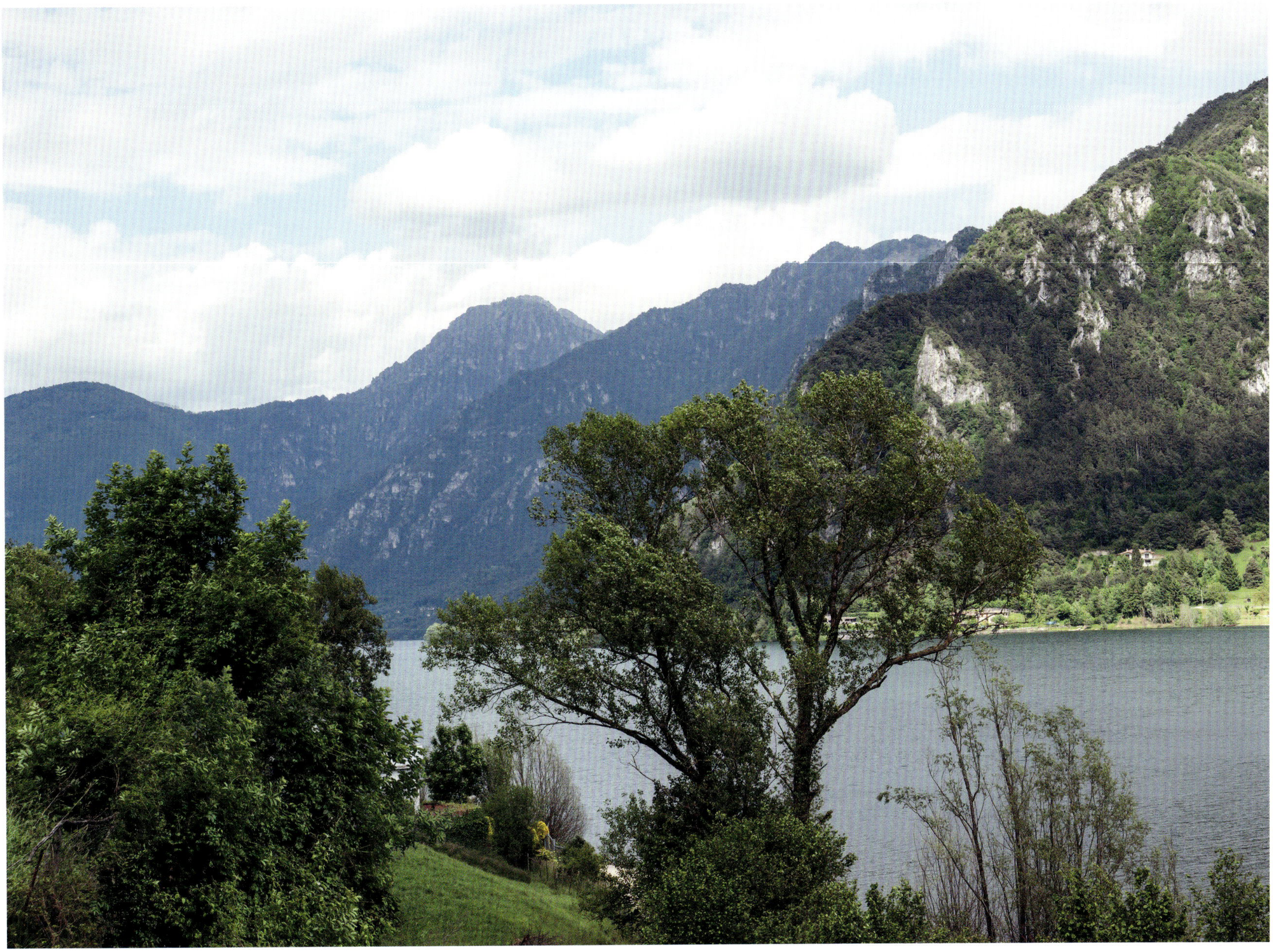

2013

Here again, there are few changes from the 1913 picture.

AMPOLAPASS

Austria

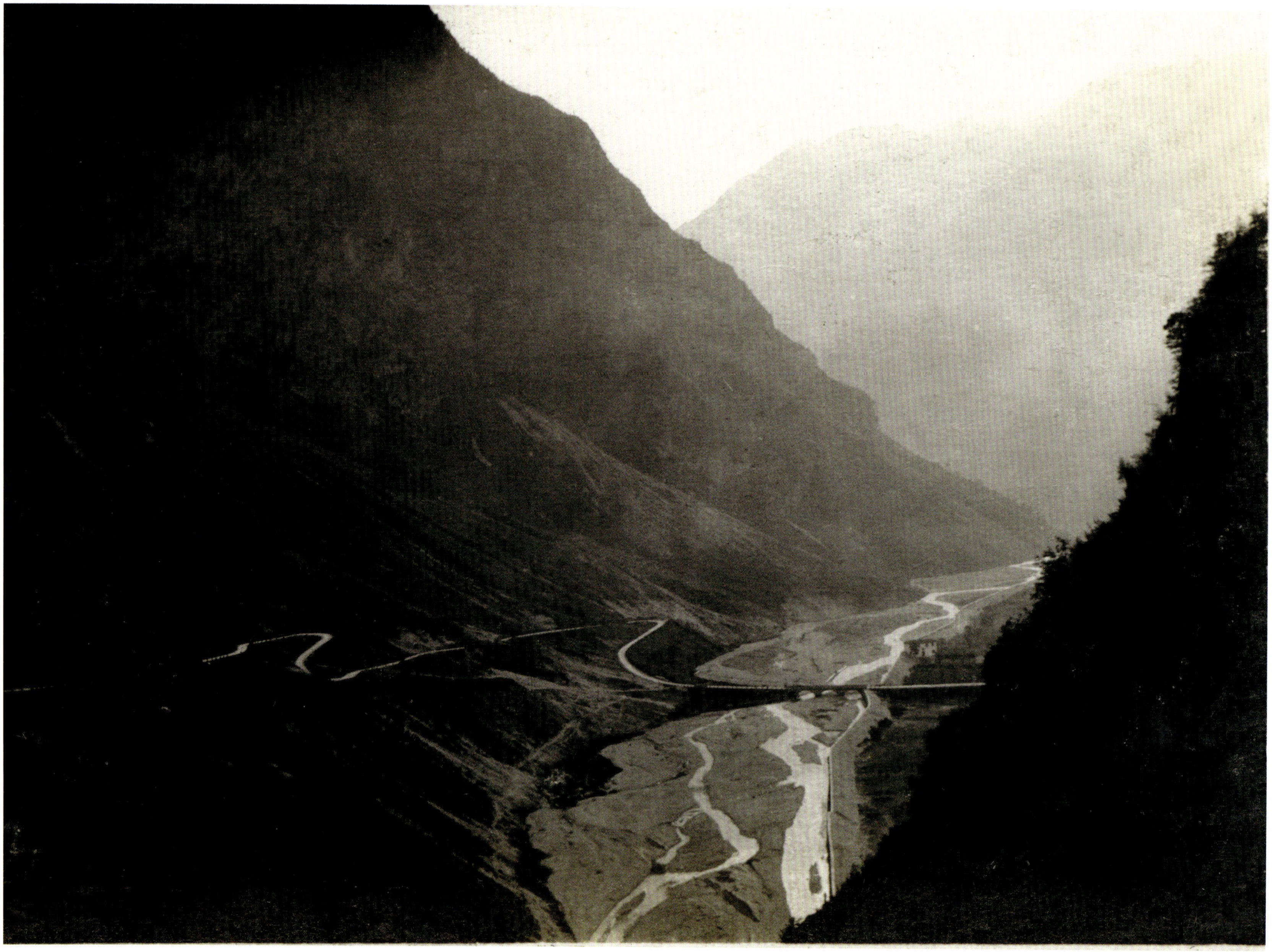

1913

Scenic view in the Ampola valley, looking back down the road to where the climb from Storo commences.

PASSO AMPOLA ROAD

Italy

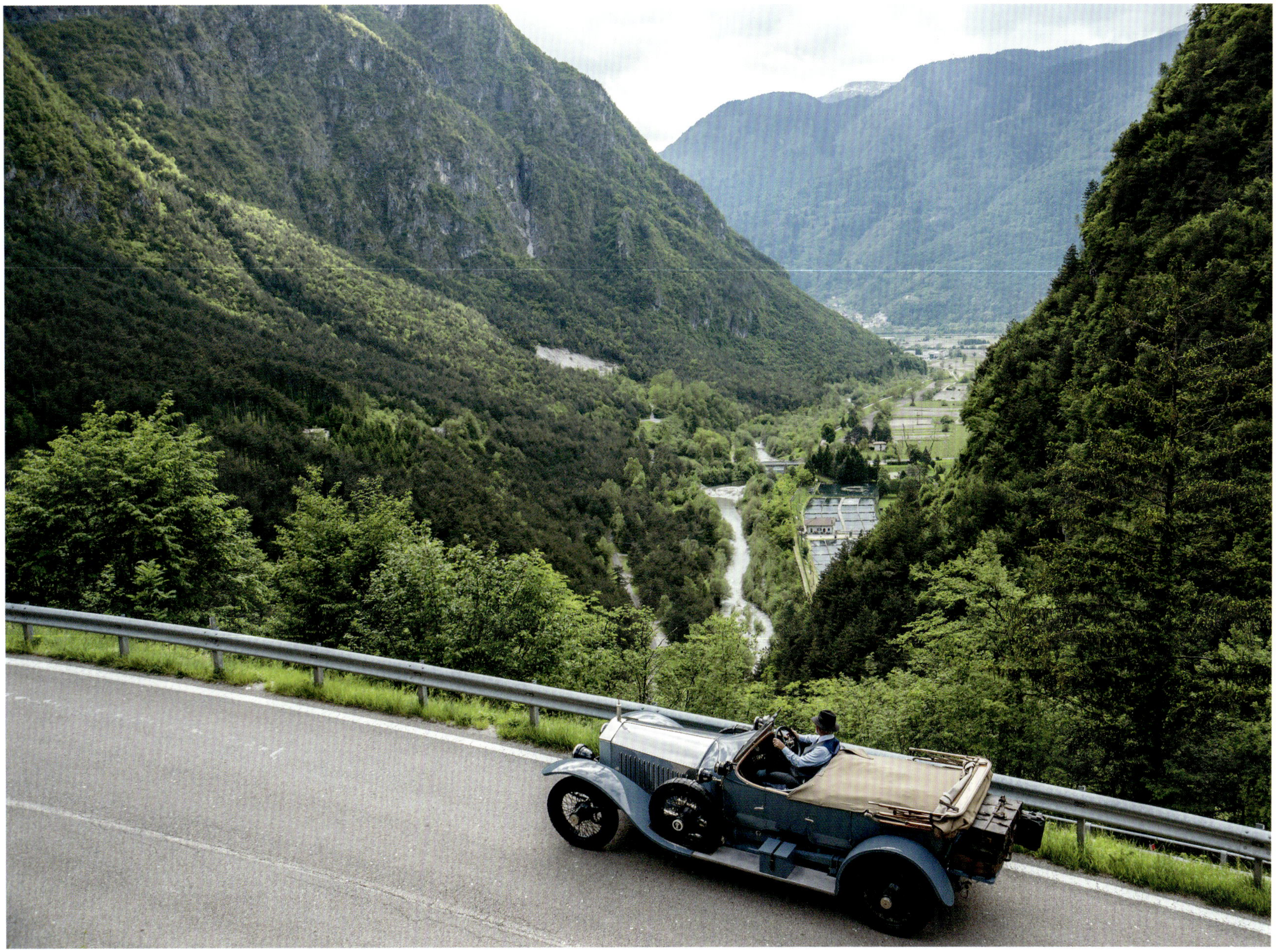

2013

Apart from extra vegetation and a wider road, the climb from Storo remains virtually the same.

THE ROAD TO RIVA

Austria

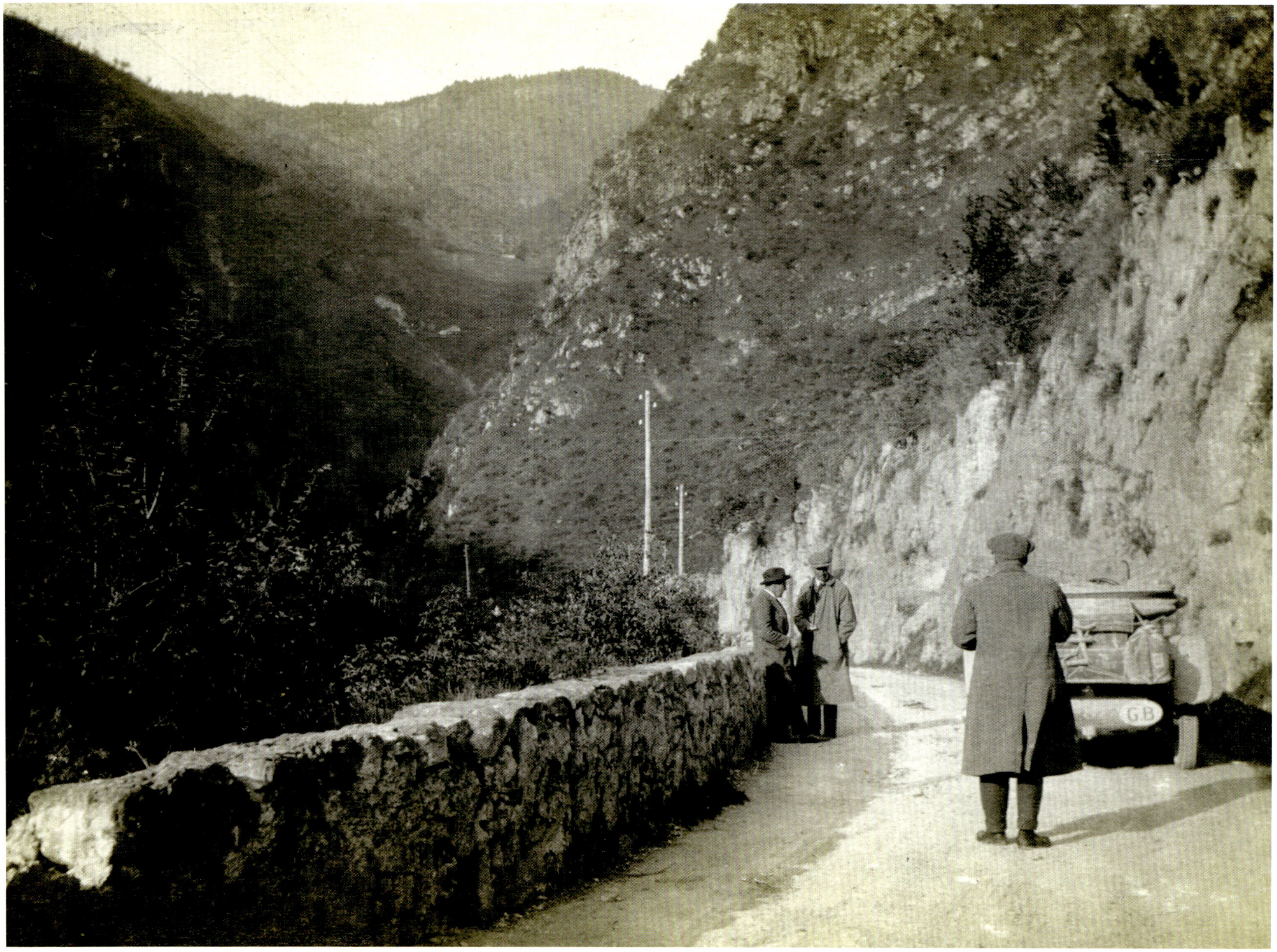

1913

Study of the car from the rear, stopped in the Ampola valley gorge road, a few kilometres to the east of Storo near the Ampola Pass; the sun is shining on the rear of the car which is heading north east towards Riva.

THE ROAD TO RIVA DEL GARDA

Italy

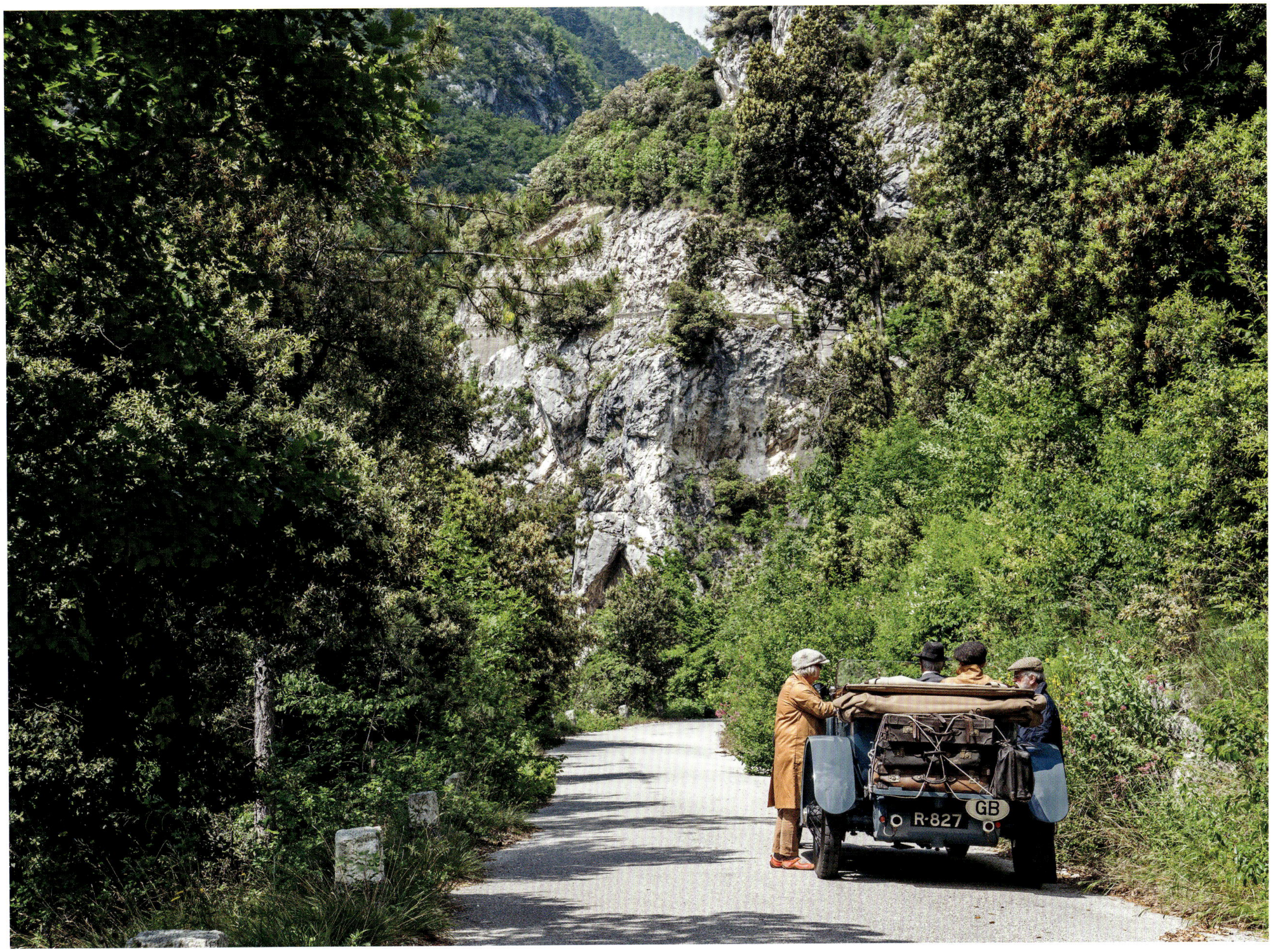

2013

The Passo Ampola road is still narrow but very busy, making it impossible to stop in the gorge. The now closed part of the route provides the ideal location to repeat the early picture.

AMPOLAPASS WATERFALL

Austria

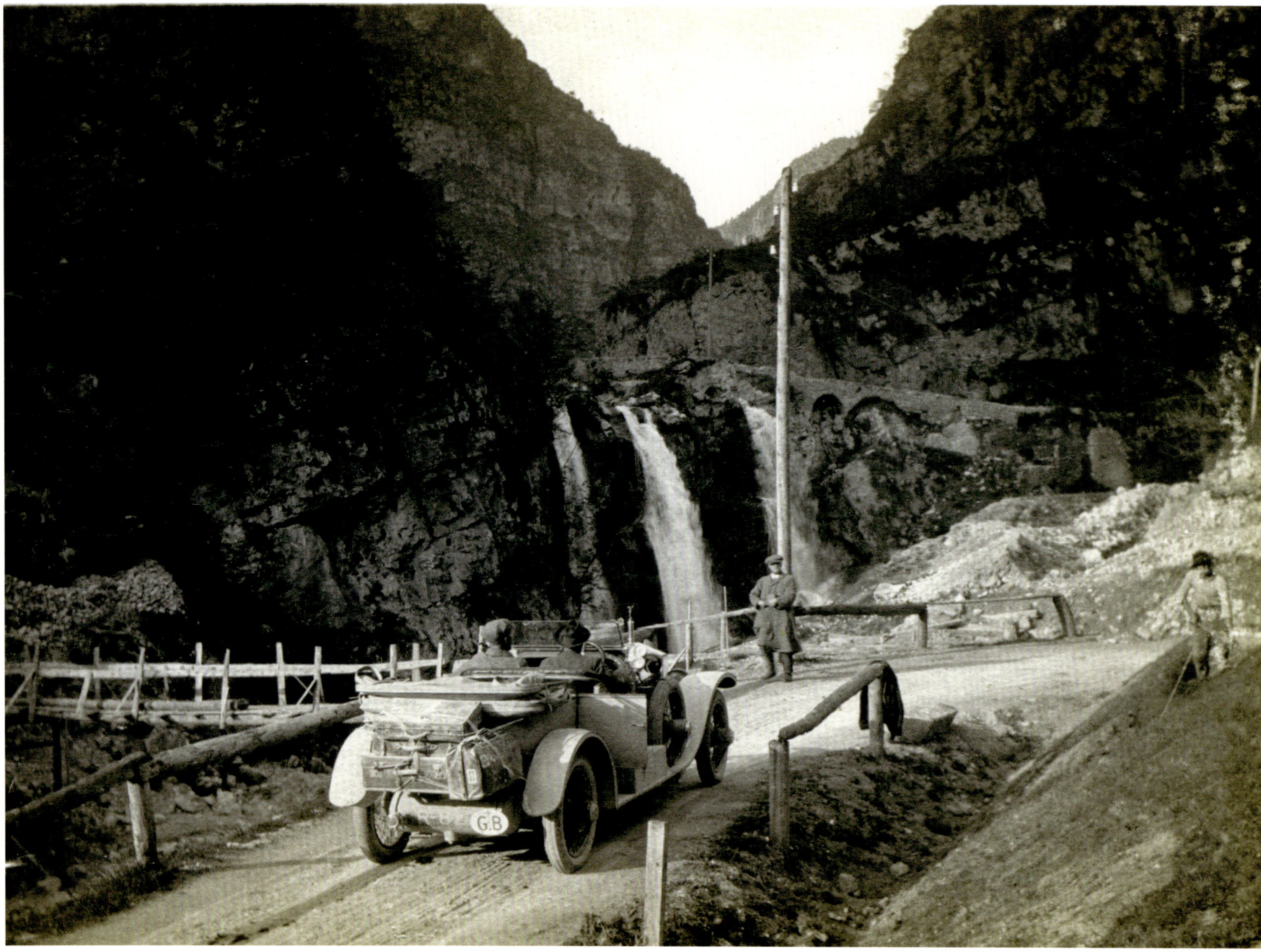

1913

Radley and co-driver pause in the car at a waterfall near the summit of the Ampola Pass (747 m). which commences a kilometre to the east of Storo.

PASSO AMPOLA WATERFALL

Italy

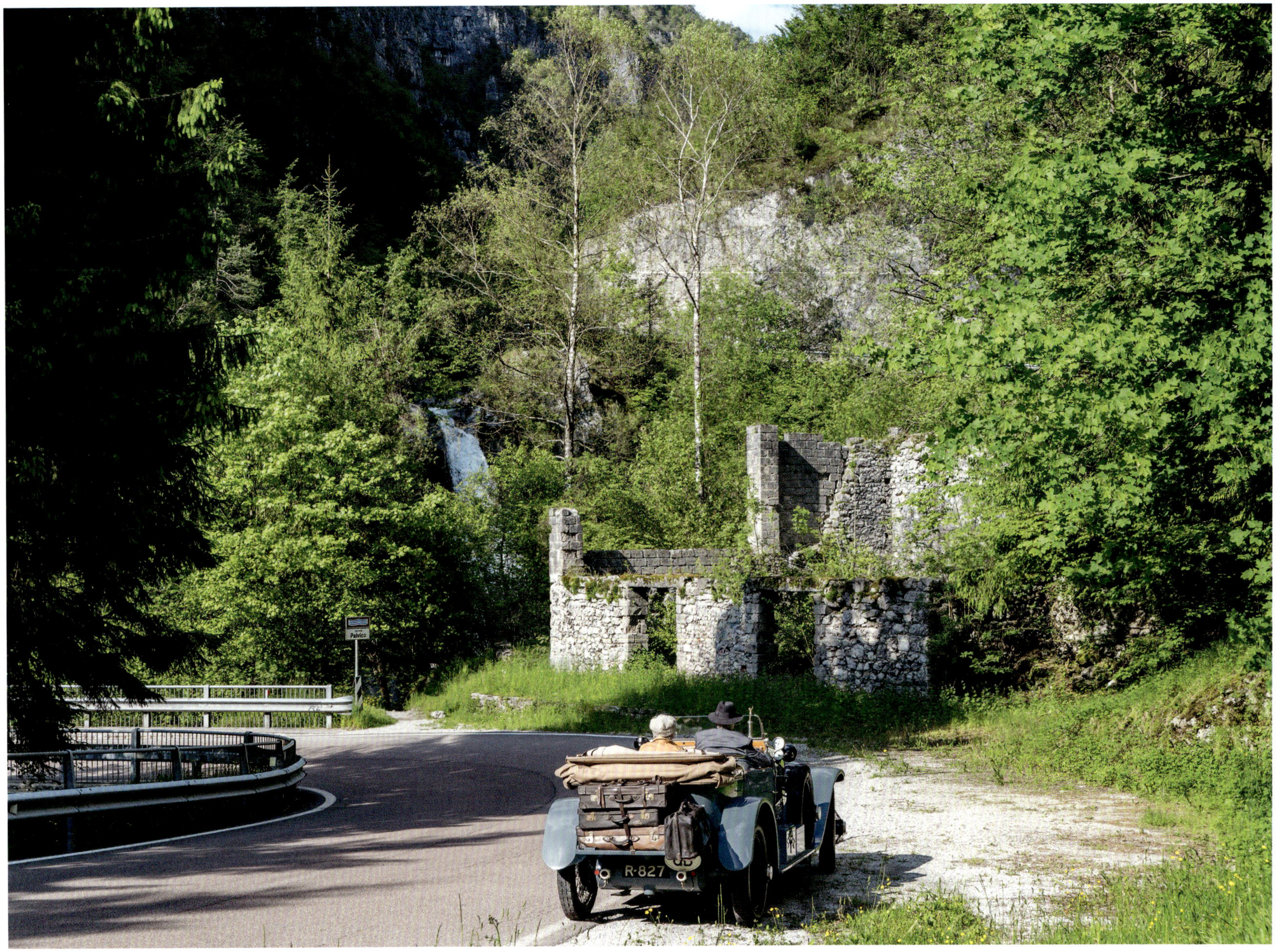

2013

The road crosses the gorge in the same location as the rickety wooden structure in the early picture.
The ruin in front of the car was built after 1913.

PONALE TUNNEL

Austria

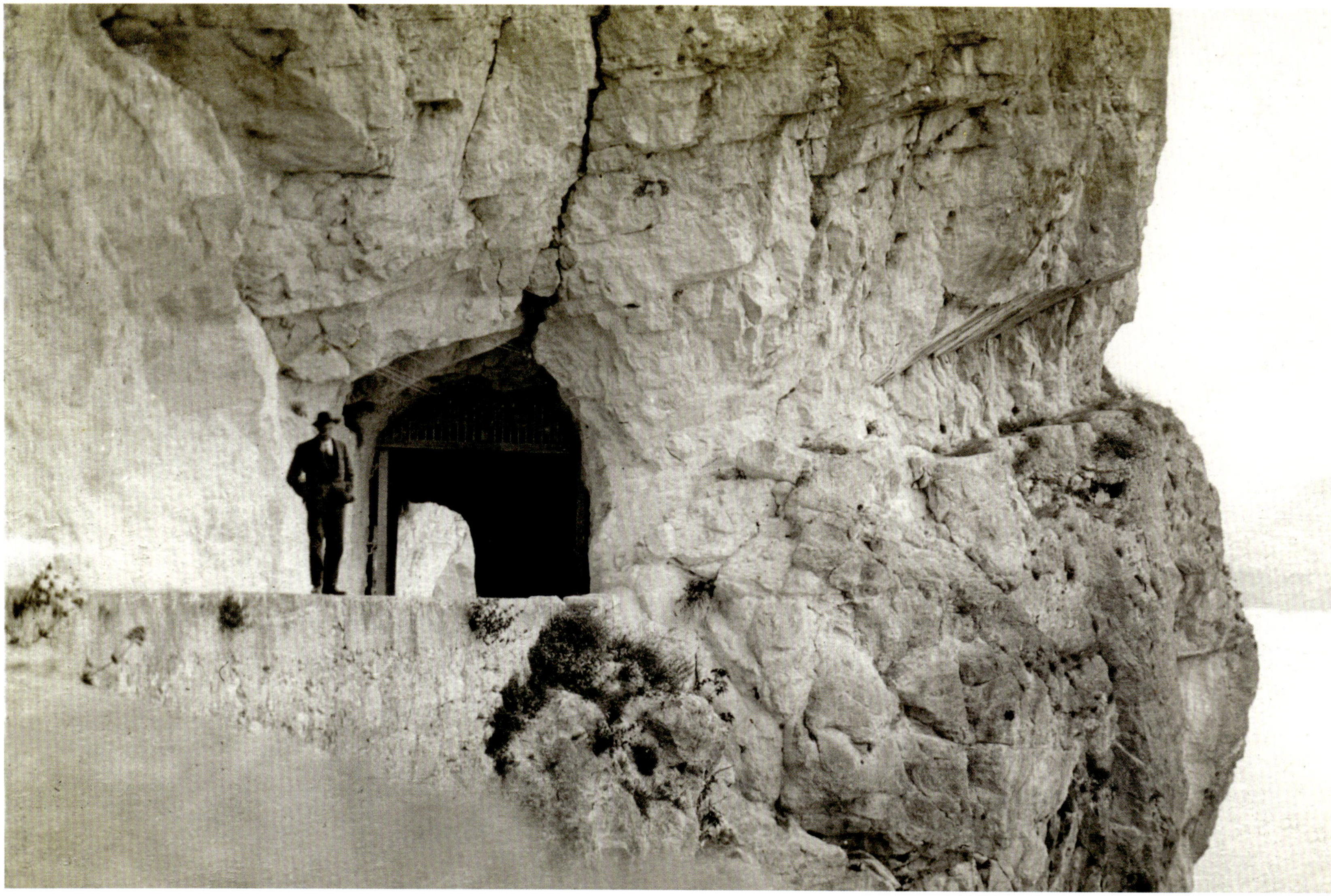

1913

Radley poses at one of the unlined rock tunnels on the famous Ponale corniche road to Riva. From where he stands, there is a sheer drop of some 200 metres to Lake Garda.

PONALE TUNNEL

Italy

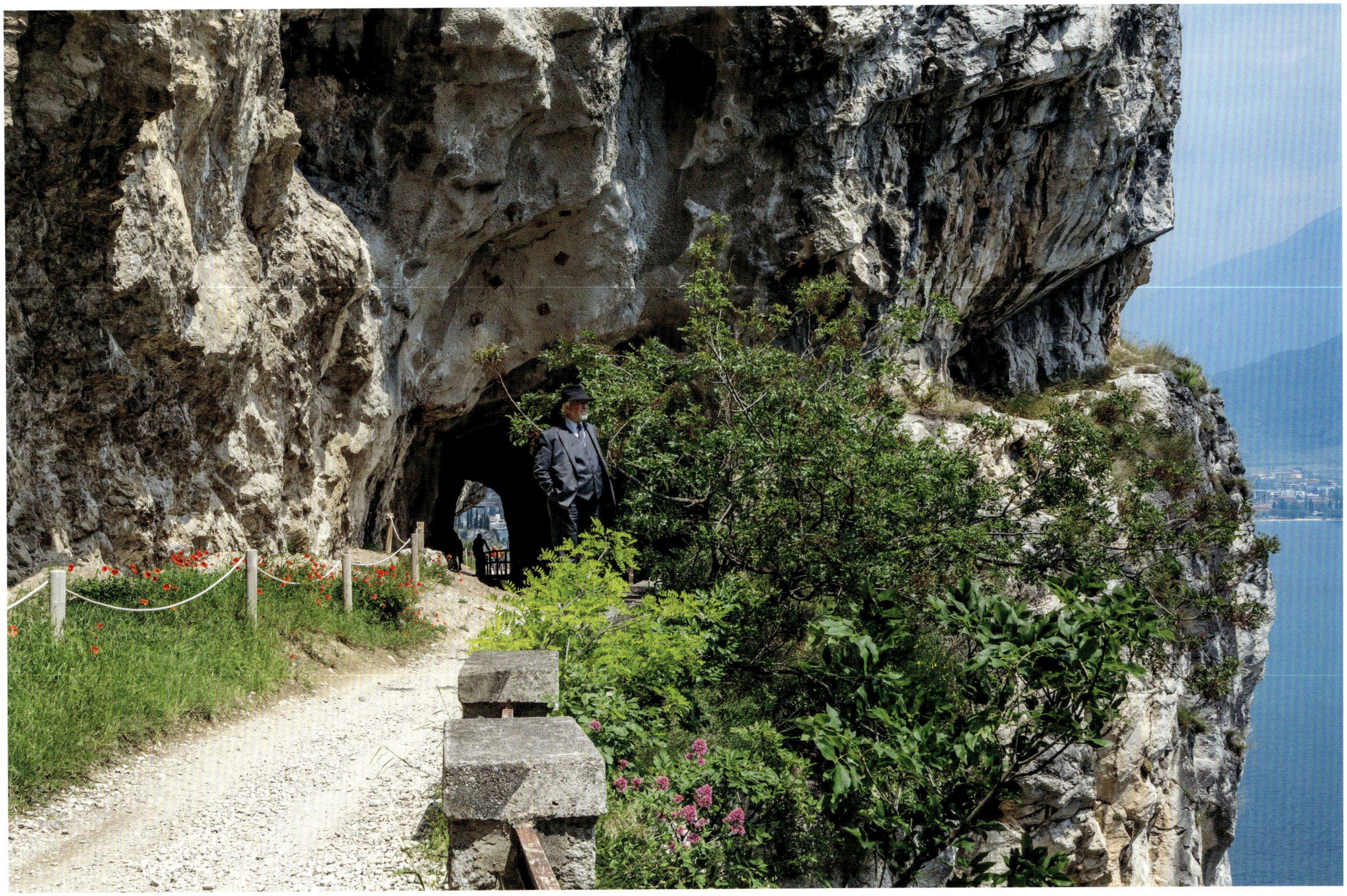

2013

The tunnel was subsequently widened and the road is now closed to motor traffic but used by walkers and mountain bikers.

PONALESTRASSE

Austria

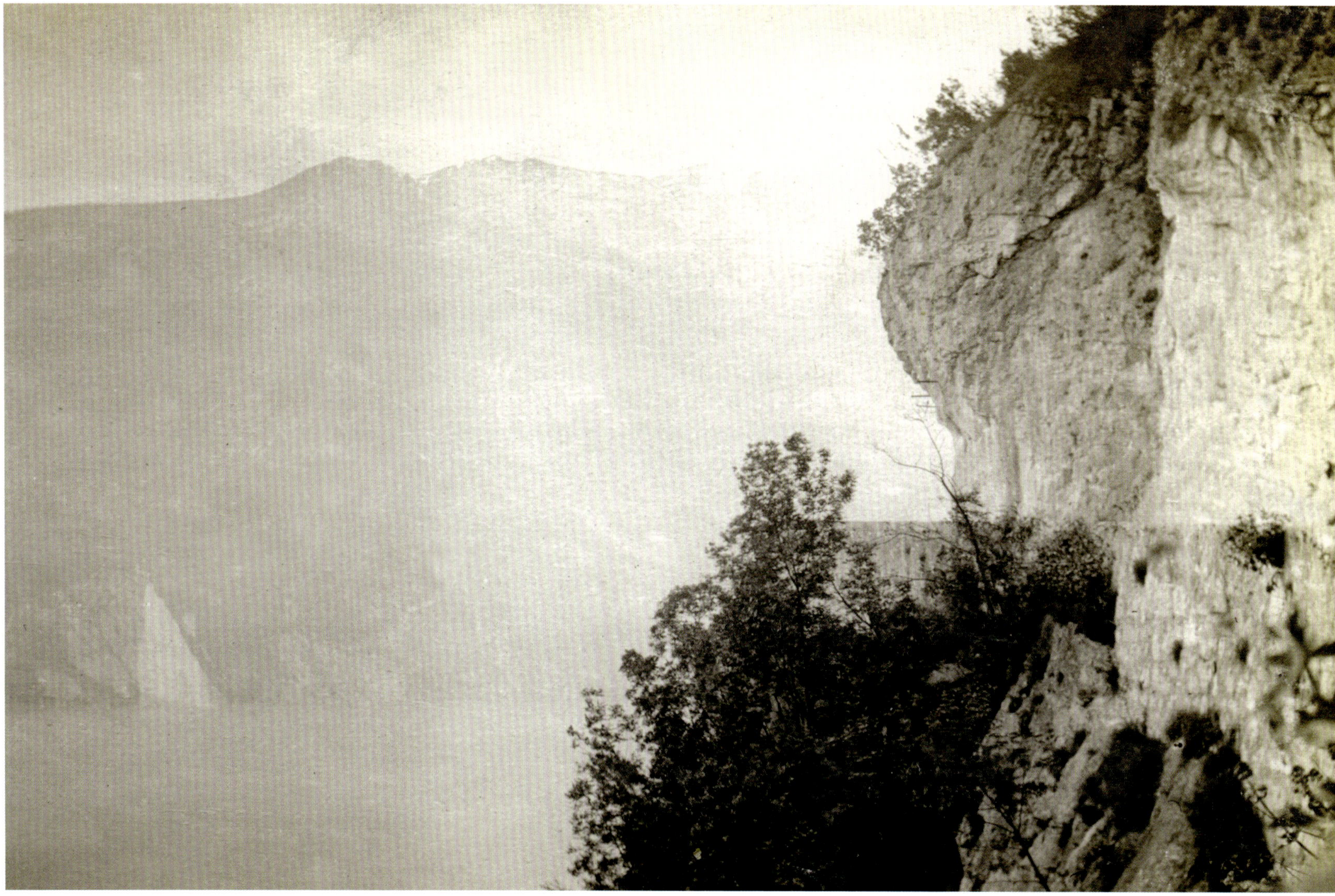

1913

View on the Ponale road taken from the same location
as the picture on the previous page but looking back up the road.

STRADA DEL PONALE

Italy

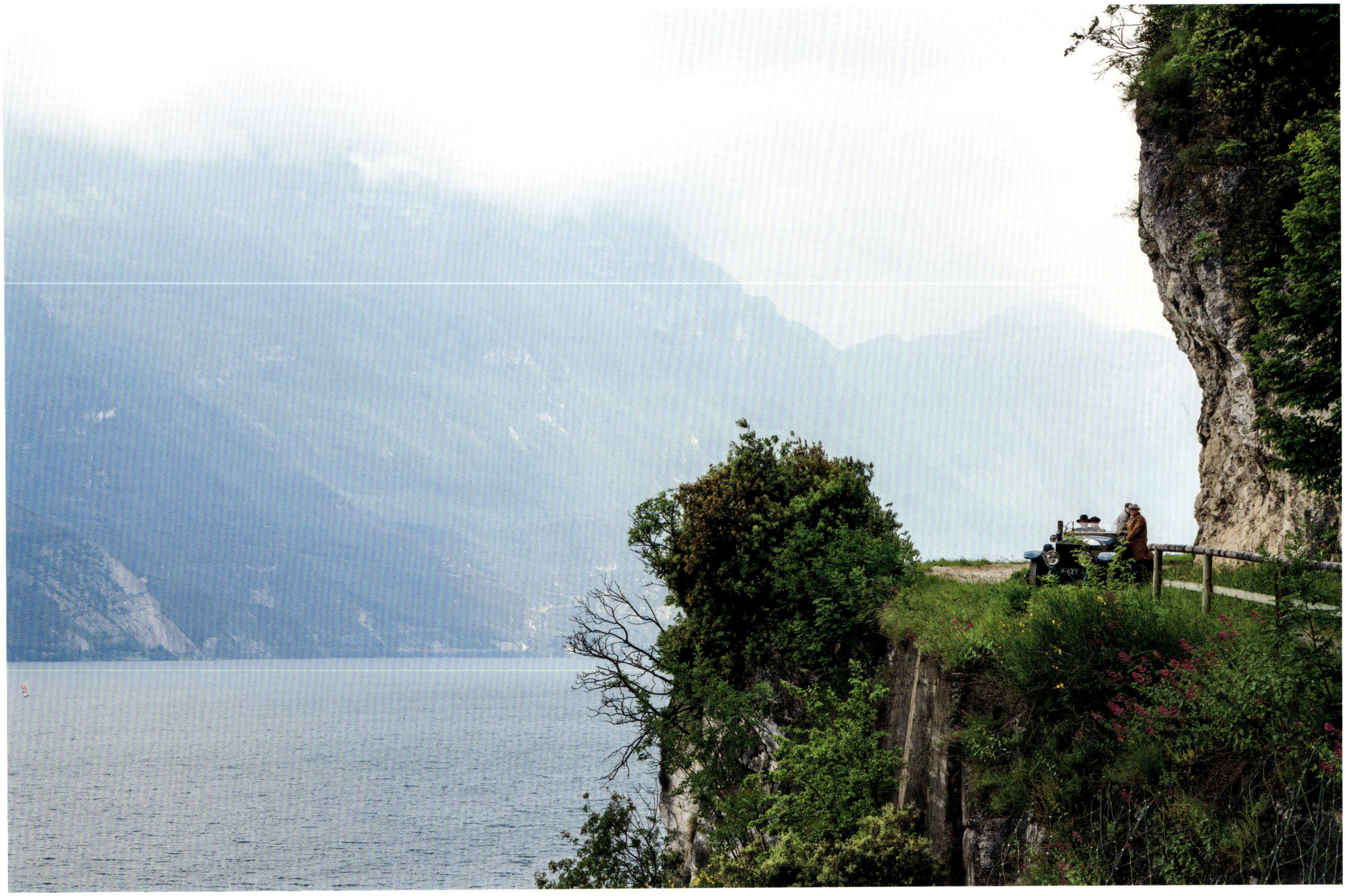

2013

The steep cliff has been cut back but the closed road again welcomes the Radley car on its centenary journey.

RIVA

Austria

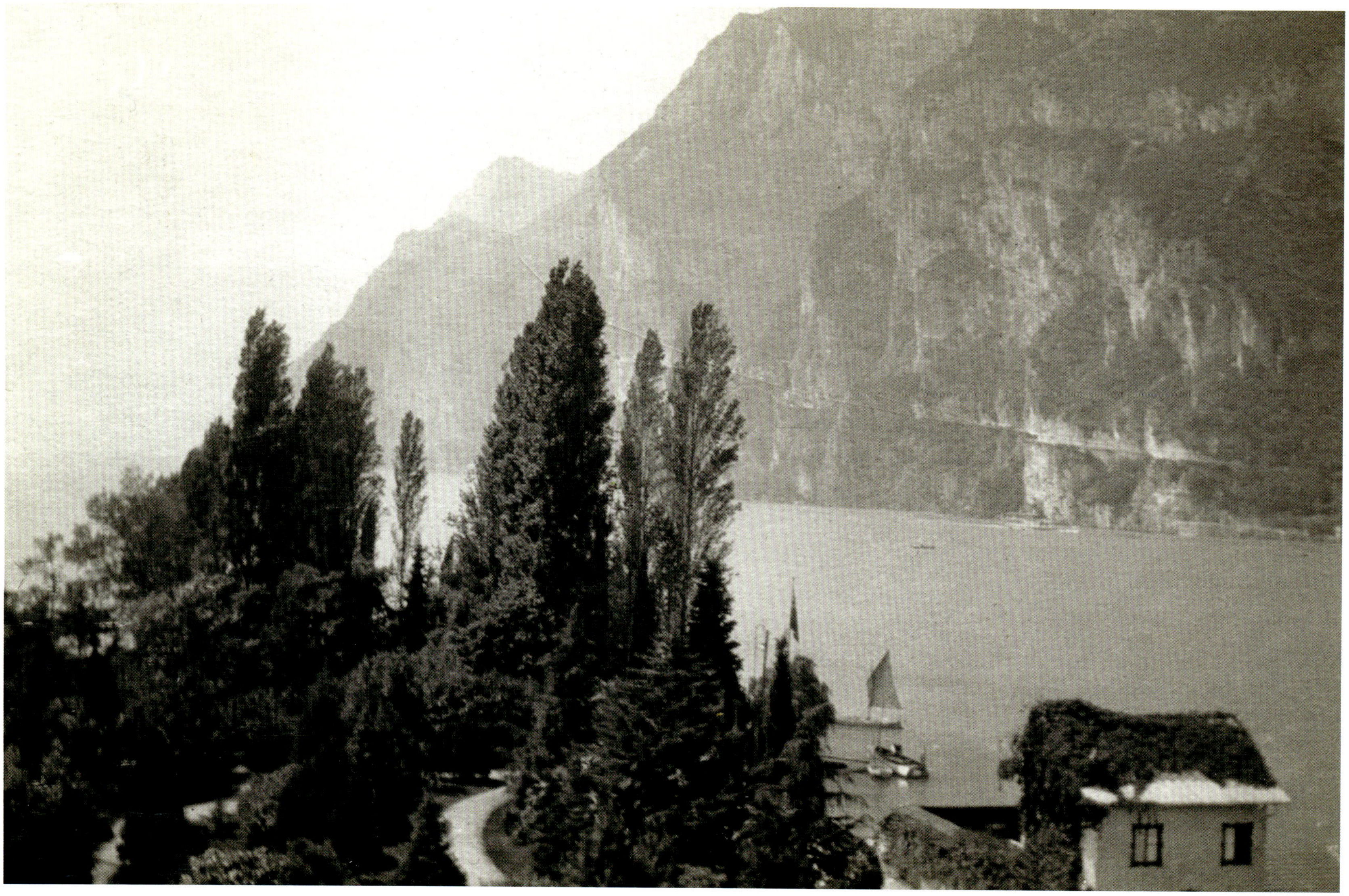

1913

Lago di Garda viewed from the Lido Palace Hotel.
Two variants of this picture have not been shown.

RIVA DEL GARDA

Italy

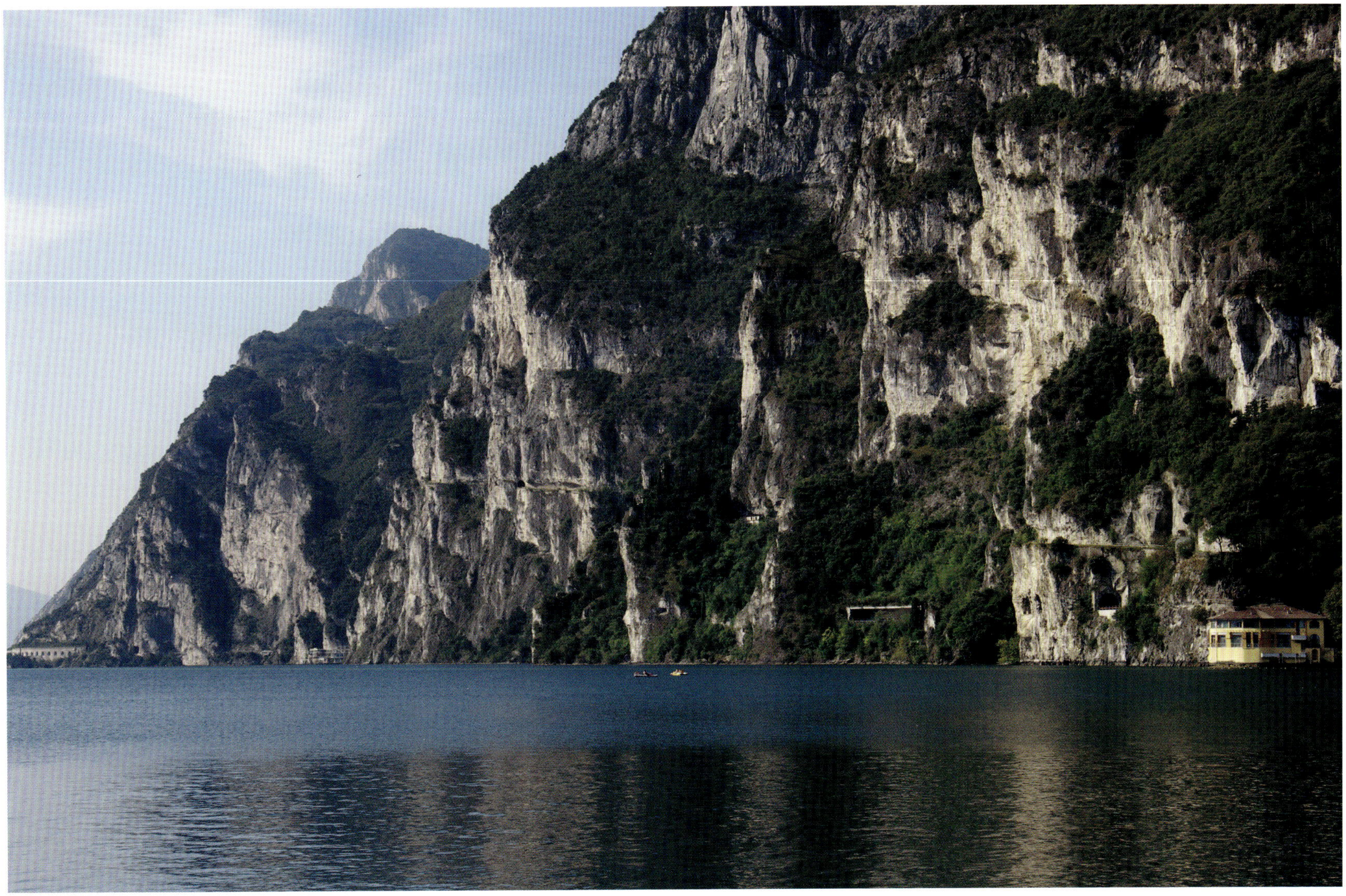

2013

Taller trees now partially obscure the view from the Lido Palace.
The view across to the Ponale corniche remains clearly visible.

RIVA

Austria

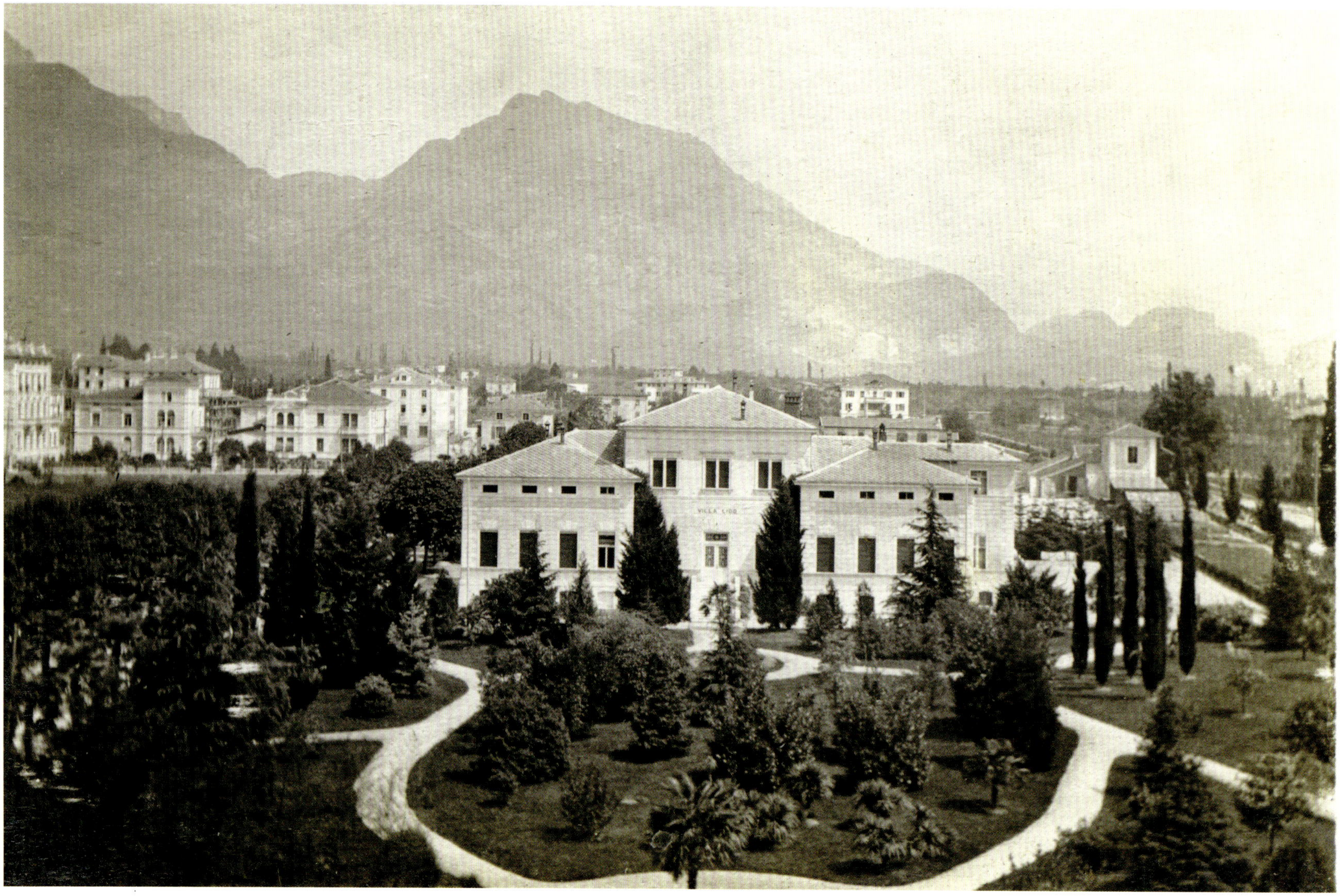

1913

Villa Lido from Lido Palace Hotel

RIVA DEL GARDA

Italy

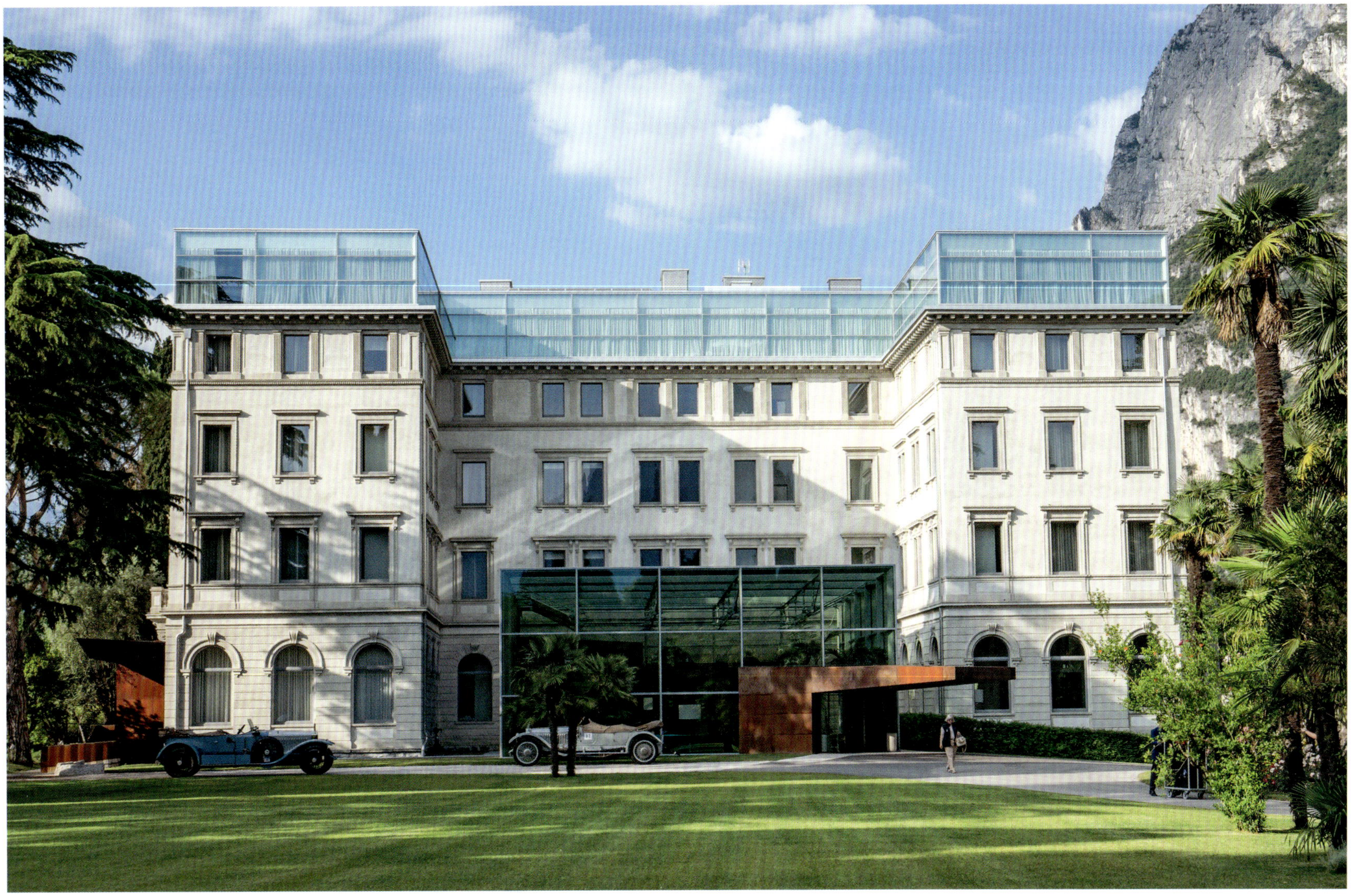

2013

Lido Palace Hotel

CASTEL TOBLINO

Austria

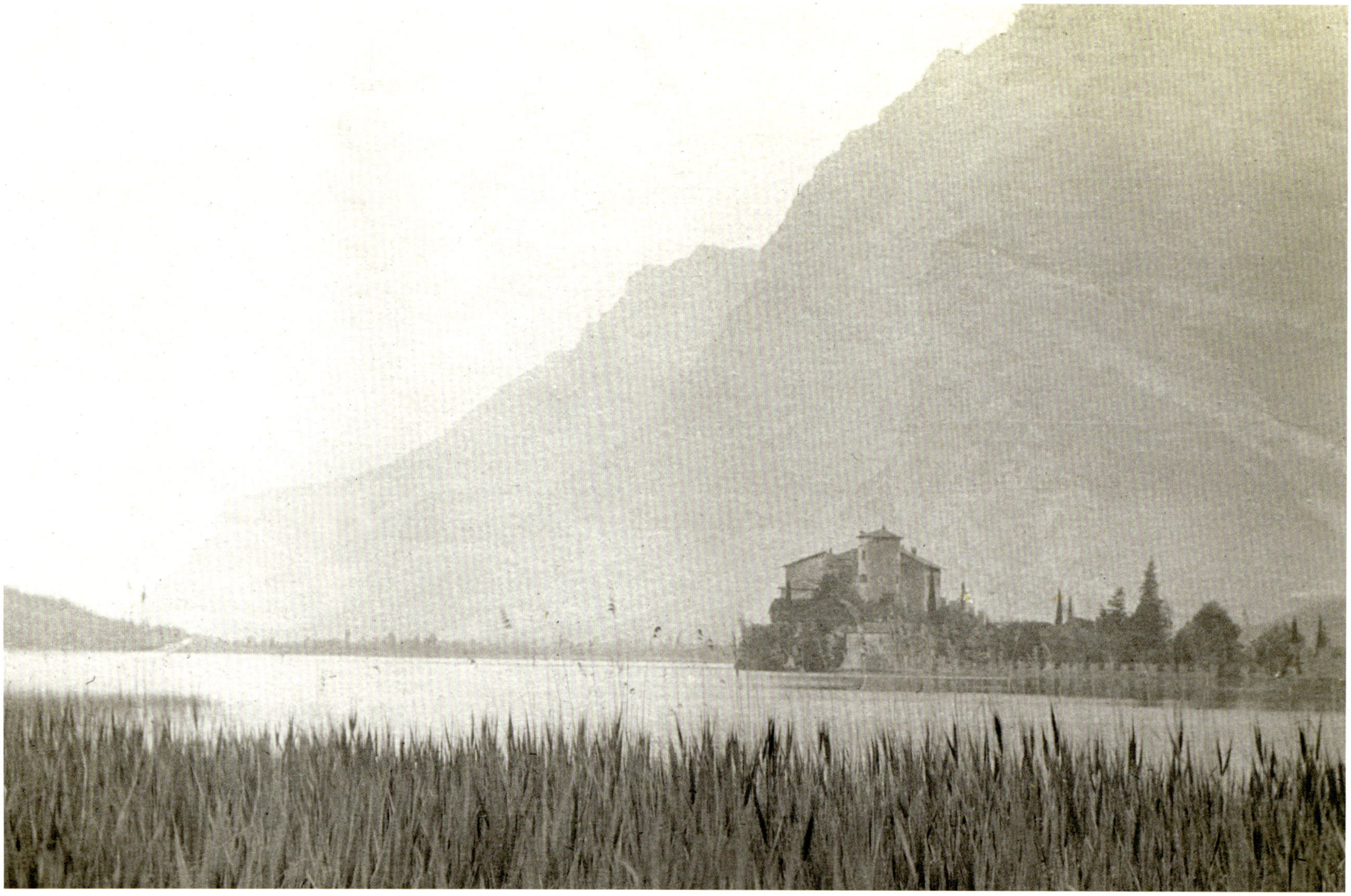

1913

The Alpenfahrt route passes the peaceful setting of Castel Toblino, north of Riva.

CASTEL TOBLINO

Italy

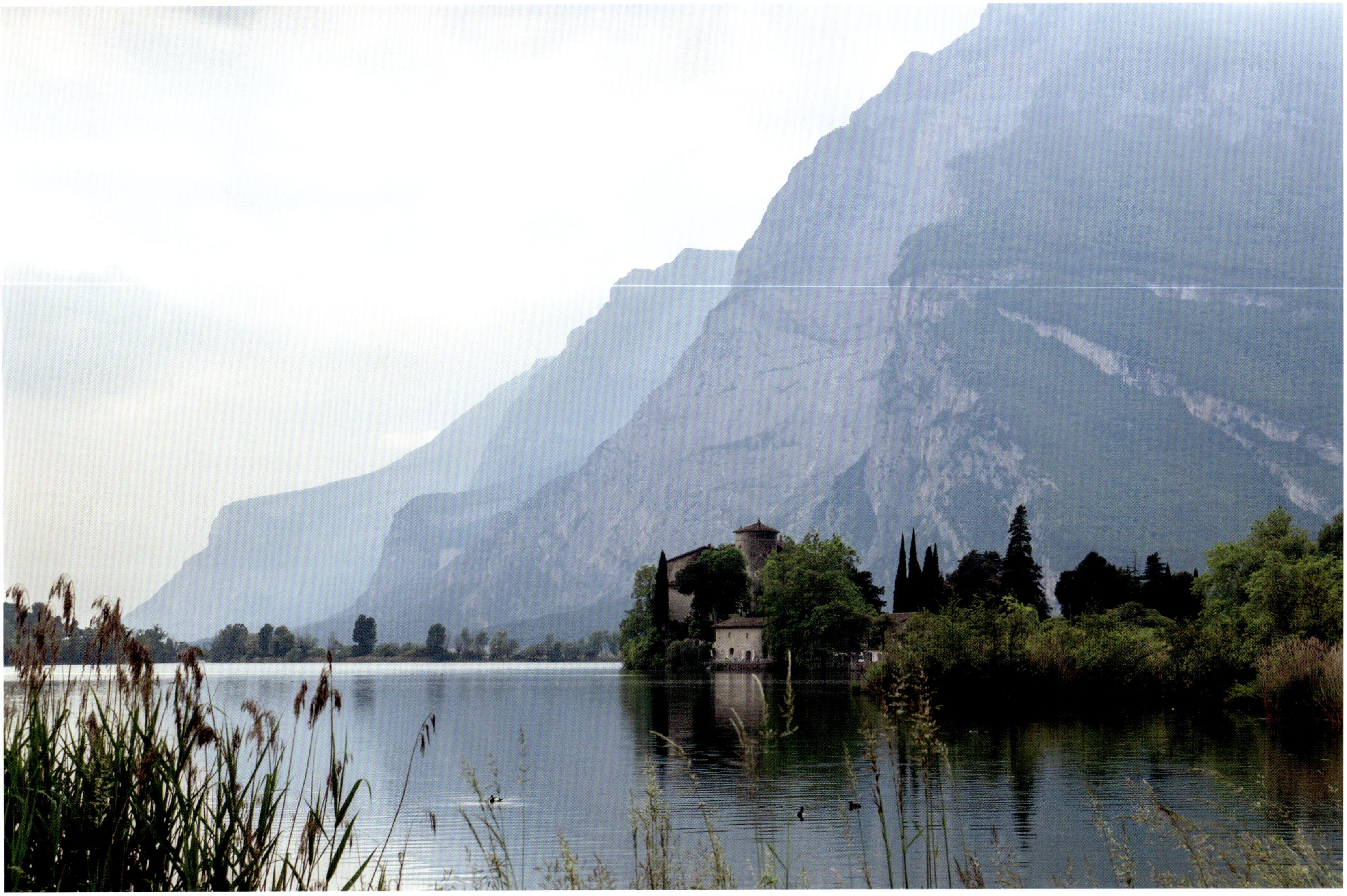

2013

A century on and Castel Toblino has become a luxury restaurant, but the view remains identical.

MORI

Austria

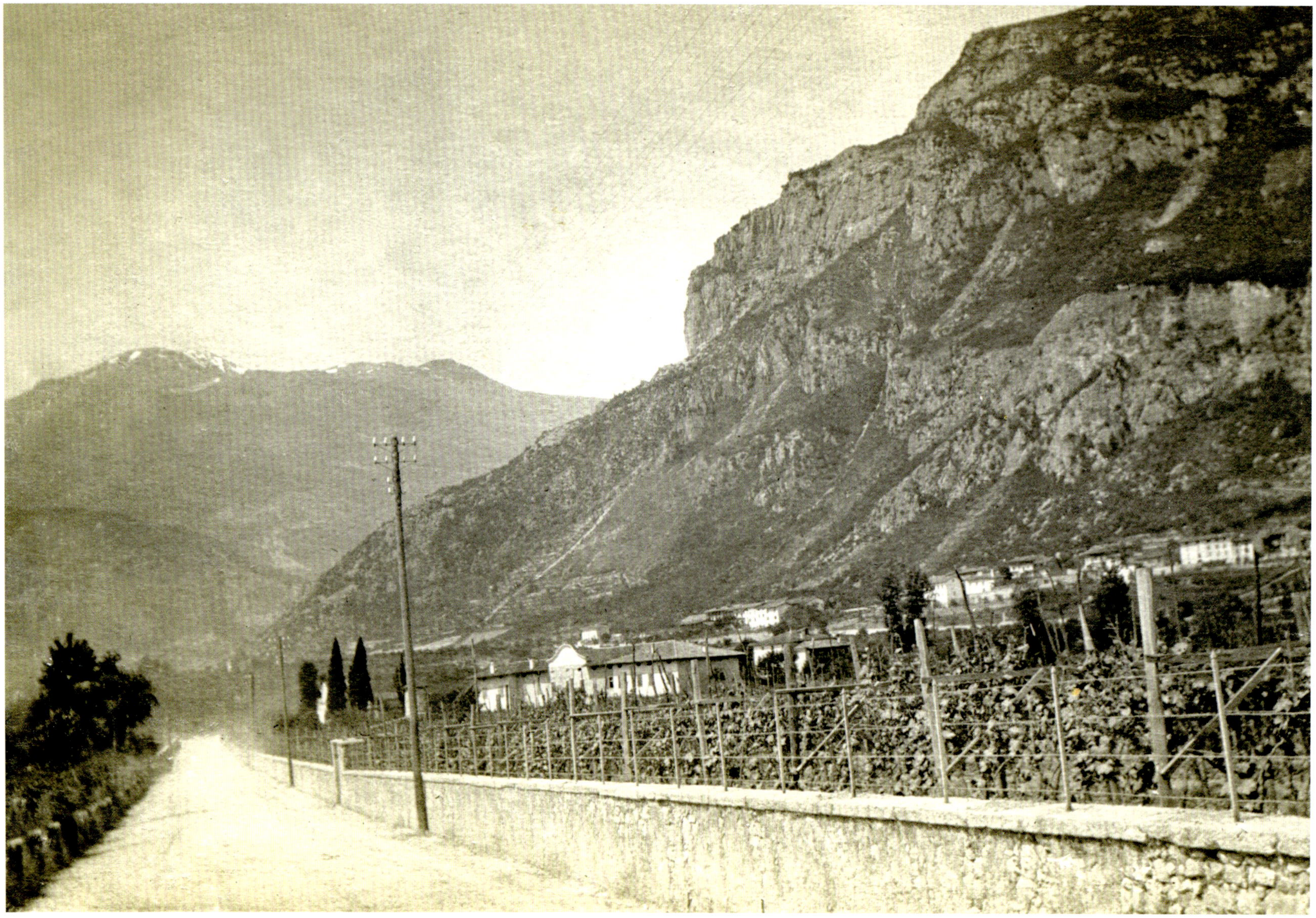

1913

On the road from Riva to Rovereto then north to the Dolomites,
while waiting for trains at the level crossing.

MORI

Italy

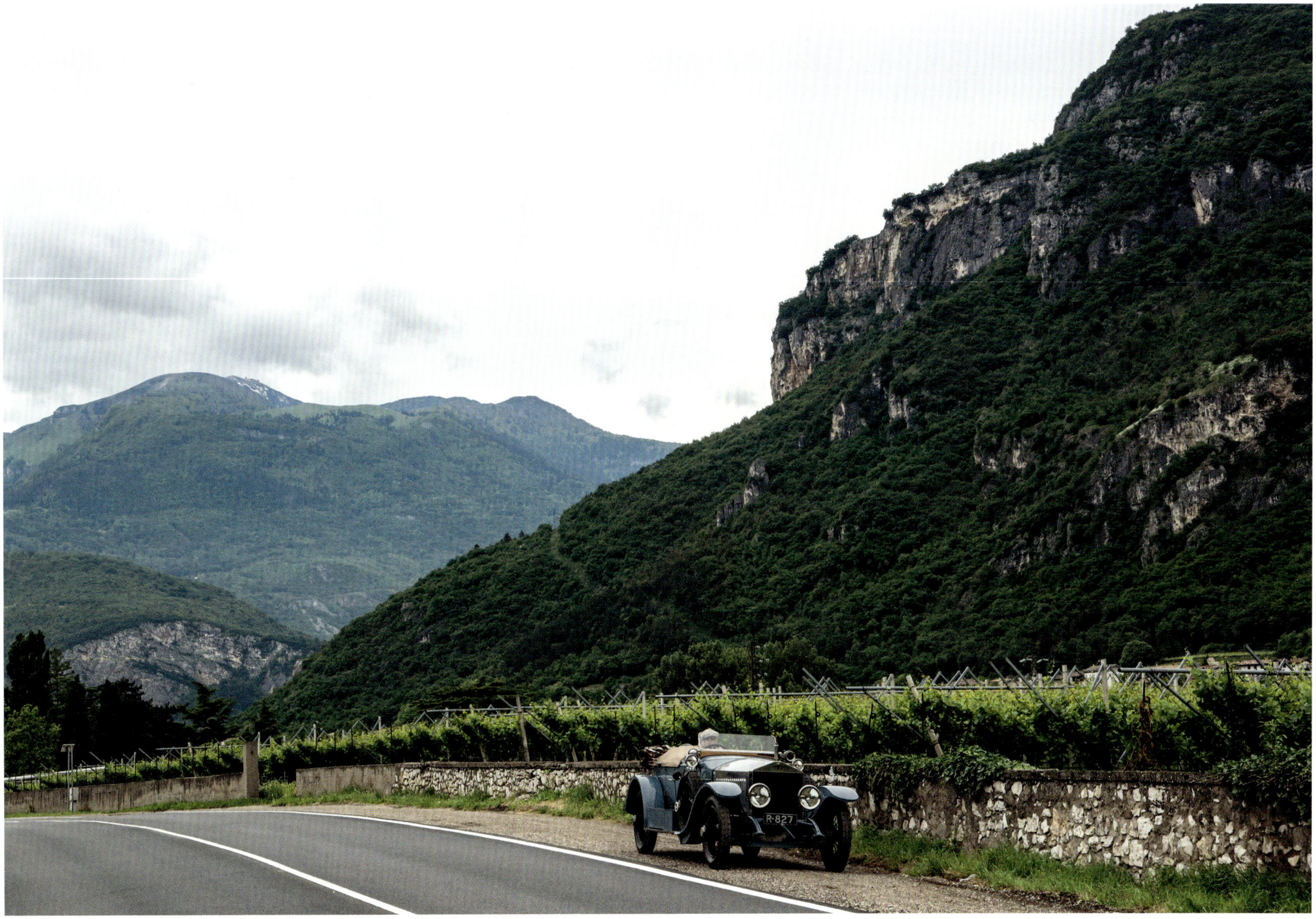

2013

The road has been realigned as there is now an Autostrada just beyond the vines.
The level crossing here has been replaced by a subway.

TRIENT / TRENTO ROAD

Austria / Italy

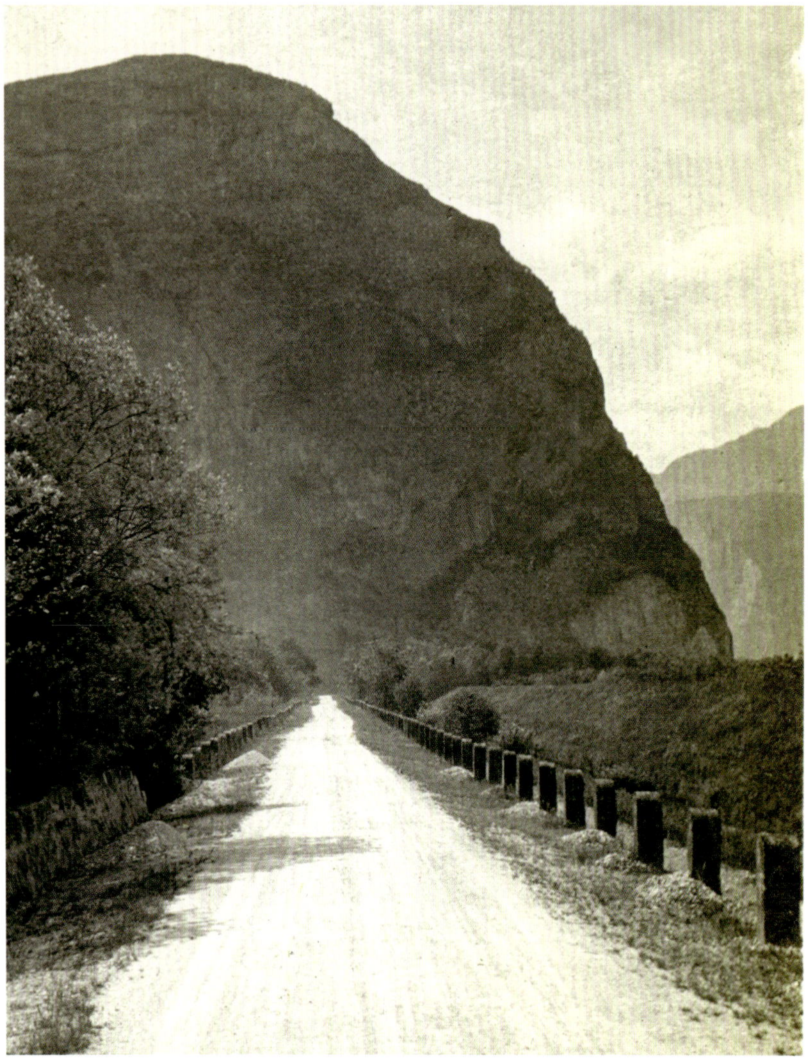

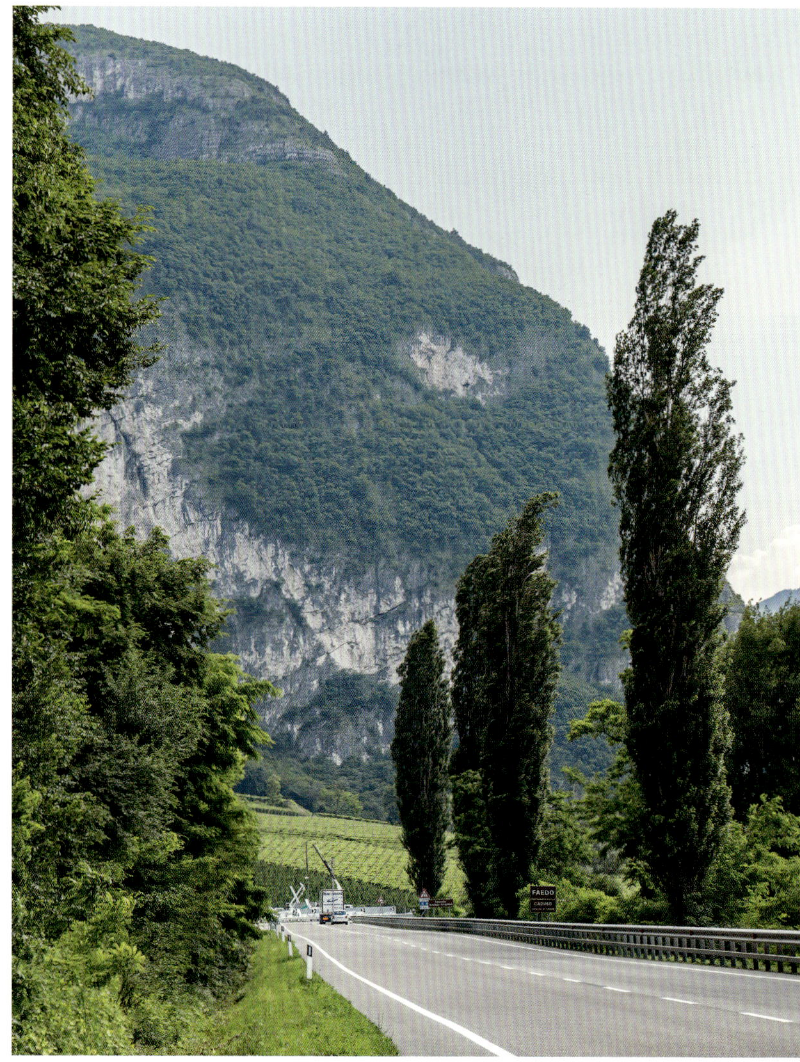

1913 Road scene taken from the back of the car on a long straight on the S12 north of Trient near Salurn, at the boundary of Trentino & Südtirol provinces, en route to Auer and San Lugano.

2013 Same location, now an extremely busy main road, in spite of the nearby Autostrada.

SAN LUGANO

Austria / Italy

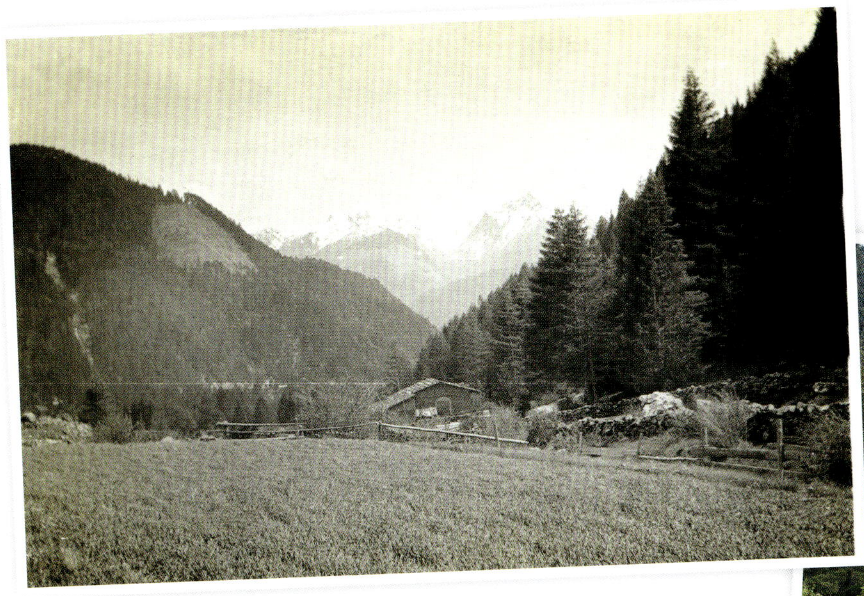

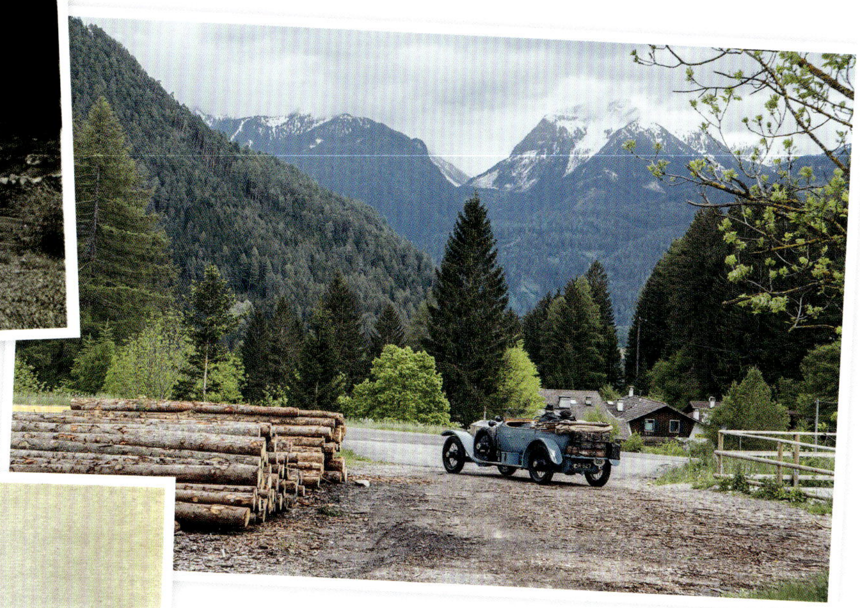

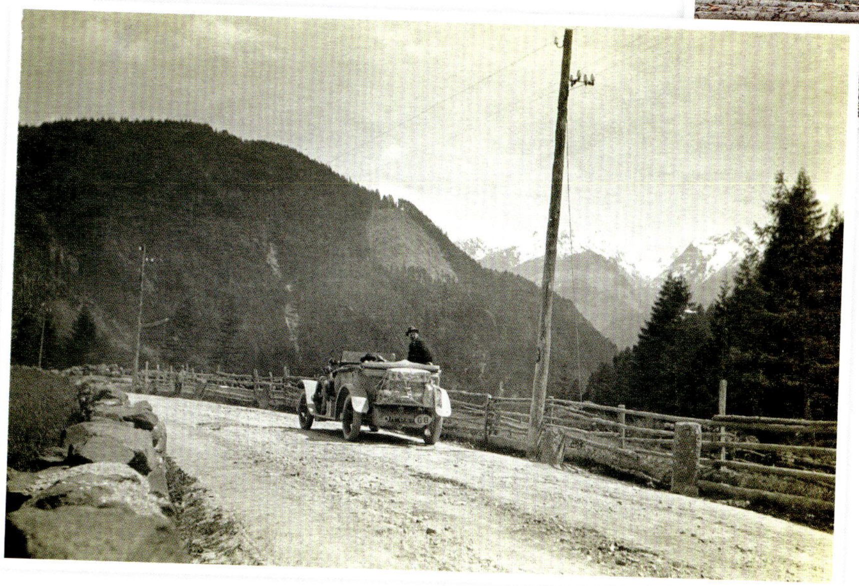

1913 Pausing at the summit of the San Lugano road (1097 m).

2013 The old road is now used for log storage. The new road junction is nearby.

MOENA

Austria

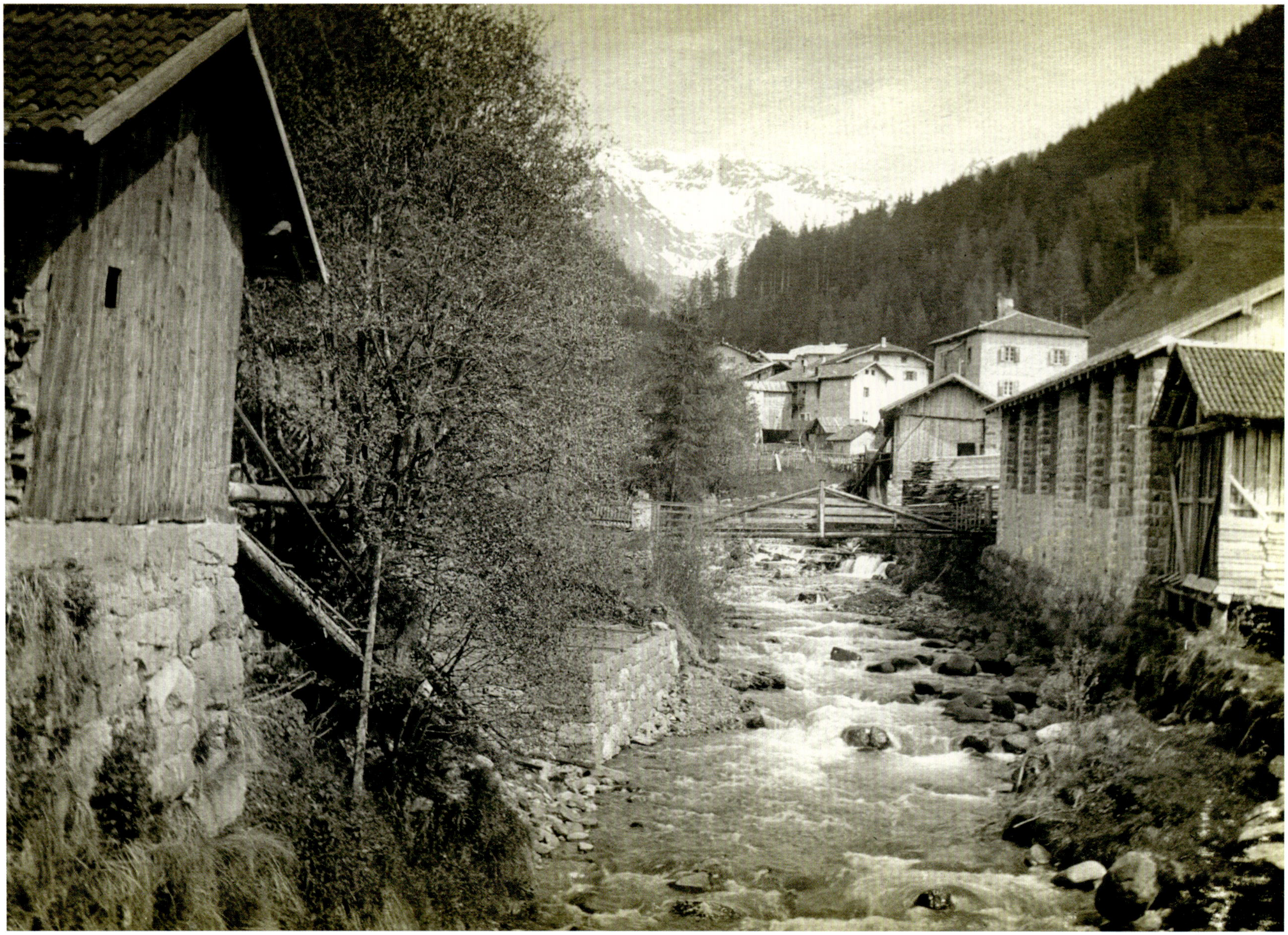

1913

Mountain scene at Moena. The main road leaving the town climbs past a narrow section.
Radley needed to slow down or briefly stop here, making it possible for a quick photograph of the mountain scene showing Rio San Pellegrino and the Dolomites in the distance to the east.

MOENA

Italy

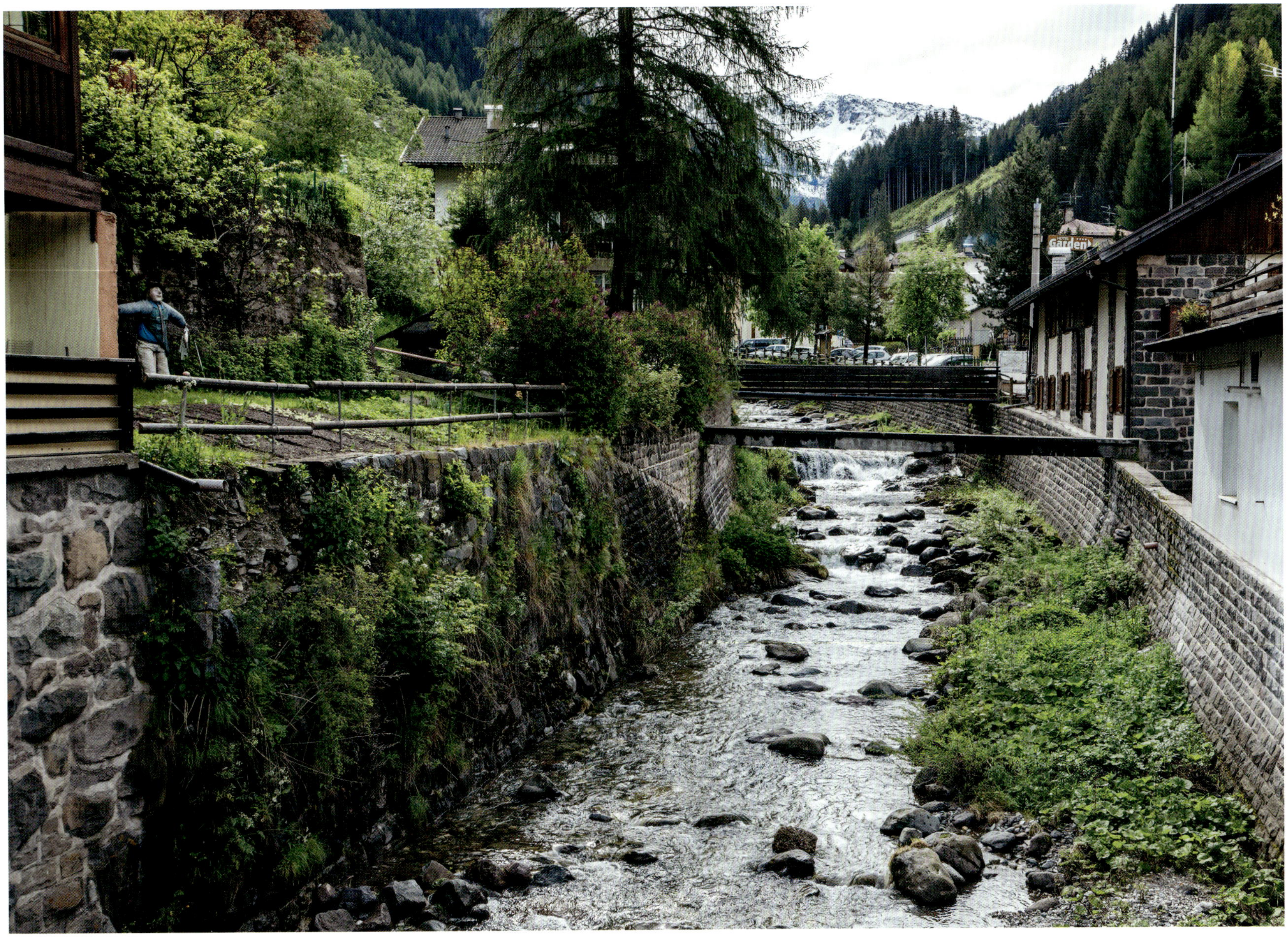

2013

The narrow gap and the one way road by the stream remain, now controlled by lights. Many of the old buildings are still there.

CAMPITELLO

Austria

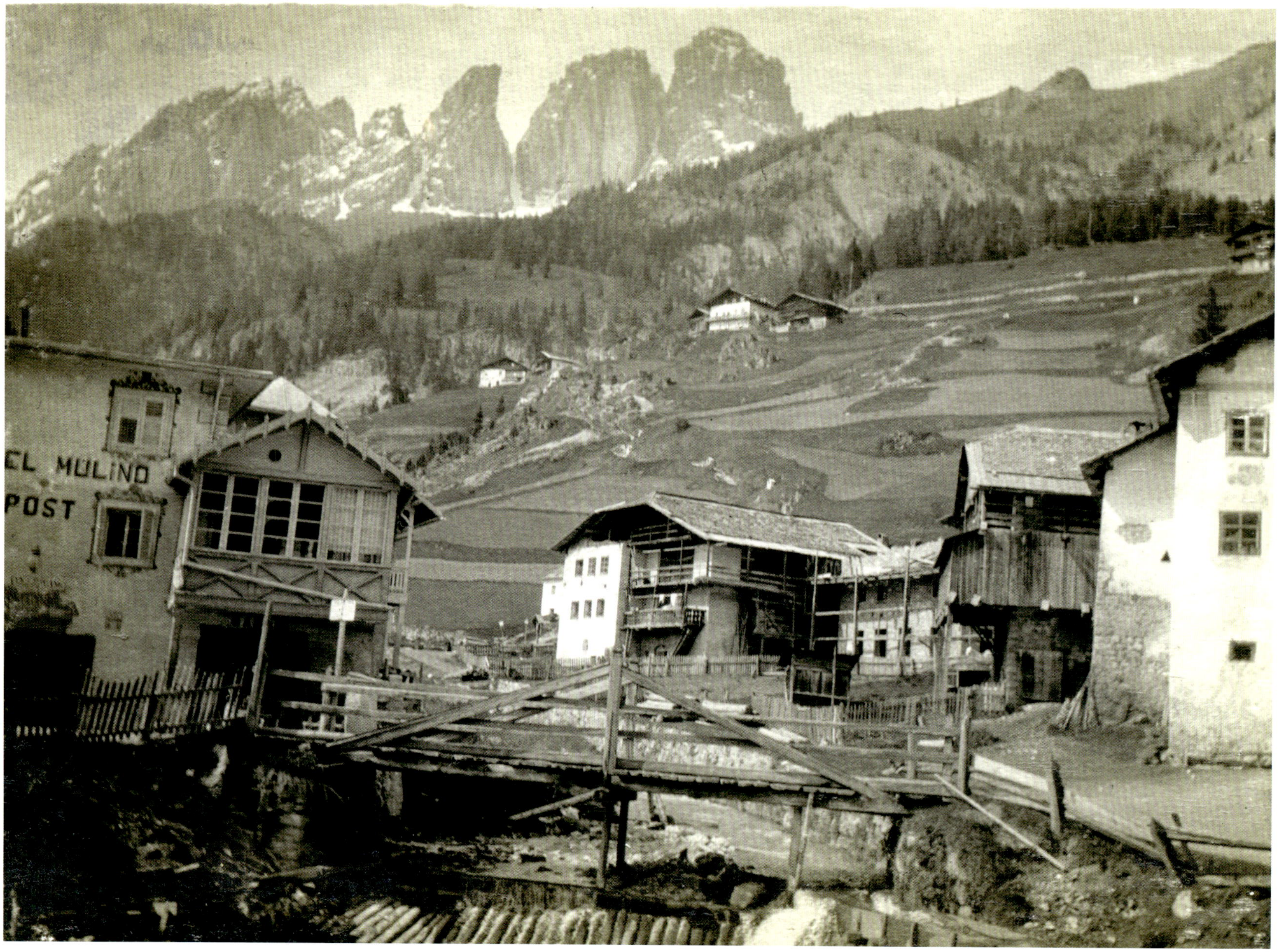

1913

Campitello with Hotel Mulino in left foreground and steep fields rising to Langkofel group in the Dolomite mountains beyond.

CAMPITELLO

Italy

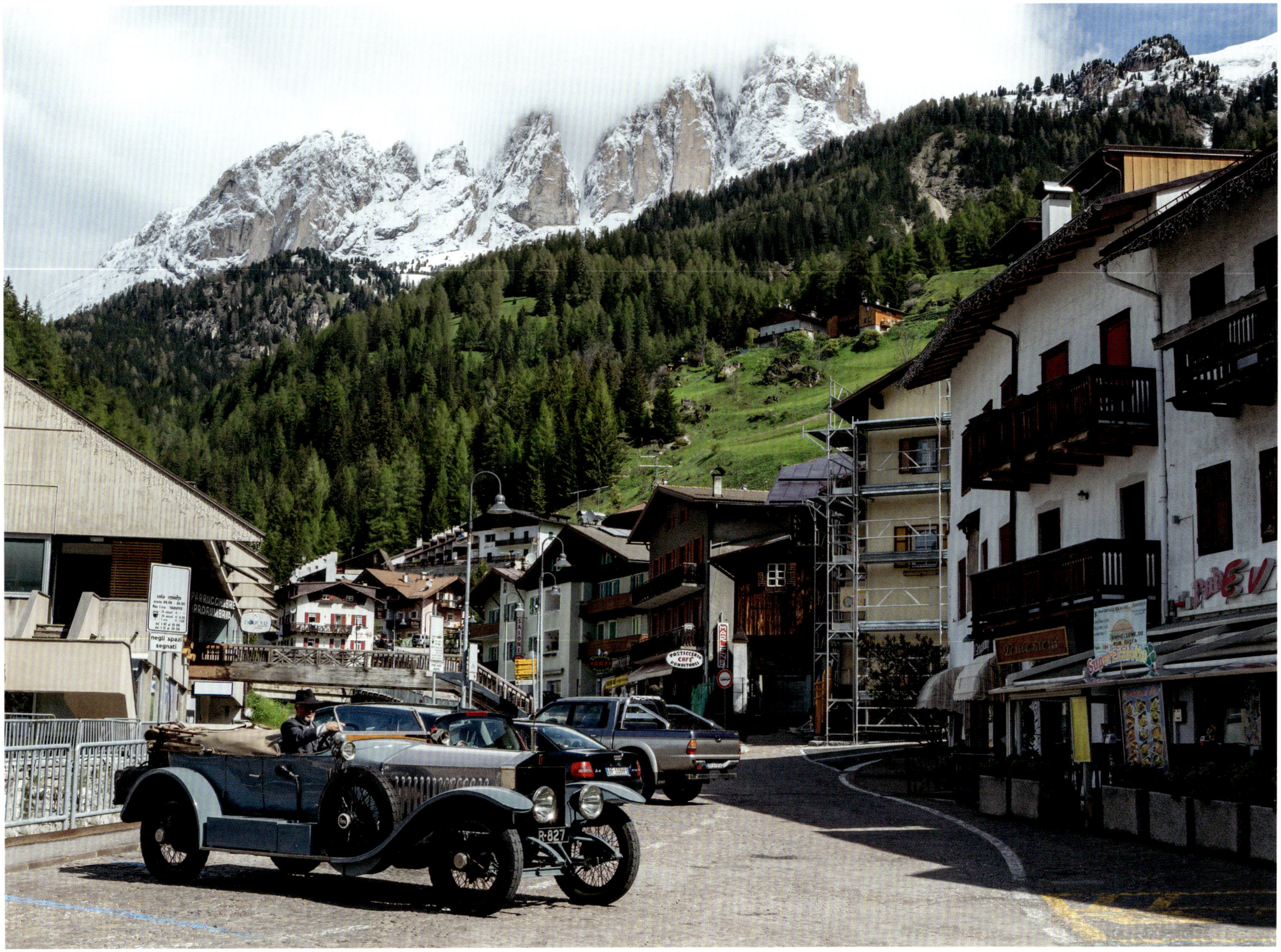

2013

An unloved modern building now replaces the hotel.
Many of the other buildings still exist.

VAL DI FASSA

Austria

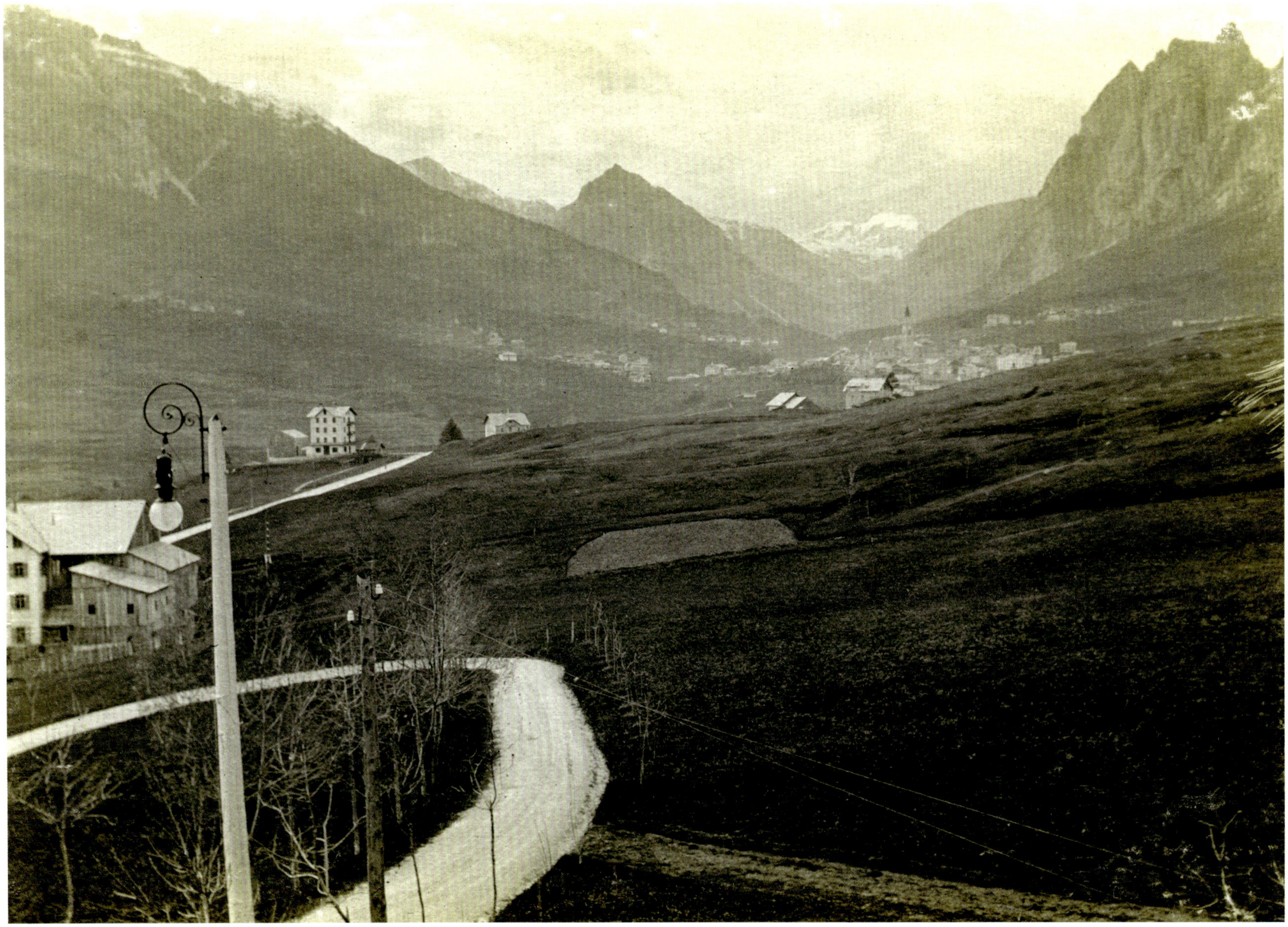

1913

Val di Fassa was an isolated valley until the opening of the Pordoi Pass road less than a decade earlier.

VAL DI FASSA

Italy

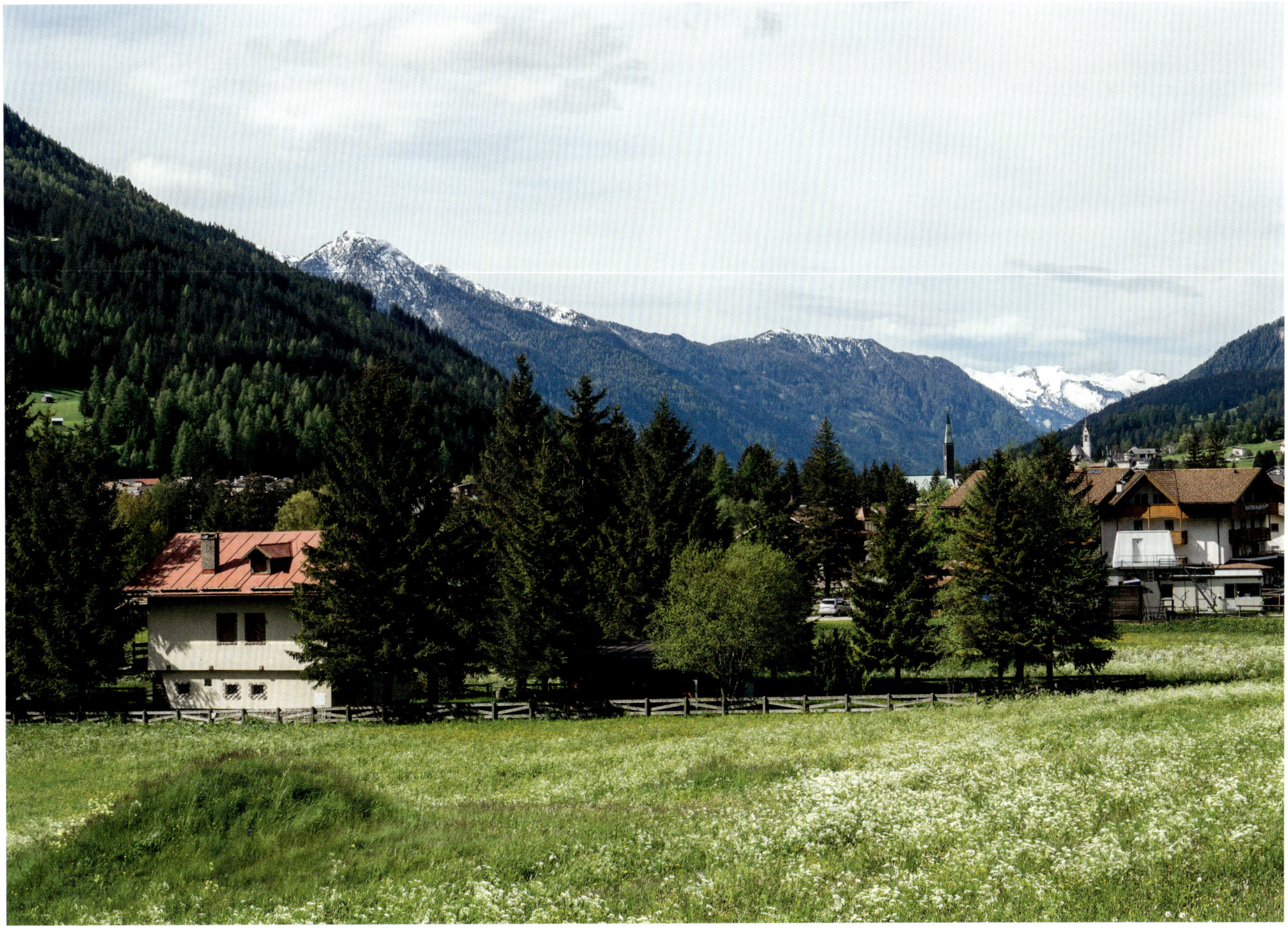

2013

Modern development and more trees make significant changes to the early views.

CANAZEI

Austria

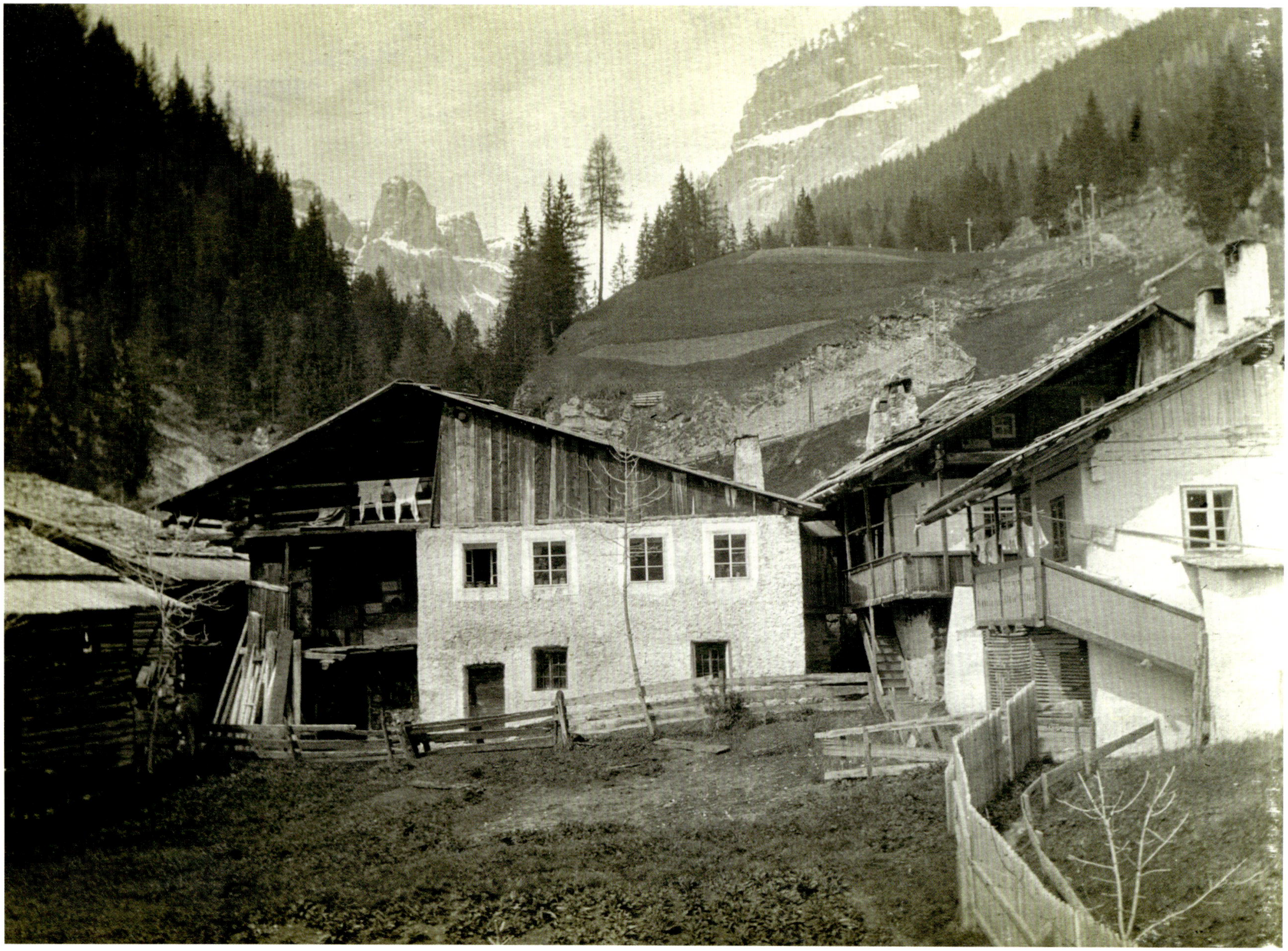

1913

Between the rustic farm houses and the high Dolomites,
the new road leading to the Pordoi Pass can be seen.

CANAZEI

Italy

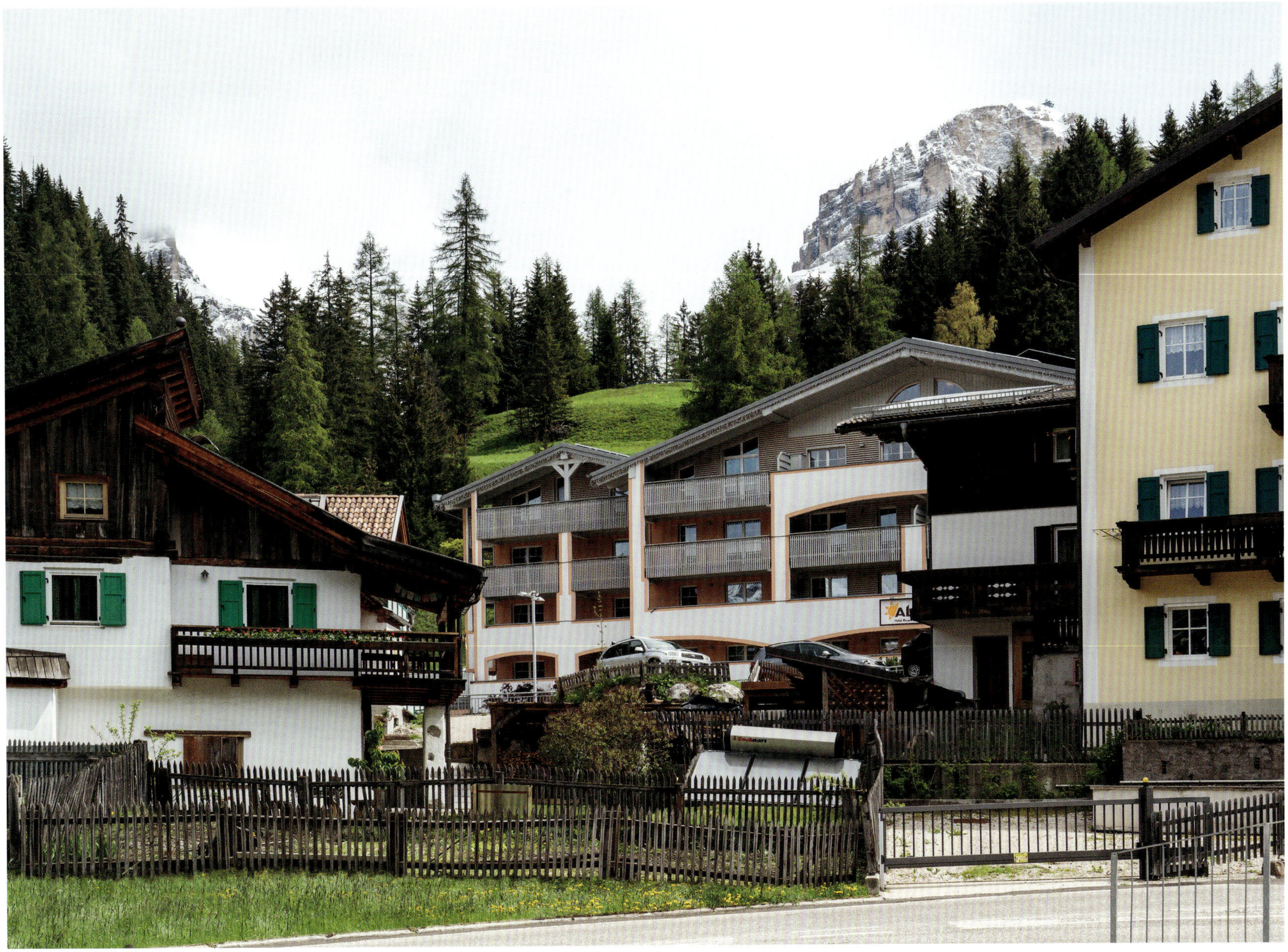

2013

Modern ski lodges have replaced some of the old farm houses and more trees almost obscure the Pordoi road.

MARMOLADA ALPS FROM CANAZEI

Austria

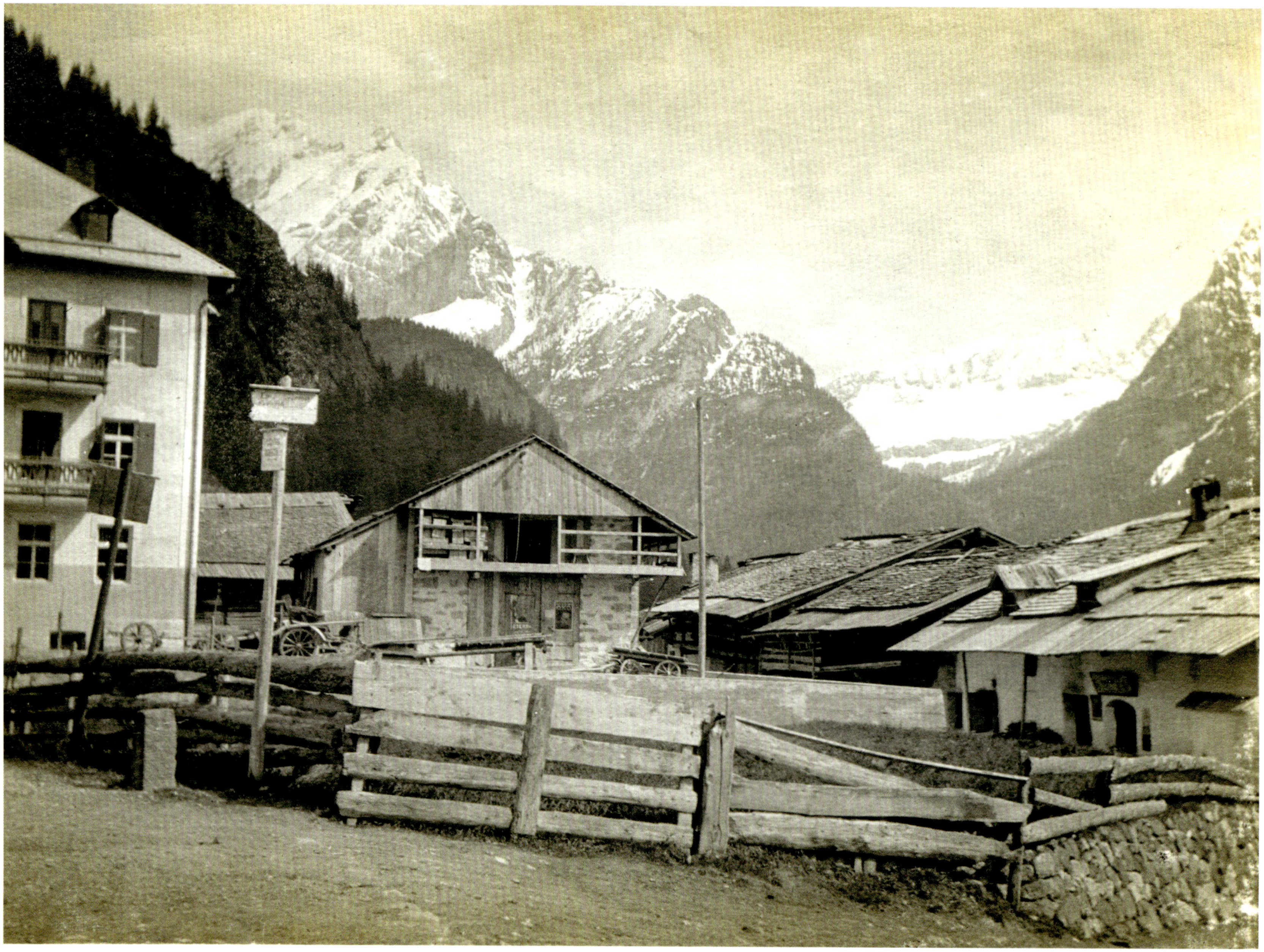

1913

The high mountains dominate the eastward view from this ancient mountain village.

MARMOLADA ALPS FROM CANAZEI

Italy

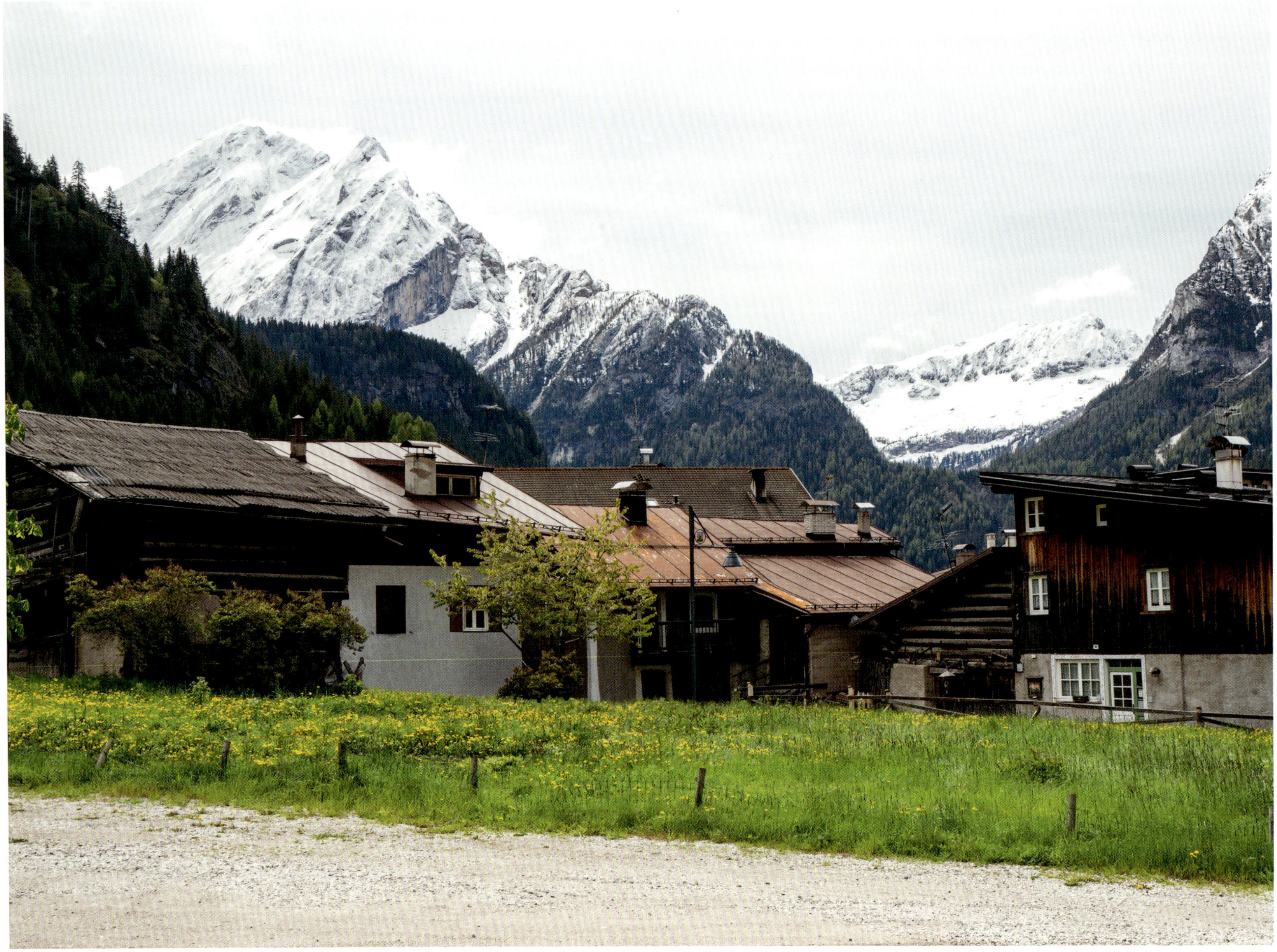

2013

Many old buildings are still seen from this view taken a century later.

PORDOIJOCH

Austria

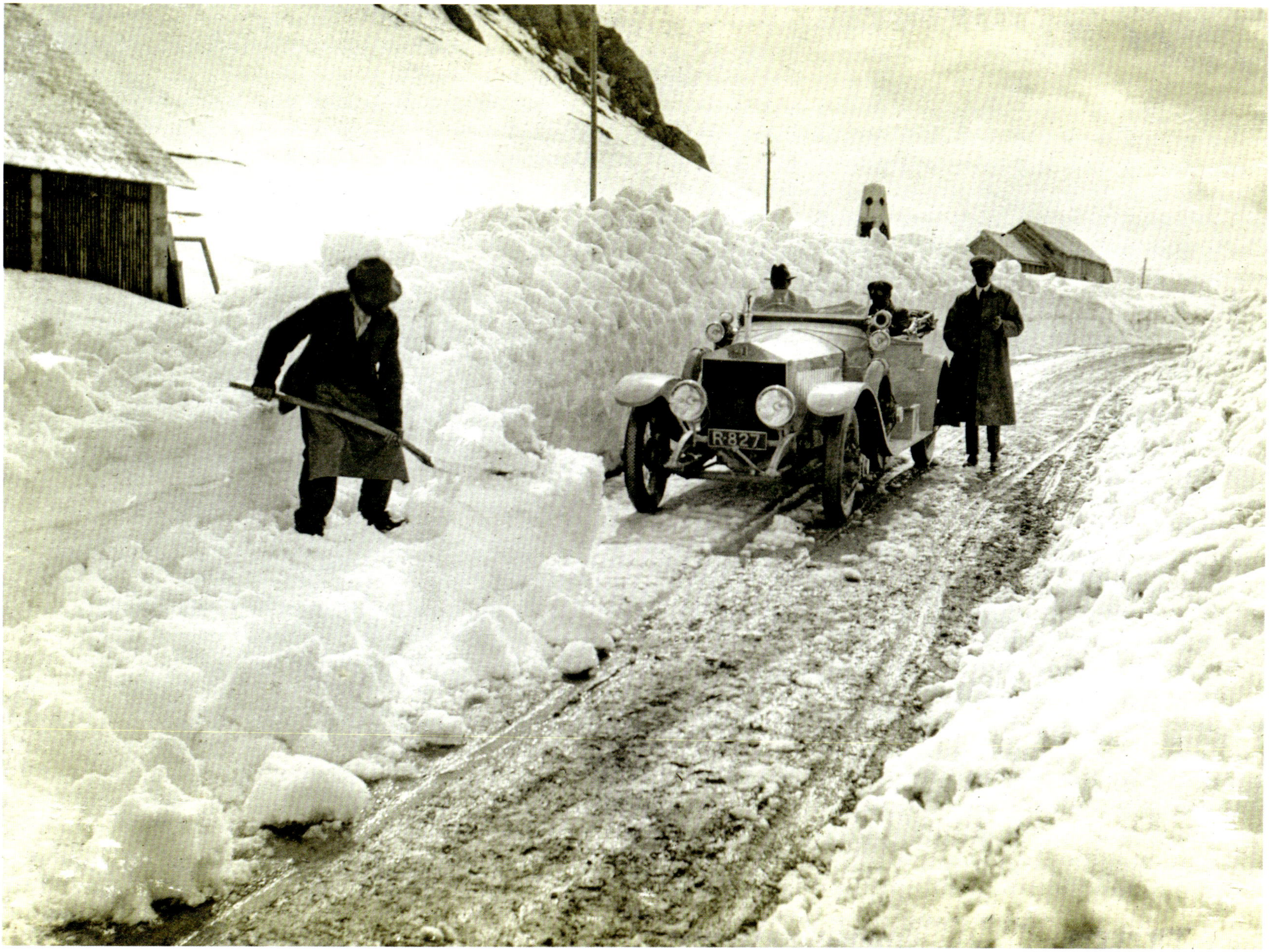

1913

Radley pauses at the Pordoi summit (2239 m).
The obelisk in the background commemorates the opening of the road in 1904.

PASSO PORDOI

Italy

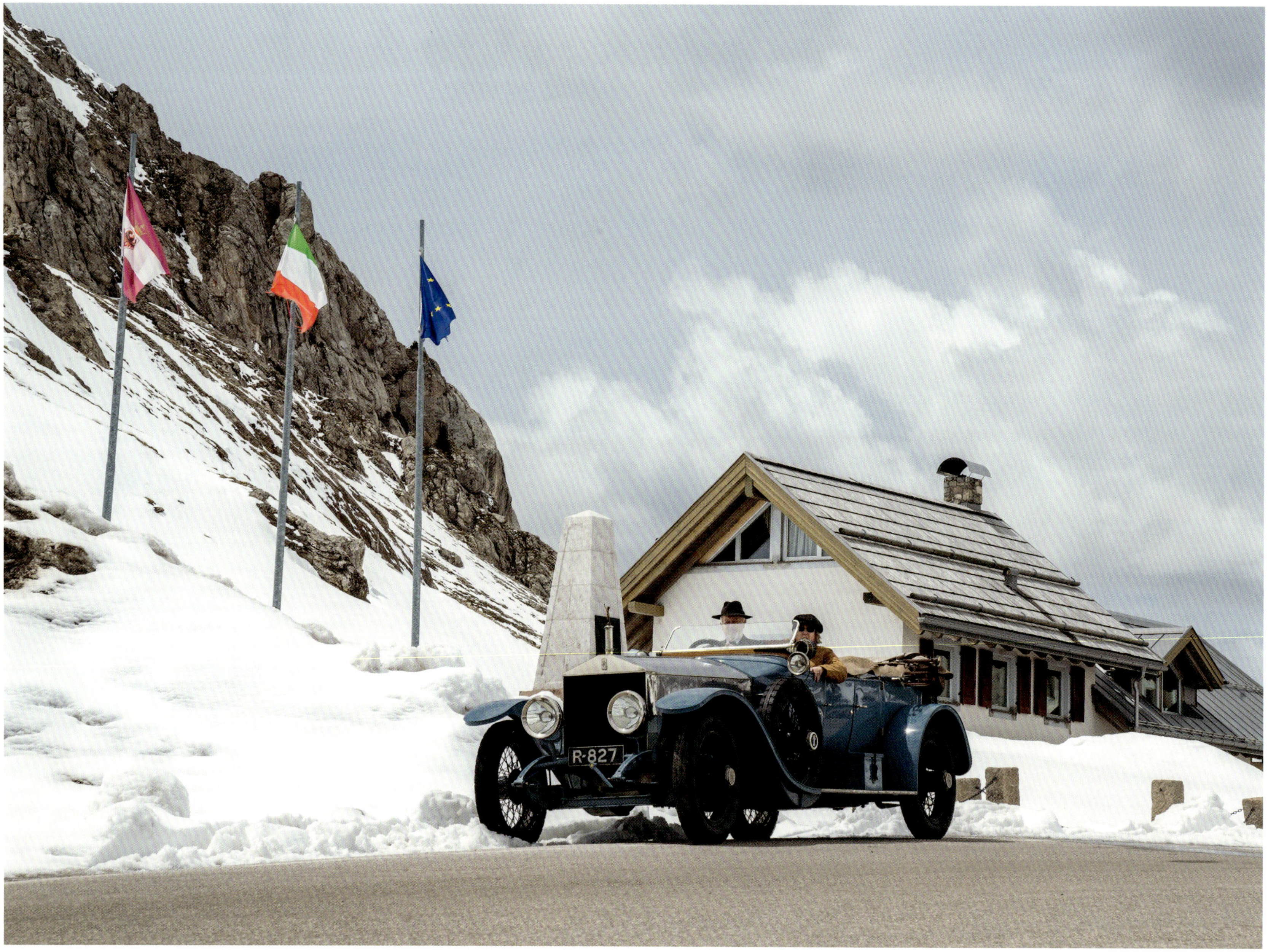

2013

The Pordoi summit now has many buildings serving this ski area. The obelisk remains.

FALZAREGO

Austria

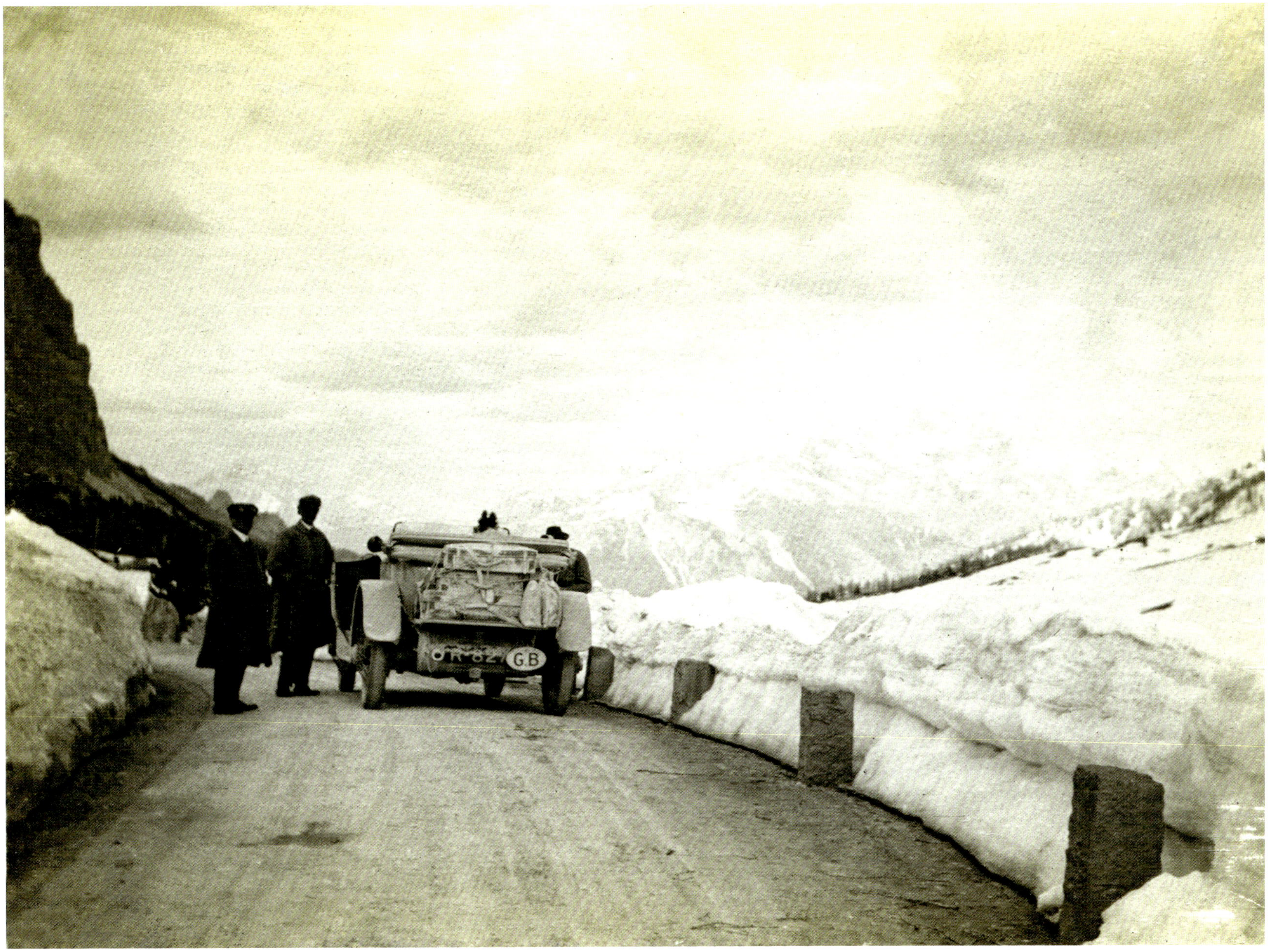

1913

At the Falzarego summit (2117 m). The road had been built in 1909.

FALZAREGO

Italy

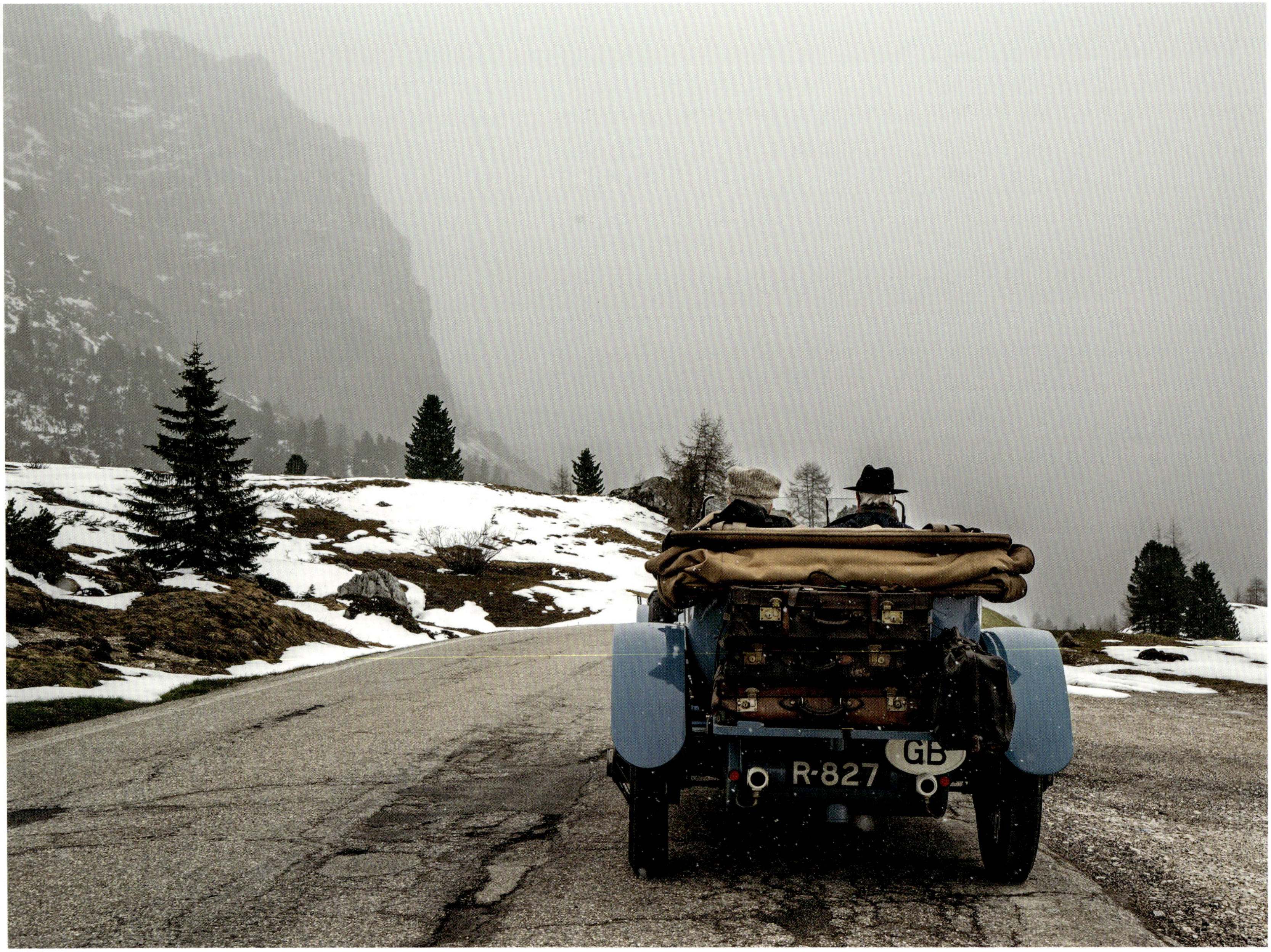

2013

Same location 100 years on. A wider road but still in the snow.

FALZAREGO

Austria

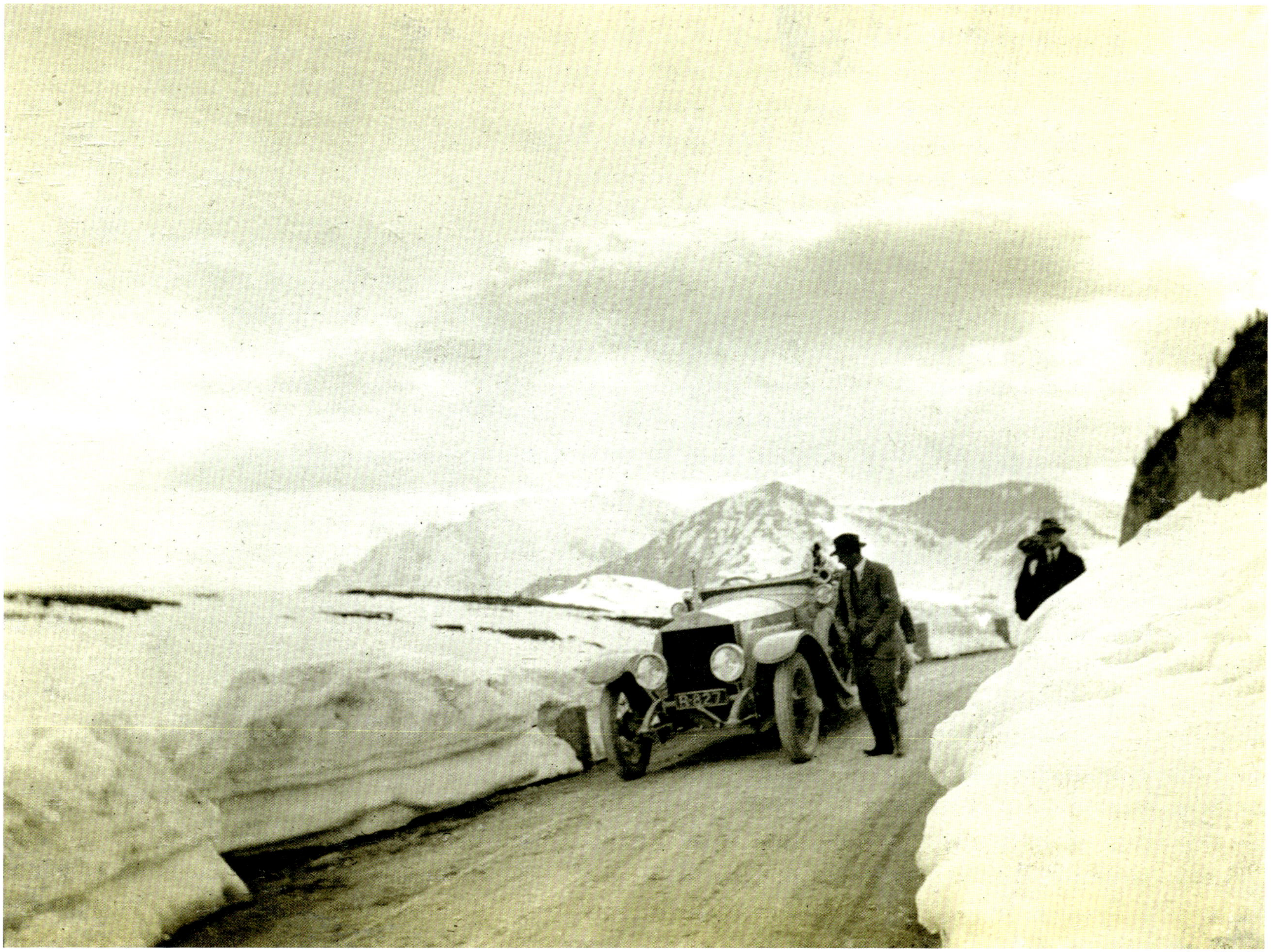

1913

Front view at the same location as the previous picture.

FALZAREGO

Italy

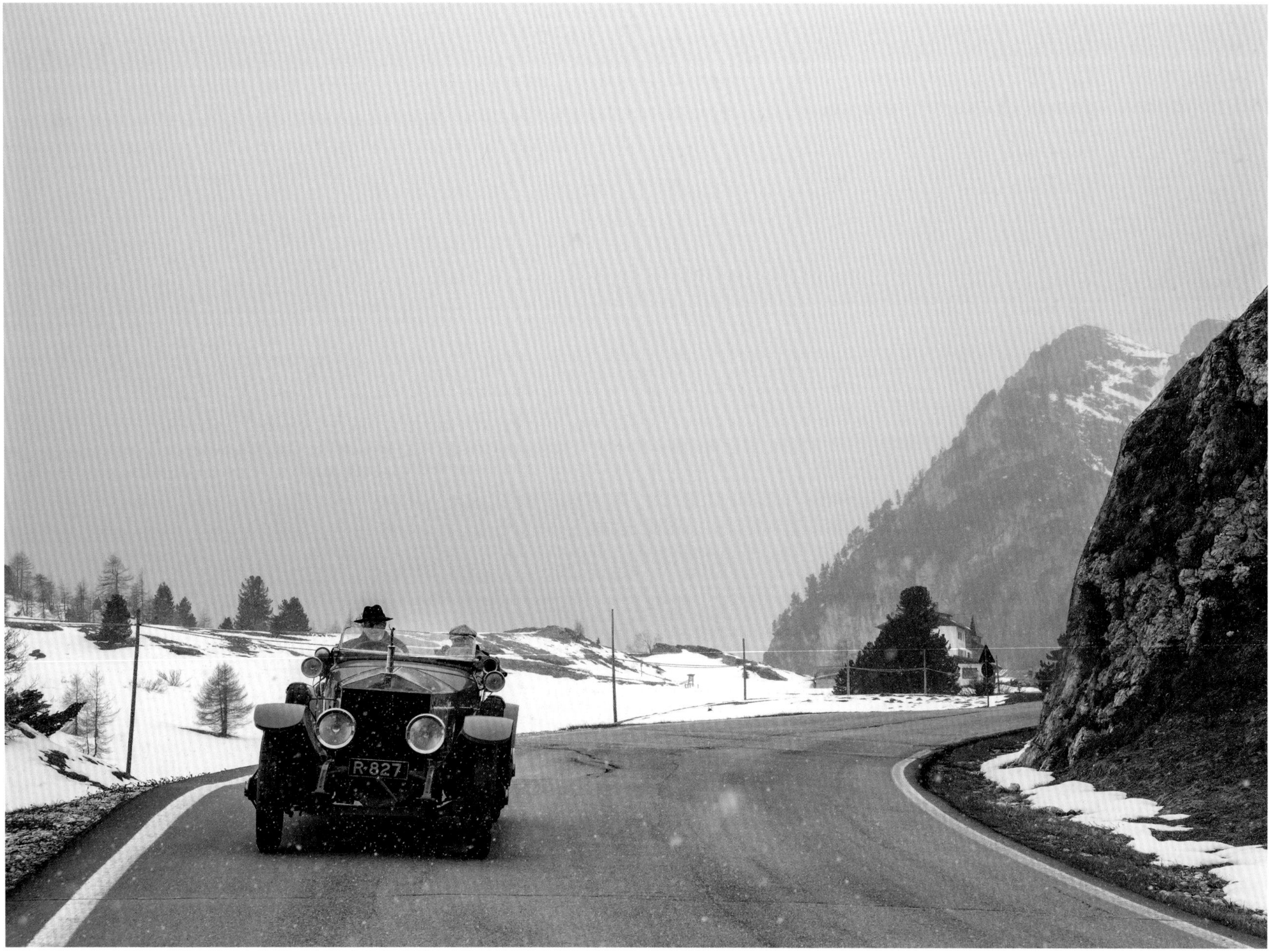

2013

Falzarego with summit hotel in the background. Same location, wider road, light snow, cold.

LOIBLPASS / LJUBELJ

Austria

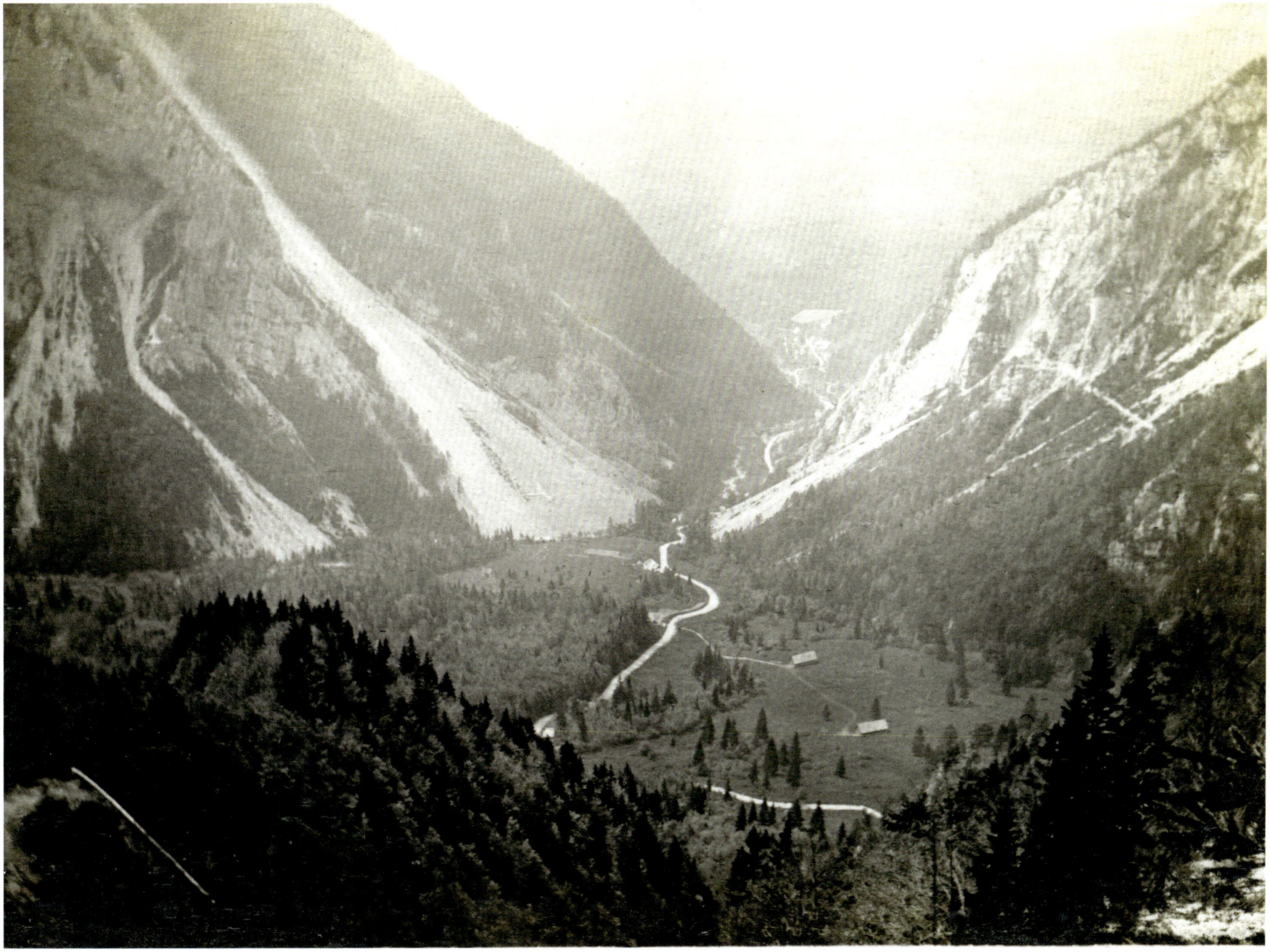

1913

Loiblpass (1370 m). The famous view looking south from the summit showing the winding road in the valley far below. The high pass was a major Alpine crossing until the Loibl tunnel was opened in the 1960s.

LOIBLPASS / LJUBELJ

Slovenia

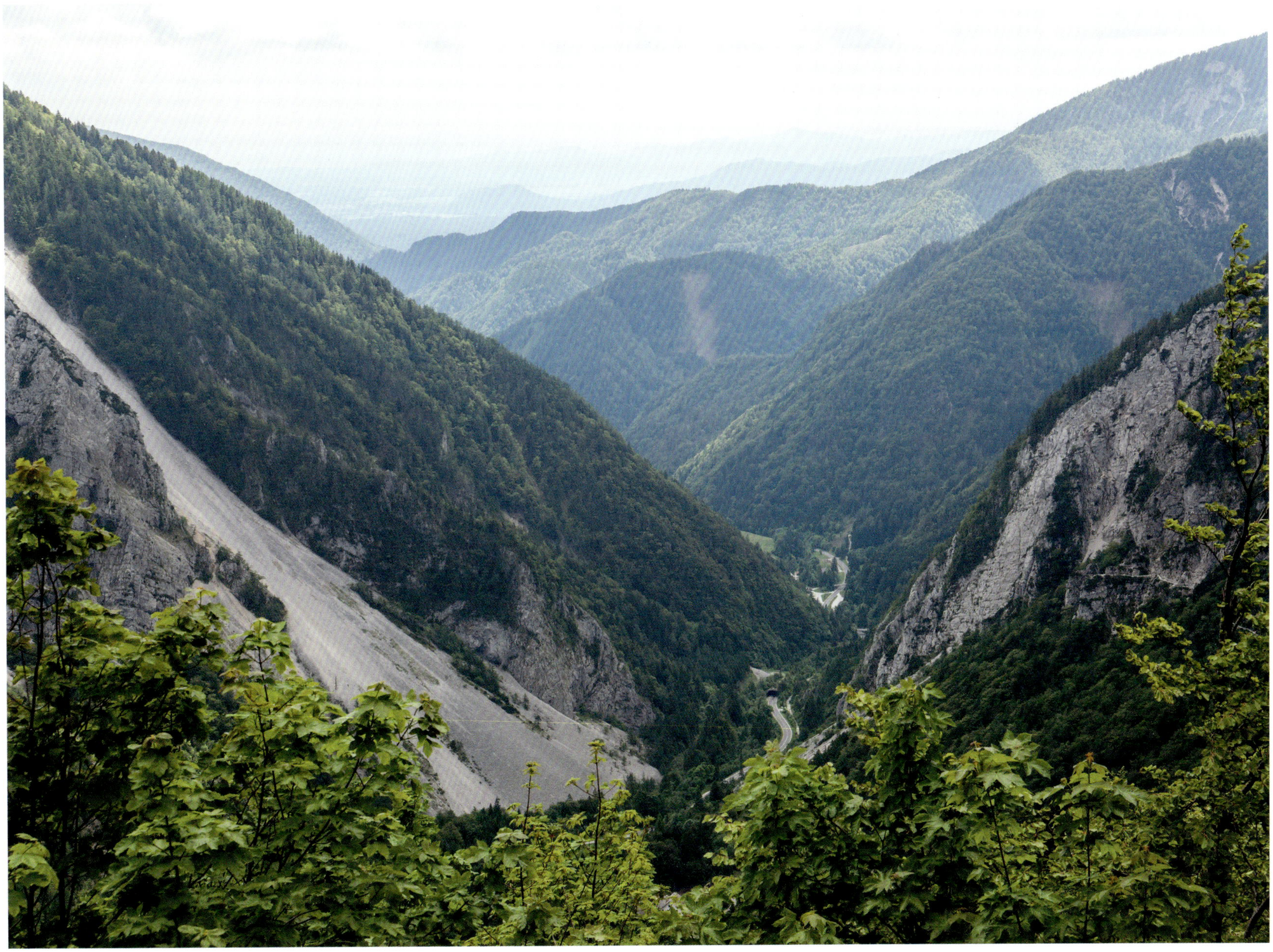

2013

The view looks south into Slovenia, from what is now the border with Austria.
Now a heritage road, the pass is open only for special events such as the visit of the Radley Silver Ghost.
The foreground view is now partly obscured by trees, as peasants no longer graze their animals on the pass.

DRAU BRIDGE

Austria

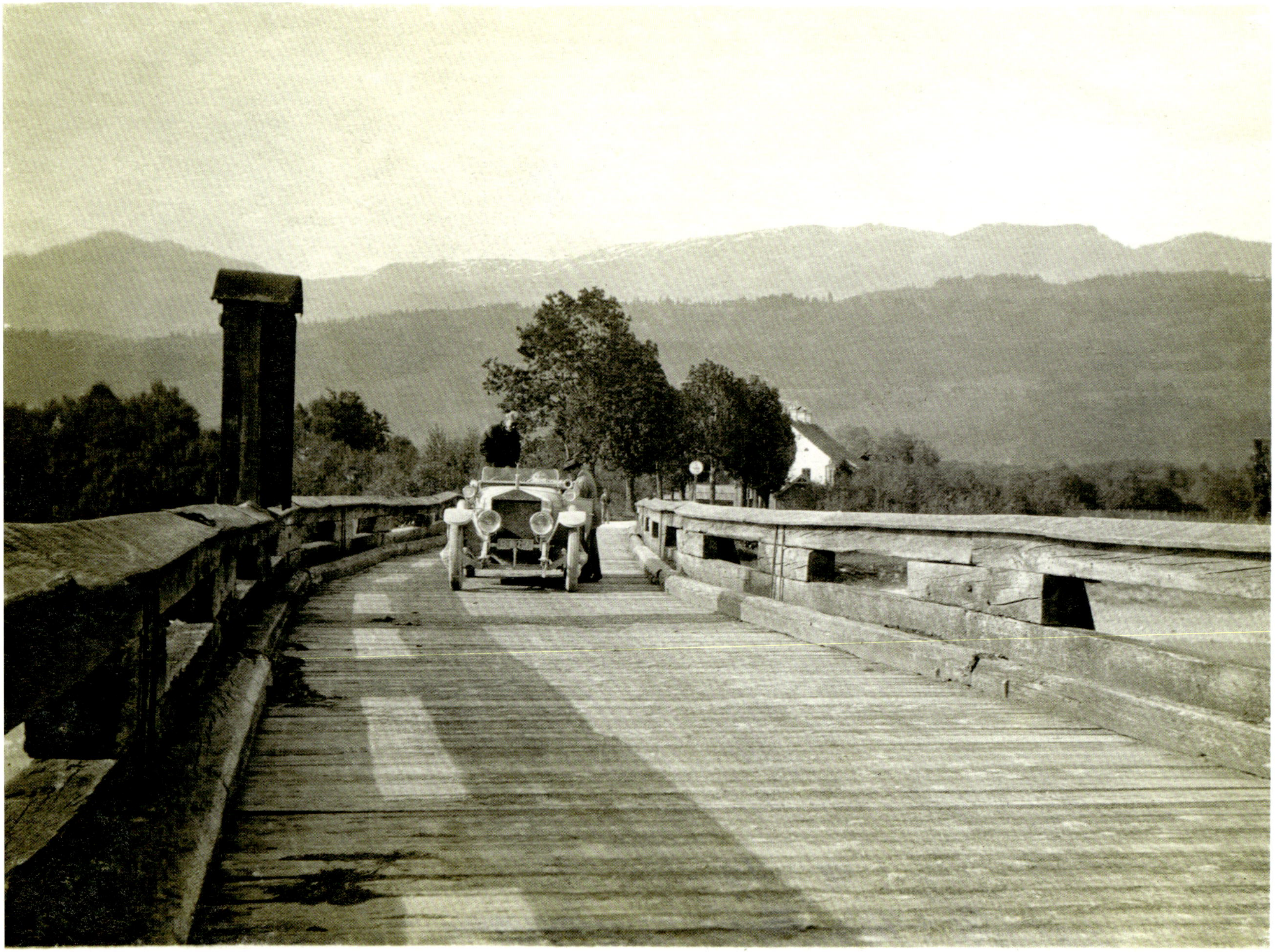

1913

The car on curved wooden bridge with Radley outside and passenger standing.
This old toll bridge at Mauthbrücken near Spittal was later submerged when a hydro dam was built.

DRAU BRIDGE

Austria

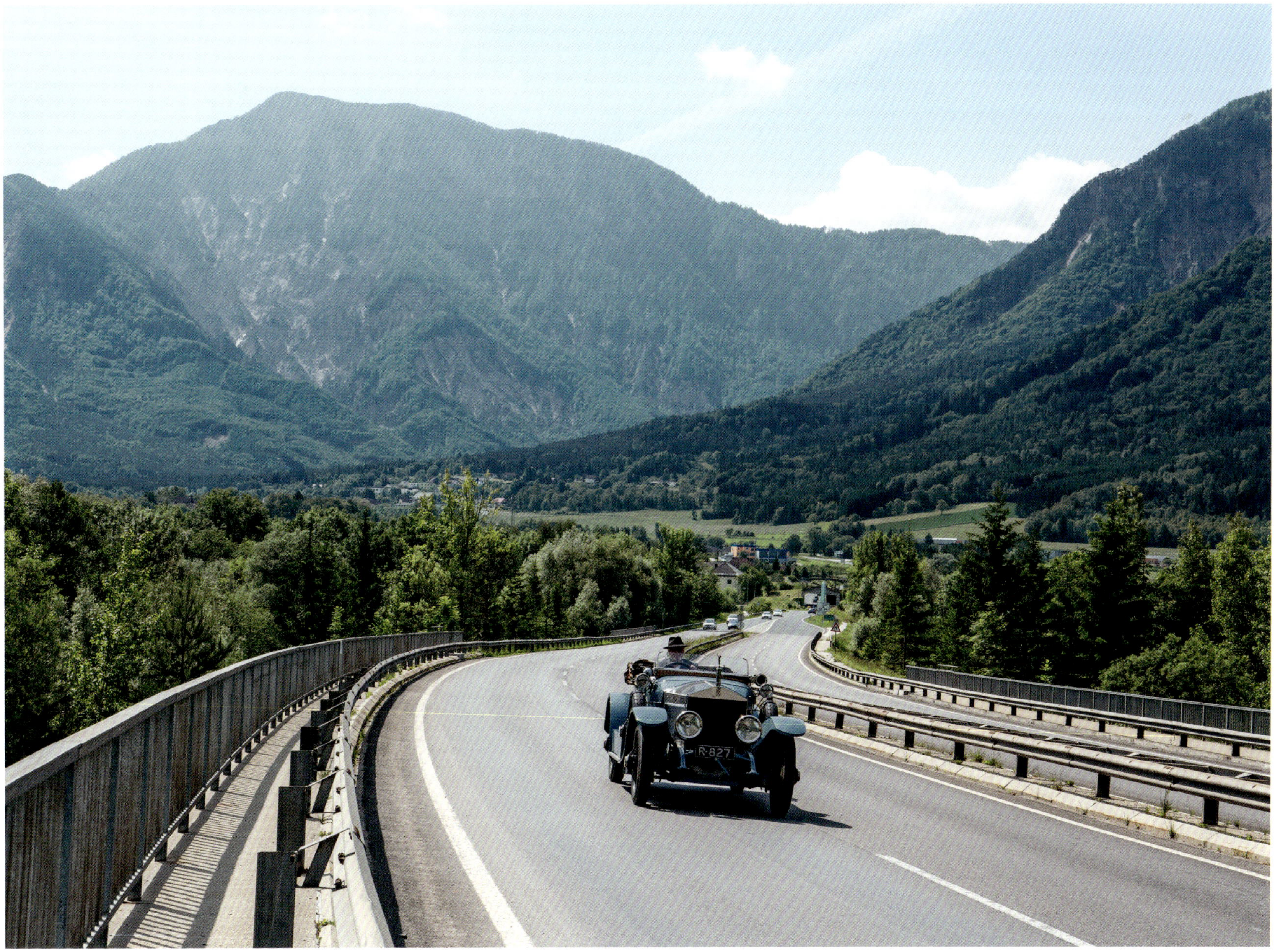

2013

Modern bridge across the Drau at Hollenburg, between the Loibl Pass and Klagenfurt. There is now a hydro dam here and this new higher level bridge has been built.

Mr Radley Drives To Vienna

Rolls-Royce and the 1913 Alpenfahrt.

BACKGROUND

The final picture from the Radley-Hope album abruptly cuts off the detailed story of the journey to Vienna. The album has blank pages at the end, which suggests that photographer Reggie Hope may have left the car in Carinthia and returned to England. The journey from Passo Ampola, near Riva to Klagenfurt is almost entirely on the route of the Alpenfahrt, so it is known that key parts of the route were tested. There is separate pictorial evidence that the Rolls-Royce team cars tested in various locations, including the Katschberg Pass, the key pass where Radley had stopped during the 1912 event. No photographs have been found showing Radley testing on this pass, but as there was exactly one month from the date Radley was at the Mont Cenis Pass, until the start date of the Alpenfahrt, it seems likely that he also tested on the Katschberg.

This section contains material relating to the Rolls-Royce and its part in the 1913 Alpenfahrt.

ROLLS-ROYCE

Der beste Wagen der Welt

Preise der Wagen (loko London):

Chassis mit Pneumatik .	£	985. 0.0	K 23.640
Touristenwagen, viersitzig (Type London-Edinburgh) ca.	£	1087.10.0	K 26.100
Torpedo-Phaethon . . ca.	£	1125. 0.0	K 27.000
Limousine, siebensitzig ca.	£	1305. 0.0	K 31.320
Limousine-Landaulet ca.	£	1235.15.0	K 29.658
Cabriolet . . . . ca	£	1240. 0.0	K 29.760

General-Repräsentanz für Oesterreich-Ungarn:

Telephon 11.958. Wien, I. Tegetthoffstraße Nr. 4. Telephon 11.958.

1913

In 1913 Rolls-Royce had opened their new depot in Vienna.

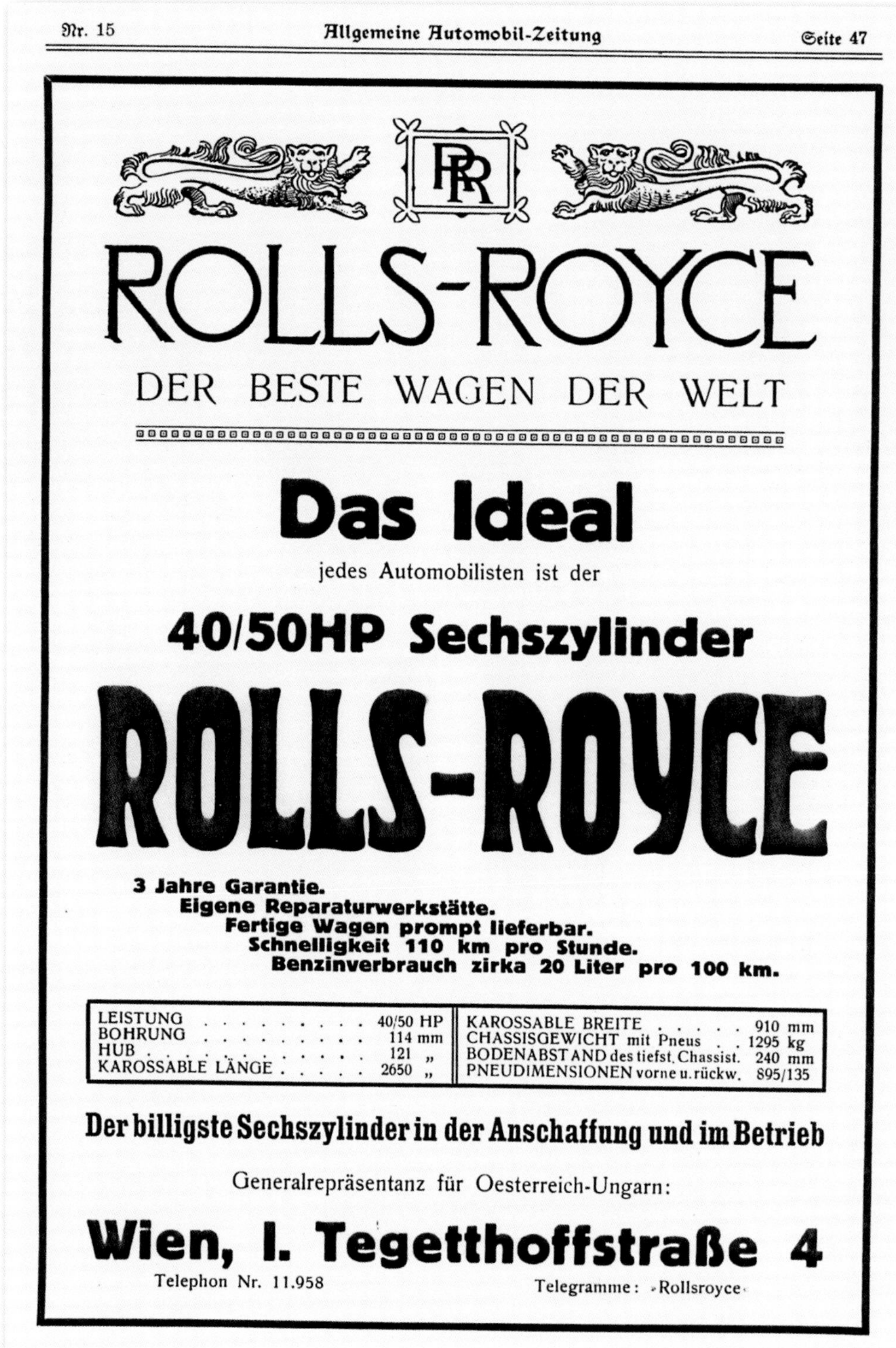

Nr. 15 Allgemeine Automobil-Zeitung Seite 47

ROLLS-ROYCE

DER BESTE WAGEN DER WELT

Das Ideal

jedes Automobilisten ist der

40/50HP Sechszylinder

ROLLS-ROYCE

3 Jahre Garantie.
Eigene Reparaturwerkstätte.
Fertige Wagen prompt lieferbar.
Schnelligkeit 110 km pro Stunde.
Benzinverbrauch zirka 20 Liter pro 100 km.

LEISTUNG	40/50 HP	KAROSSABLE BREITE	910 mm
BOHRUNG	114 mm	CHASSISGEWICHT mit Pneus	1295 kg
HUB	121 „	BODENABSTAND des tiefst. Chassist.	240 mm
KAROSSABLE LÄNGE	2650 „	PNEUDIMENSIONEN vorne u. rückw.	895/135

Der billigste Sechszylinder in der Anschaffung und im Betrieb

Generalrepräsentanz für Oesterreich-Ungarn:

Wien, I. Tegetthoffstraße 4

Telephon Nr. 11.958 Telegramme: »Rollsroyce«

1913

They marketed the Silver Ghost as 'The Best Car in the World'.

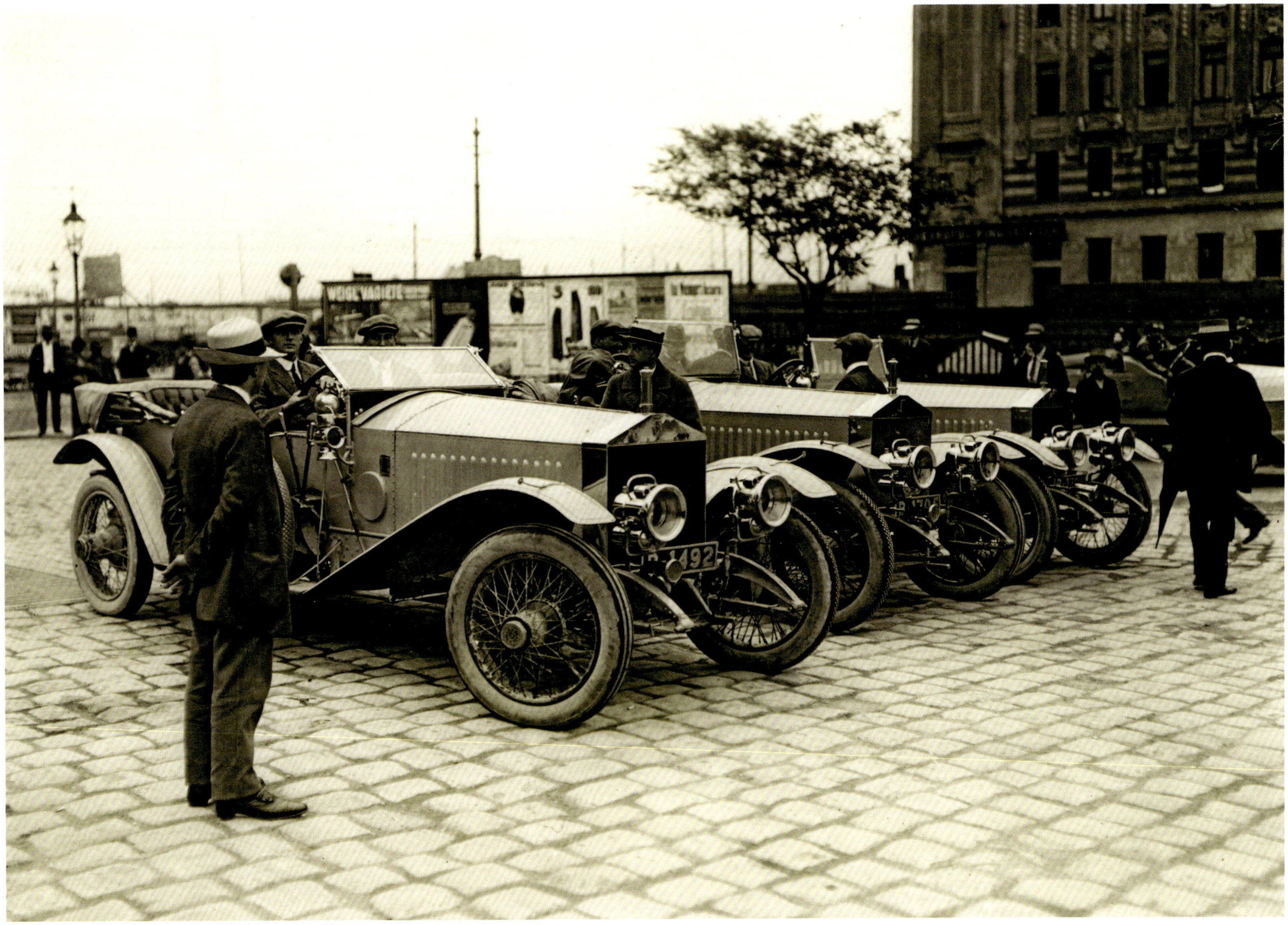

1913

The Rolls-Royce team arrive in Vienna.

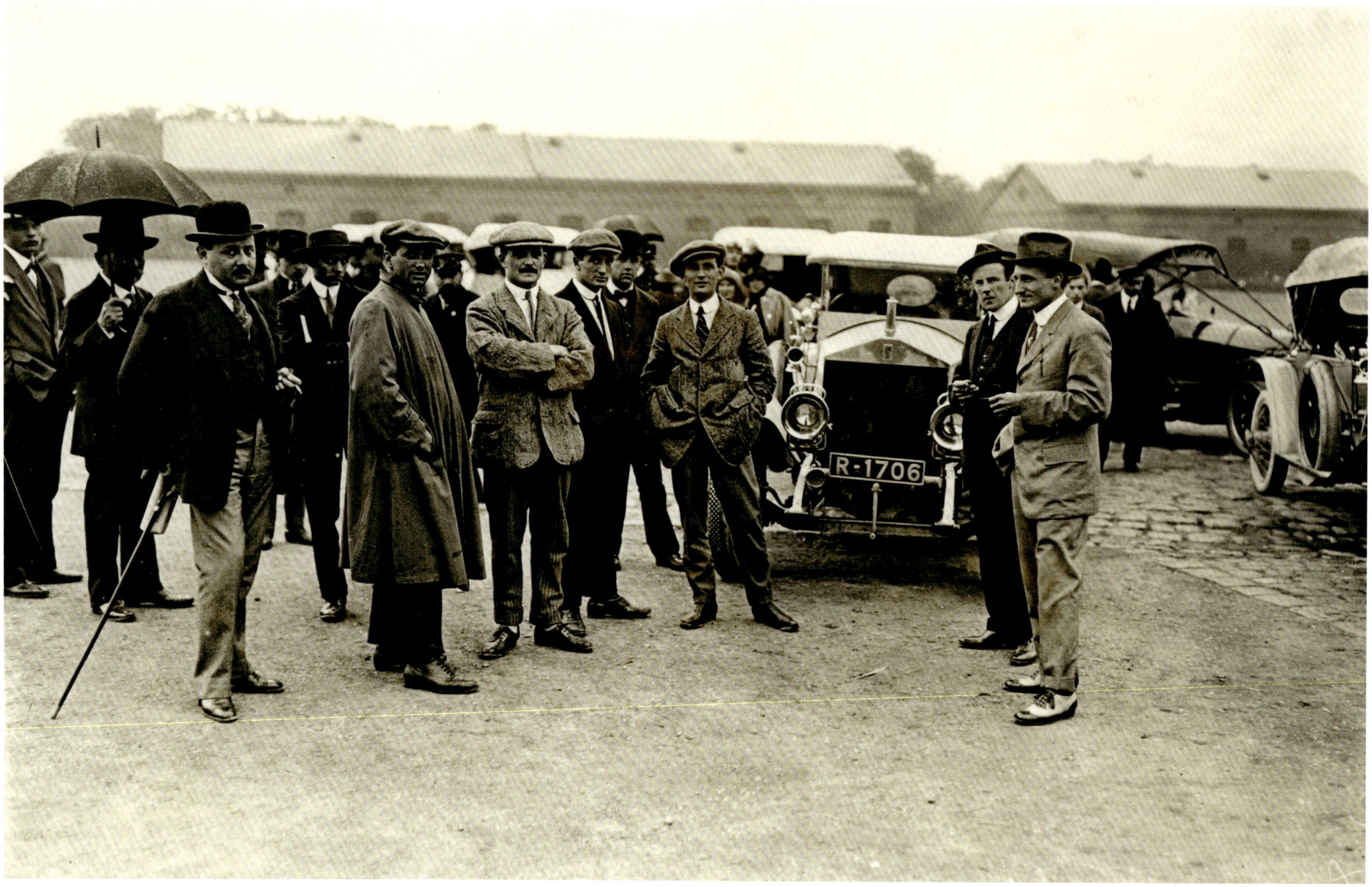

1913

Mr Radley joins the Rolls-Royce team in Vienna.

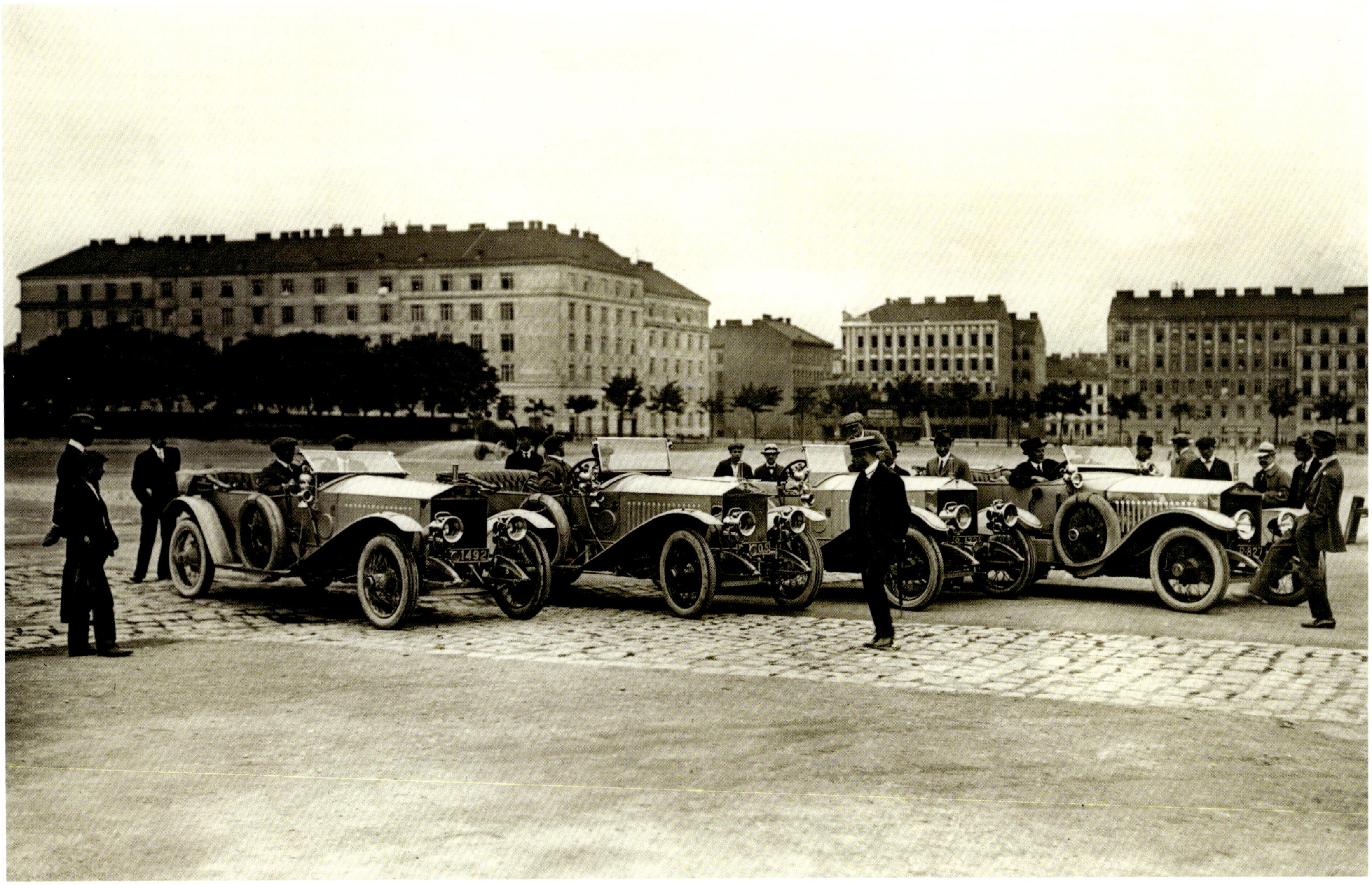

1913

All the Rolls-Royce cars prepare to depart from Vienna on the 1913 Alpenfahrt.

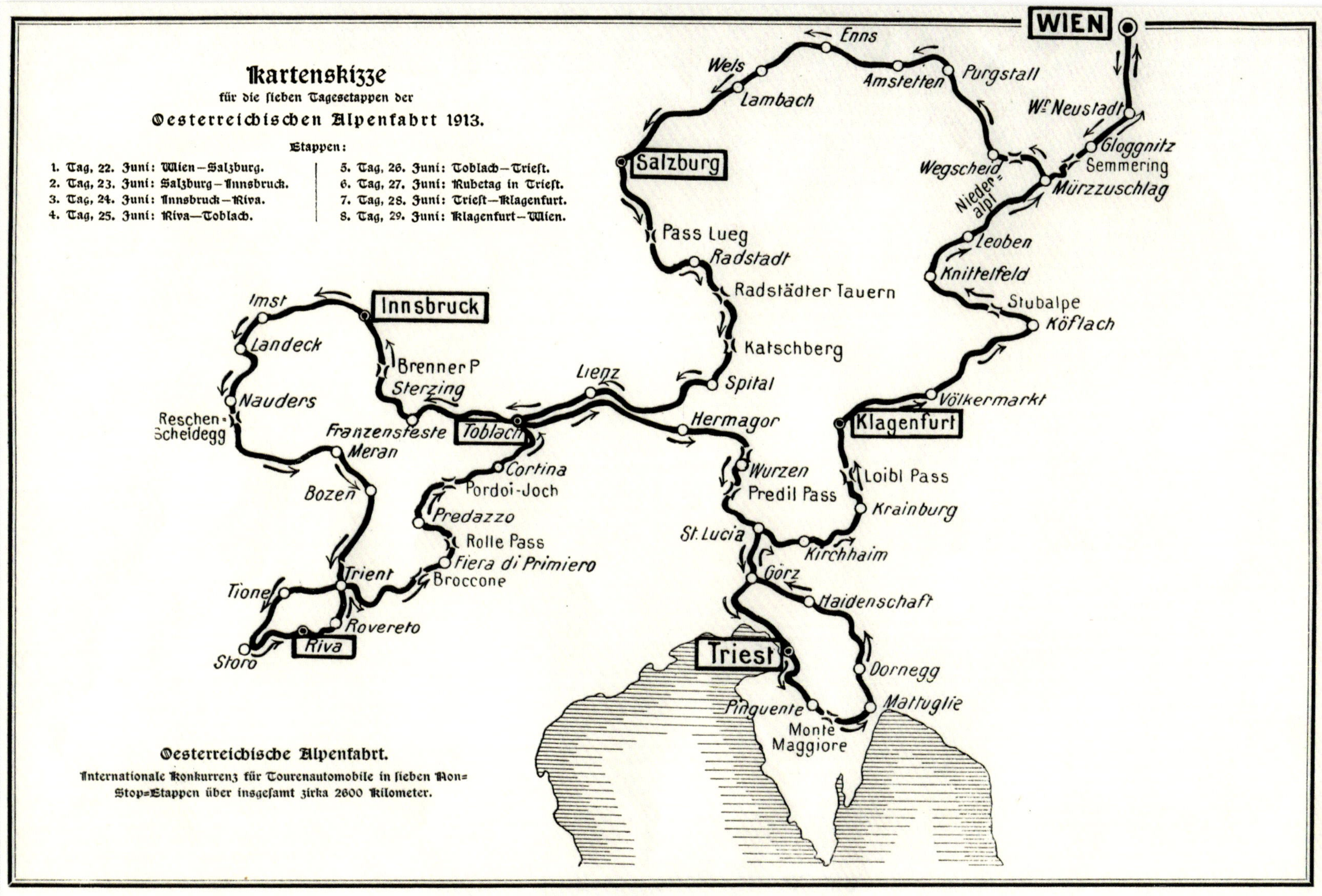

1913

Map of the 1913 Alpenfahrt route.

The Great Alpine Contest.

Facts and Figures about one of the Great Events of the Year. An Extended Route. The Conditions of the Competition. By C. L. Freeston, F.R.G.S.

THERE is no gainsaying the fact that the Oesterreichische Alpenfahrt, or Austrian Alpine contest, has effected the miraculous in automobile history. Year by year, since the thousand miles trial of 1900, the annual competitions in one country or another had gradually become more and more strenuous, but the efficiency of the motor car itself increased to a still greater degree, and first in Great Britain, with its reliability trials, and then abroad, with its Herkomer and Prince Henry contests, the day of abandonment arrived because there seemed no obstacle to put before the all-conquering car which it could not easily surmount.

But there remained the Alps! To western minds these are so frequently associated with Switzerland alone, and the hostility of the average Swiss to motor vehicles is so well known, that, to Englishmen at all events, the idea of an annual contest being feasible in that region had hardly suggested itself, and even when the Alpine contest was established by the Imperial and Royal Automobile Club of Austria in 1911 the event passed almost unnoticed, from sheer lack of knowledge as to the highly interesting nature of the competition and the territory through which it passed. An English car was entered, however, for last year's Alpenfahrt, and another accompanied it as a free lance; as a result, the event received the publicity which was its due in the English press, and its all but epic character came to be understood.

The route of this year's contest differs somewhat from that of 1912, but is no less strenuous, and even on the score of long distances alone its formidable nature may be gathered from the following itinerary:

			Kiloms.		Miles.
June 22nd.	Vienna to Salzburg	... ...	413.6	=	255
,, 23rd.	Salzburg to Innsbruck	...	417.9	=	259¼
,, 24th.	Innsbruck to Riva	... ...	393.1	=	244
,, 25th.	Riva to Toblach	... ...	306.2	=	191
,, 26th.	Toblach to Trieste	... ...	329.3	=	203½
,, 27th.	Rest day in Trieste ...	...	——		——
,, 28th.	Trieste to Klagenfurt	...	389.6	=	241
,, 29th.	Klagenfurt to Vienna	...	418.1	=	259¼
	Totals	... ...	2,667.8	=	1,654

Now these figures give an average of 372 kilometres, or 230½ miles *per diem*, and that of itself is no light undertaking for the competitors. But mere figures as to mileage are absolutely delusive in this connection unless they are also accompanied by further details as to the heights of the Alpine passes which have to be traversed. Of these, as a reference to the map will show, there are no fewer than nineteen, and they may be set out as follows in the order in which they occur: Semmering, 3,149ft.; Niederalpl, 4,130ft.; Pass Lueg, 1,829ft.; Tauern, 5,695ft.; Katschberg, 5,383ft.; Brenner, 4,495ft.; Reschen-Scheidegg, 4,901ft.; Broccone, 5,305ft.; Gobbera, 3,339ft.; Rolle, 6,424ft.; Pordoi, 7,382ft.; Falzarego, 6,913ft.; Ampezzo, 5,065ft.; Kreuzberg, 3,596ft.; Wurzen, 3,512ft.; Predil, 3,629ft.; Monte Maggiore, 4,275ft.; Loibl, 4,494ft.; and the Stubalpe, 5,416ft. It is not to be assumed, of course, that each of these summits has to be attained from sea level; but on the other hand it must be borne in mind that in the case of passes within measurable distance of each other, such as the Rolle, the Pordoi, and the Falzarego, there is a considerable drop from one before the ascent of the next is begun, and that the negotiation of "hair-pin" corners is more difficult on the down grade than on the up, for in addition to the nicety of control required for the steering round the corners in either case, the question of brake control has to be taken into account on the descending side.

Still, it is the ability to climb which is the most impressive factor in the case of the car itself, as apart from the skill required in its control, and a mere glance at the itinerary for each day will show the stiff nature of the task which the competitors in the coming contest have to face. On the fourth day, for example, they have to ascend from Riva, which is almost on the level of the sea, to the summit of the Broccone Pass, a rise of from 230ft. to 5,315ft.; they then descend to Canale S. Boro, 2,490ft.; cross the saddle of the Gobbera, descend to Imer, 2,133ft., and rise to the Rolle summit, 6,424ft. Descending to Predazzo

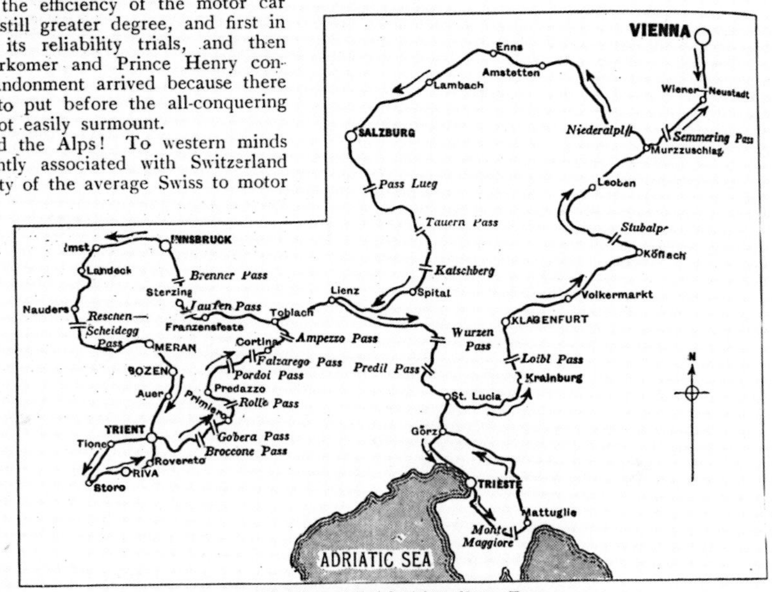

The route of the Austrian Alpine Tour.

1913

The Alpenfahrt is described as 'One of the Great Events of the Year'.

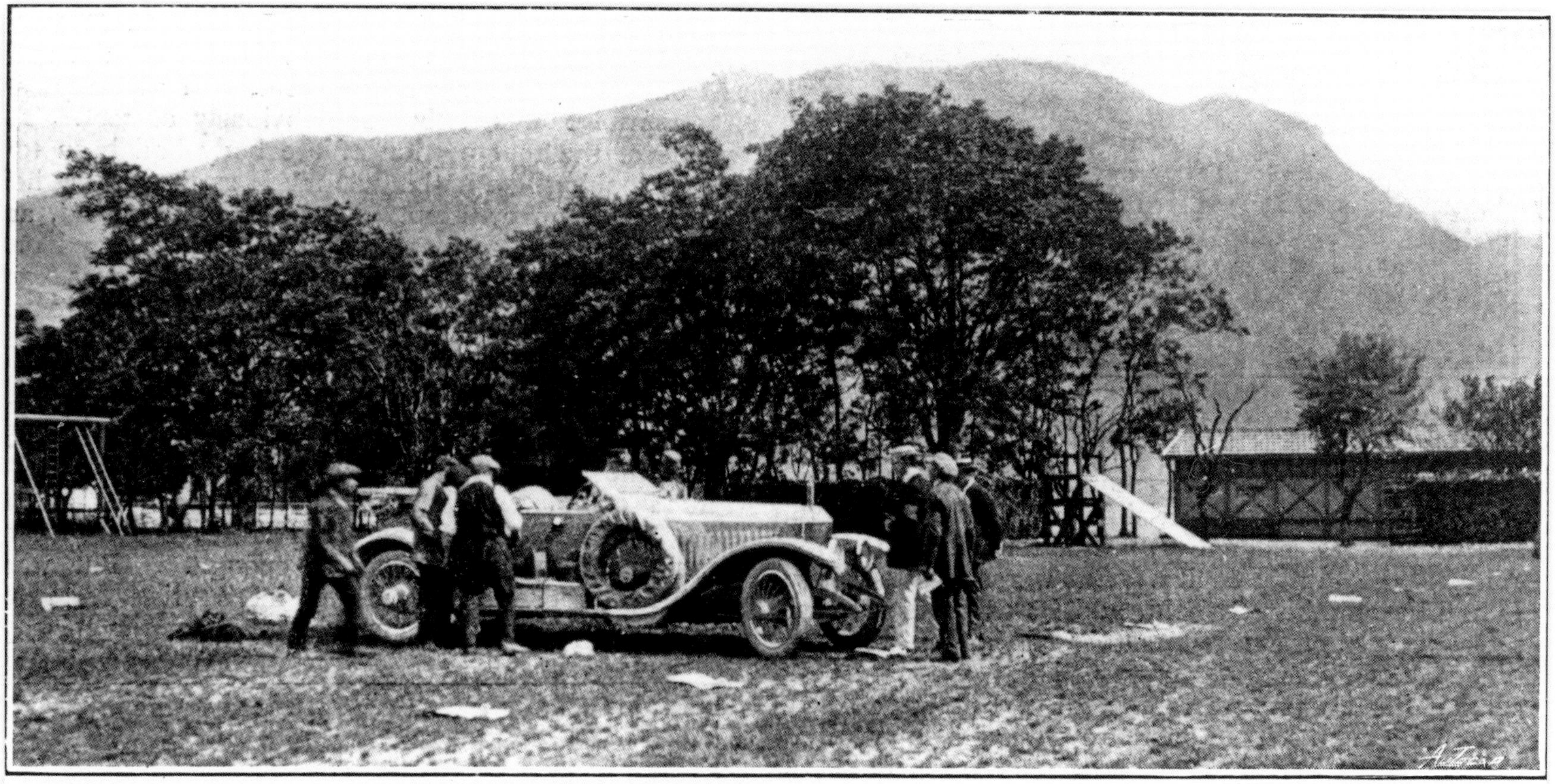

The first arrival at Riva. The Rolls Royce No. 4, belonging to and driven by Mr. James Radley.

1913

Mr. Radley's performance is notable.

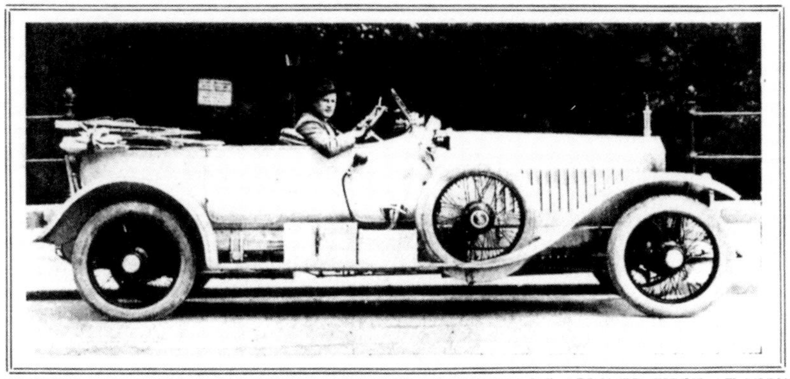

MR. JAMES RADLEY AND HIS ROLLS-ROYCE CAR, ON WHICH HE ARRIVED FIRST AT VIENNA.

1st DAY
Vienna to Salzburg.

ROLLS-ROYCE CARS finished 1st, 2nd, 3rd and 4th.

Mr. Radley, who arrived first, completed the distance of 260 miles in eight hours.

2nd DAY.
Salzburg to Innsbruck.

ROLLS-ROYCE CARS finished 1st, 2nd, 3rd and 4th.

So fast were these cars up the Katschberg that they even passed the official pacemaker, which afterwards was unable to catch them, and they arrived at Innsbruck about an hour ahead of the official car.

3rd DAY.
Innsbruck to Riva.

ROLLS-ROYCE CARS finished 1st, 2nd, 3rd and 4th.

Mr. Radley's Rolls-Royce came in at the heels of the official pacemaker, which he was not allowed to pass, and the other Rolls-Royces followed after an interval.

4th DAY.
Riva to Toblach.

ROLLS-ROYCE CARS finished 1st, 2nd, 3rd and 4th.

"The regular running of the Rolls-Royce cars is exciting praise on all sides."—
The Daily Mail.

5th DAY.
Toblach to Trieste.

ROLLS-ROYCE CARS finished 1st, 2nd, 3rd and 4th.

The Autocar, July 5th, states :—"As usual, the Rolls-Royce cars reached the finishing point in front of the other competitors, and there is certainly nothing in the trial to hold them as regards speed."

The Autocar, July 12th, adds :—"The only thing that had become monotonous being the regularity with which the Rolls-Royce cars kept in the van."

6th DAY.

Competitors resting at Trieste.

7th DAY.
Trieste to Klagenfurt.

ROLLS-ROYCE CARS continue to lead the field, and climb the Loibl Pass with its numerous turns in record time, finishing at Klagenfurt 1st, 2nd, 3rd and 4th.

The following is taken from "THE AUTOCAR," July 12th :—

> "By the majority of the competitors, the Loibl was feared more than the Katschberg itself, because, though the latter is slightly steeper, it has no corners, whereas the Loibl has a great many. The best time ever known to have been accomplished up the hill was 6½ minutes, but Radley (Rolls-Royce) went up in 5."

8th DAY.
FINAL.
Klagenfurt to Vienna.

ROLLS-ROYCE CARS maintain the lead throughout and finish first at Vienna. Only an accident to one of the Rolls-Royce cars, which was run into by a non-competing car, prevented the Rolls-Royce quartette's record of arriving first at every terminal point throughout the contest.

1913

Mr Radley finishes first on every day of the contest. The Rolls-Royce team were the next to finish.

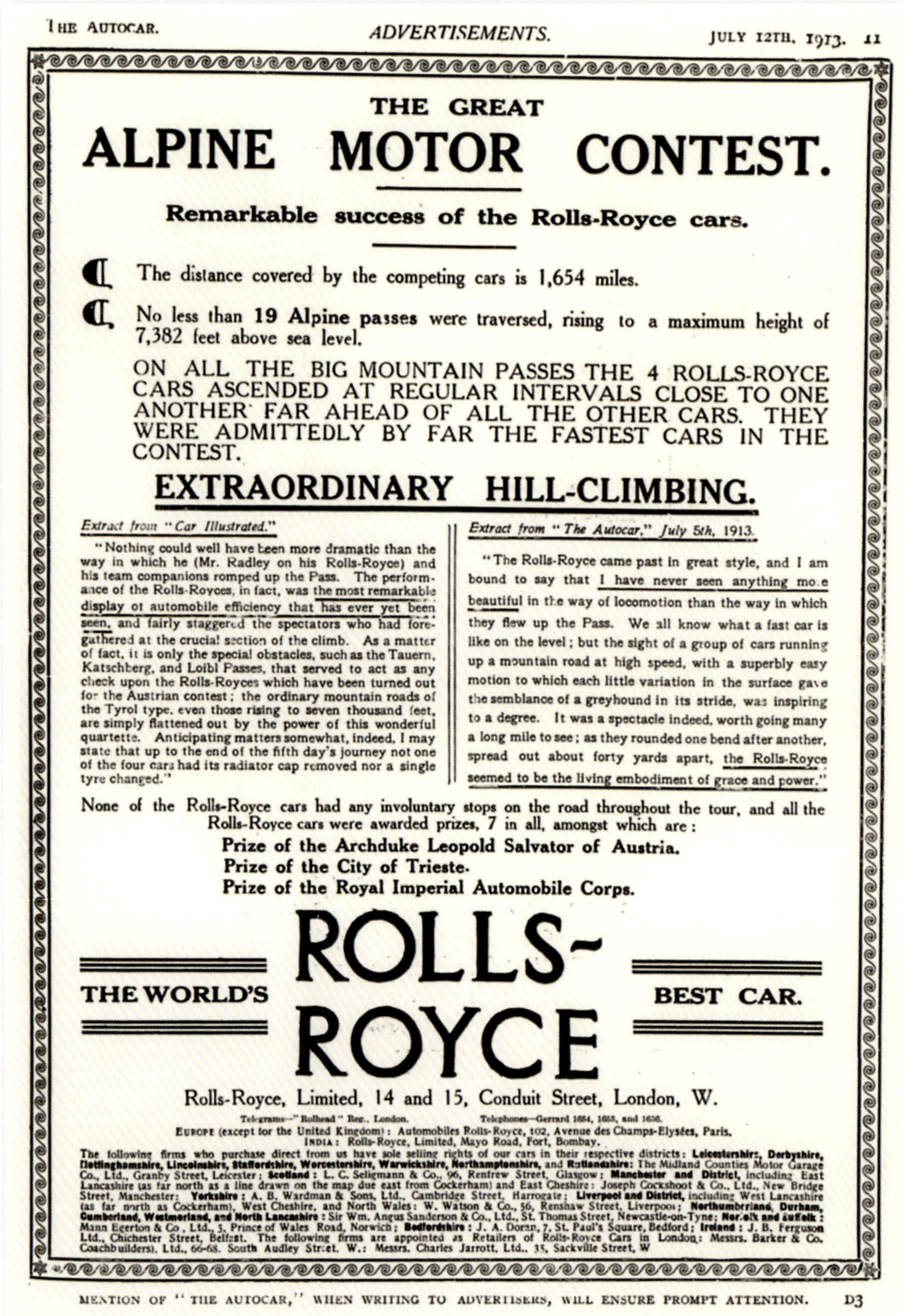

THE AUTOCAR. ADVERTISEMENTS. JULY 12TH, 1913. 11

THE GREAT

ALPINE MOTOR CONTEST.

Remarkable success of the Rolls-Royce cars.

The distance covered by the competing cars is 1,654 miles.

No less than **19 Alpine passes** were traversed, rising to a maximum height of 7,382 feet above sea level.

ON ALL THE BIG MOUNTAIN PASSES THE 4 ROLLS-ROYCE CARS ASCENDED AT REGULAR INTERVALS CLOSE TO ONE ANOTHER FAR AHEAD OF ALL THE OTHER CARS. THEY WERE ADMITTEDLY BY FAR THE FASTEST CARS IN THE CONTEST.

EXTRAORDINARY HILL-CLIMBING.

Extract from "Car Illustrated."

"Nothing could well have been more dramatic than the way in which he (Mr. Radley on his Rolls-Royce) and his team companions romped up the Pass. The performance of the Rolls-Royces, in fact, was the most remarkable display of automobile efficiency that has ever yet been seen, and fairly staggered the spectators who had foregathered at the crucial section of the climb. As a matter of fact, it is only the special obstacles, such as the Tauern, Katschberg, and Loibl Passes, that served to act as any check upon the Rolls-Royces which have been turned out for the Austrian contest; the ordinary mountain roads of the Tyrol type, even those rising to seven thousand feet, are simply flattened out by the power of this wonderful quartette. Anticipating matters somewhat, indeed, I may state that up to the end of the fifth day's journey not one of the four cars had its radiator cap removed nor a single tyre changed."

Extract from "The Autocar," July 5th, 1913.

"The Rolls-Royce came past in great style, and I am bound to say that I have never seen anything more beautiful in the way of locomotion than the way in which they flew up the Pass. We all know what a fast car is like on the level; but the sight of a group of cars running up a mountain road at high speed, with a superbly easy motion to which each little variation in the surface gave the semblance of a greyhound in its stride, was inspiring to a degree. It was a spectacle indeed, worth going many a long mile to see; as they rounded one bend after another, spread out about forty yards apart, the Rolls-Royce seemed to be the living embodiment of grace and power."

None of the Rolls-Royce cars had any involuntary stops on the road throughout the tour, and all the Rolls-Royce cars were awarded prizes, 7 in all, amongst which are:

Prize of the Archduke Leopold Salvator of Austria.
Prize of the City of Trieste.
Prize of the Royal Imperial Automobile Corps.

THE WORLD'S ROLLS-ROYCE BEST CAR.

Rolls-Royce, Limited, 14 and 15, Conduit Street, London, W.

Telegrams—"Rolhead" Reg., London. Telephones—Gerrard 1654, 1655, and 1656.

EUROPE (except for the United Kingdom): Automobiles Rolls-Royce, 102, Avenue des Champs-Elysées, Paris.
INDIA: Rolls-Royce, Limited, Mayo Road, Fort, Bombay.

The following firms who purchase direct from us have sole selling rights of our cars in their respective districts: **Leicestershire, Derbyshire, Nottinghamshire, Lincolnshire, Staffordshire, Worcestershire, Warwickshire, Northamptonshire,** and **Rutlandshire:** The Midland Counties Motor Garage Co., Ltd., Granby Street, Leicester; **Scotland:** L. C. Seligmann & Co., 96, Renfrew Street, Glasgow; **Manchester and District,** including East Lancashire (as far north as a line drawn on the map due east from Cockerham) and East Cheshire: Joseph Cockshoot & Co., Ltd., New Bridge Street, Manchester; **Yorkshire:** A. B. Wardman & Sons, Ltd., Cambridge Street, Harrogate; **Liverpool and District,** including West Lancashire (as far north as Cockerham), West Cheshire, and North Wales: W. Watson & Co., 56, Renshaw Street, Liverpool; **Northumberland, Durham, Cumberland, Westmorland, and North Lancashire:** Sir Wm. Angus Sanderson & Co., Ltd., St. Thomas Street, Newcastle-on-Tyne; **Norfolk and Suffolk:** Mann Egerton & Co., Ltd., 5, Prince of Wales Road, Norwich; **Bedfordshire:** J. A. Doran, 7, St. Paul's Square, Bedford; **Ireland:** J. B. Ferguson Ltd., Chichester Street, Belfast. The following firms are appointed as Retailers of Rolls-Royce Cars in London: Messrs. Barker & Co. (Coachbuilders), Ltd., 66-68, South Audley Street, W.: Messrs. Charles Jarrott, Ltd., 35, Sackville Street, W

MENTION OF "THE AUTOCAR," WHEN WRITING TO ADVERTISERS, WILL ENSURE PROMPT ATTENTION. D3

1913

The success of Rolls-Royce assures their status.

Nr. 24 — Allgemeine Automobil-Zeitung — Seite 41

ROLLS-ROYCE

Der beste Wagen der Welt!

3 Jahre Garan-tie

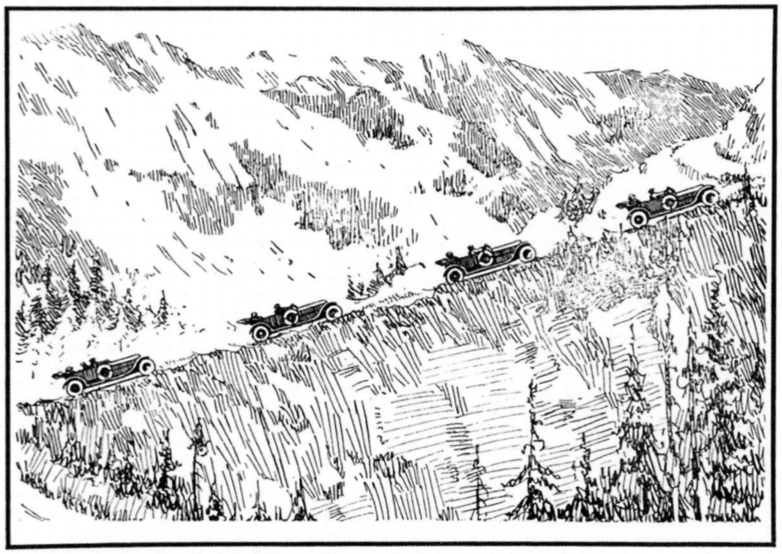

40|50 HP 6 Zyl.

Ein interessanter Rückblick!

ALPENFAHRT 1913

Punktelos! Sieben Preise!

. . . . Tag für Tag erklommen die vier Rolls-Royce Wagen, knapp hintereinander fahrend, diese Steigungen nicht nur viel schneller, sondern auch mit viel größerer Leichtigkeit und Geräuschlosigkeit als alle anderen Konkurrenten . . . (Financial Times, 15. Juli 1913)

. . . . Die Rolls-Royce Wagen flogen den Katschberg mühelos hinan, der Anblick einer Gruppe von Wagen, welche die Bergstraßen gleich Windspielen hinanflogen, war wirklich begeisternd. . . . . (The Autocar, 12. Juli 1913)

. . . . Alle vier unserer steilsten Bergpässe mühelos erklommen, kehrten alle vier Rolls-Royce Wagen nach Wien mit der gleichen Plombe am Kühler zurück. . . . (Neue Freie Presse, 6. Juli 1913)

. . . . Das brillante Abschneiden der Rolls-Royce . . . . (Fremdenblatt, 6. Juli 1913)

General-Repräsentanz für Oesterreich-Ungarn

Telegr.-Adresse Rollsroyce.

Wien, I. Tegetthoffstraße Nr. 4.

Telephon Nr. 11.958.

1913

Rolls-Royce - The Best Car in the World.

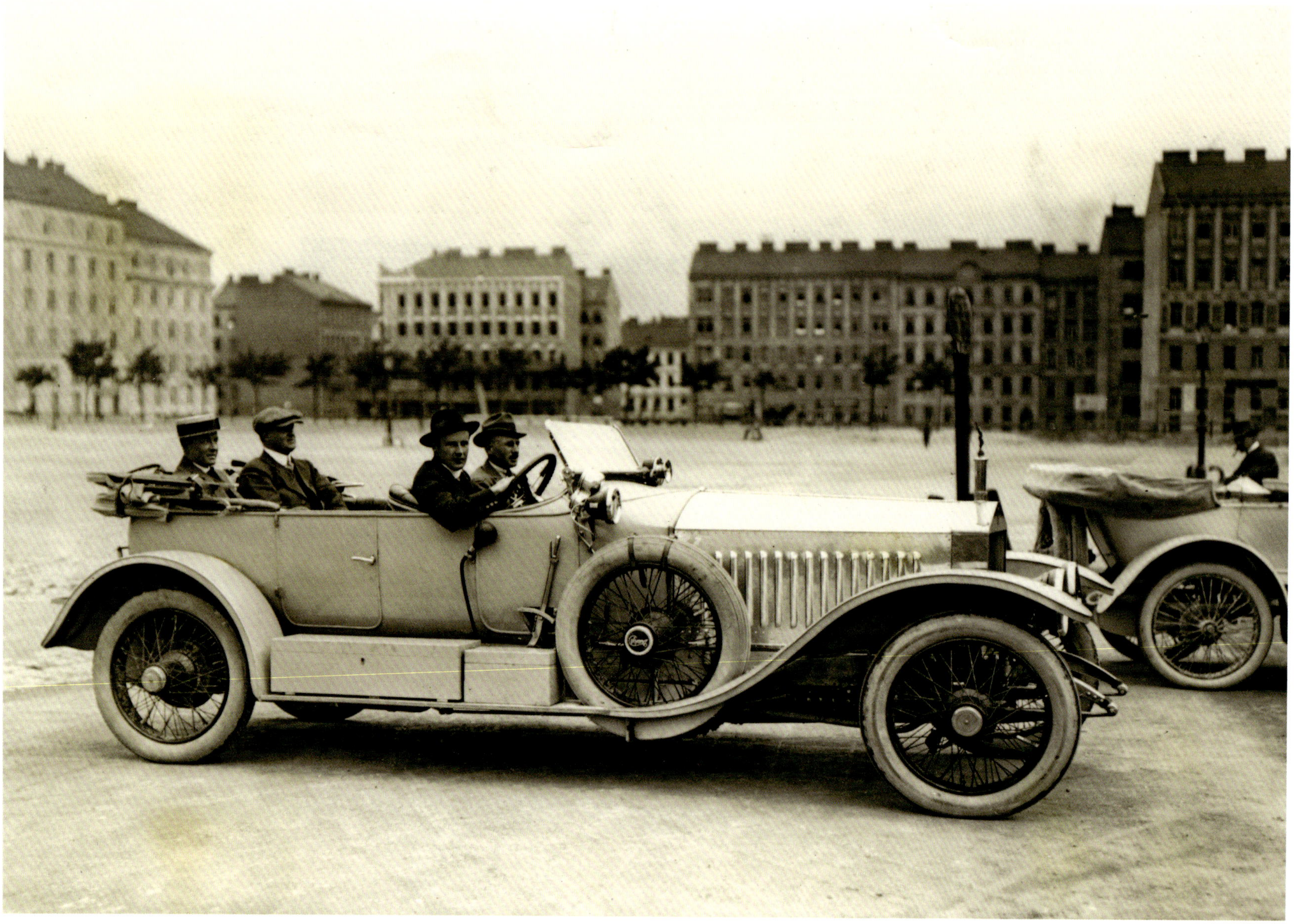

1913

Mr Radley at Vienna in June 1913.

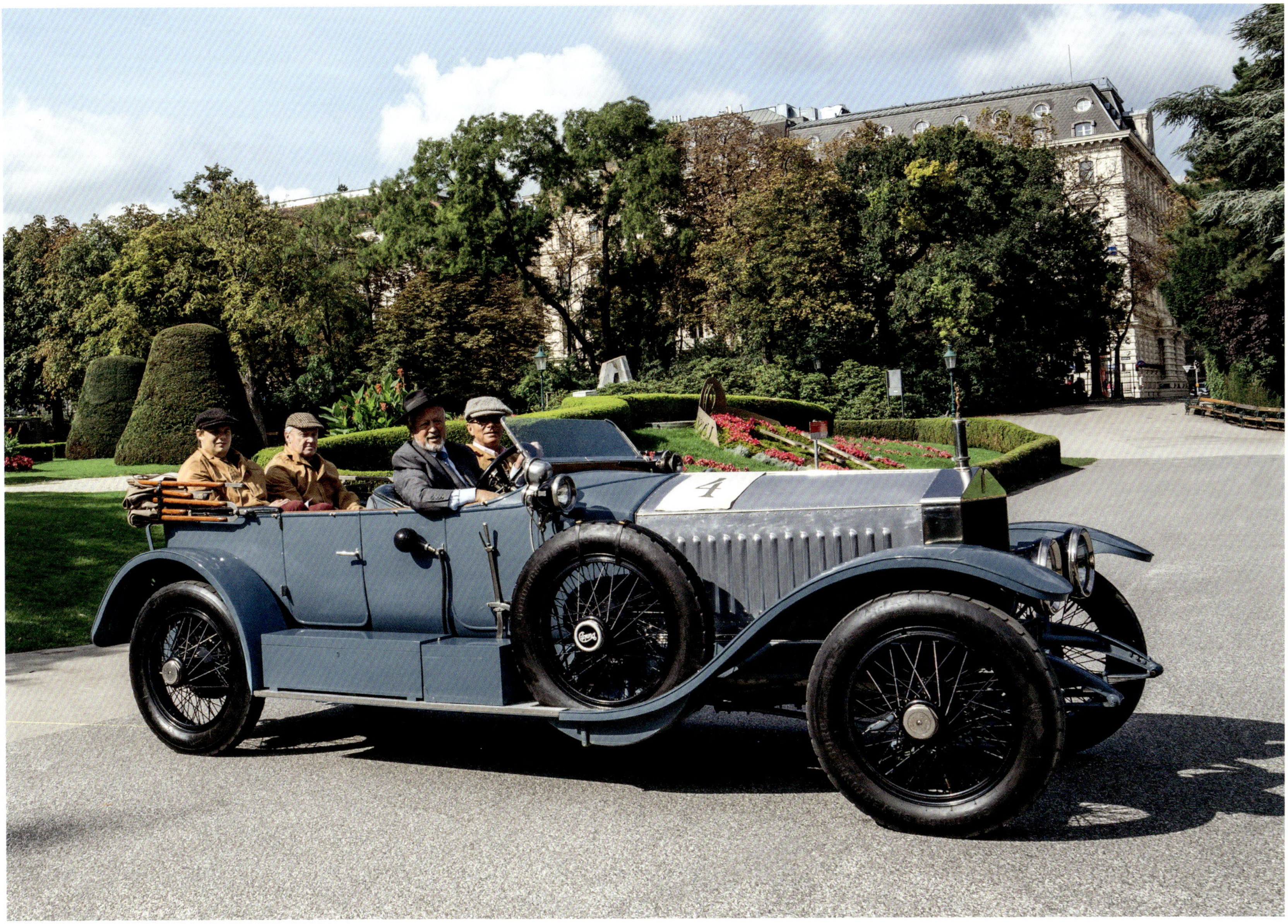

2013

The Radley car repeated the journey a century later.

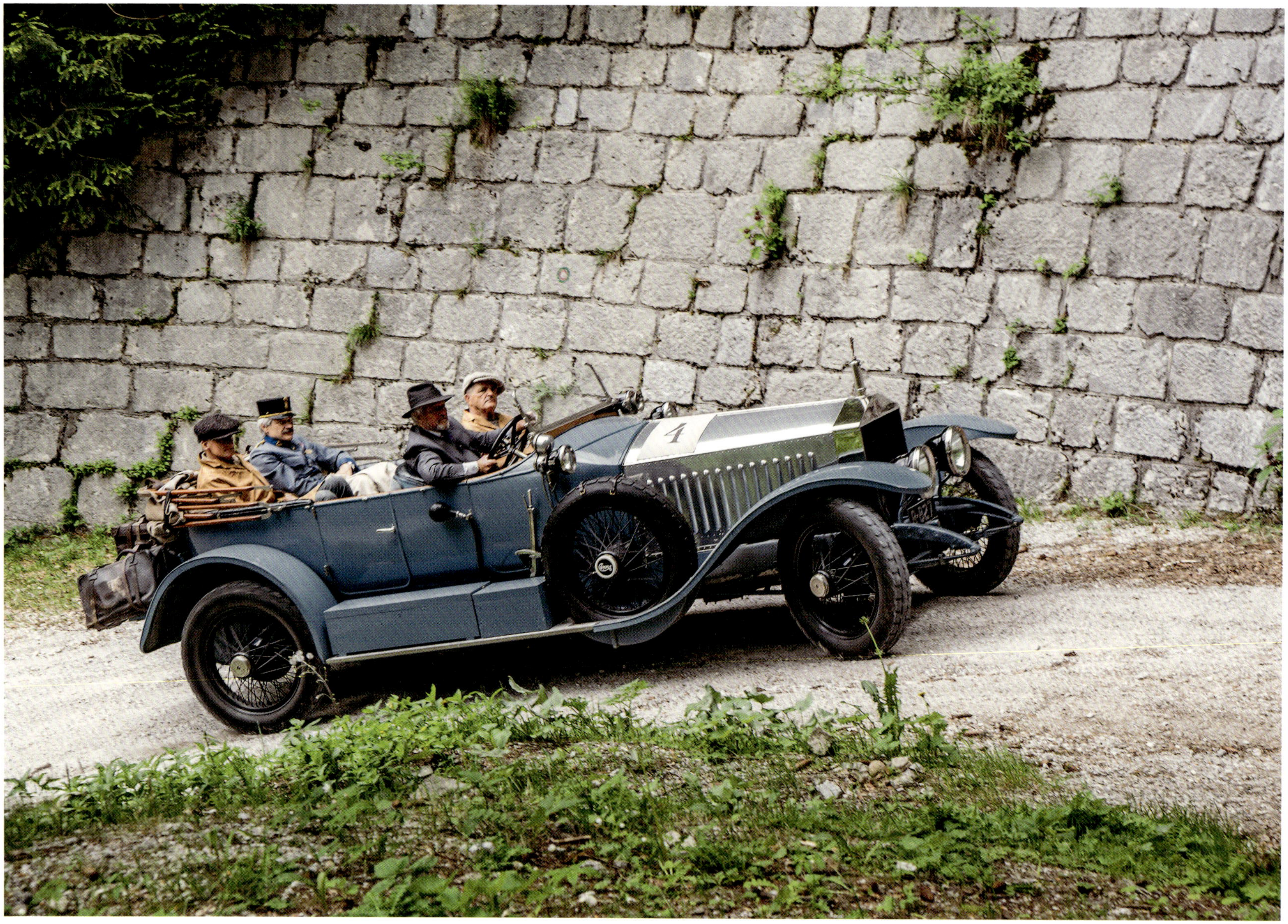

2013

All the mountain passes were climbed once again.
The historic performance of 1913 was repeated.

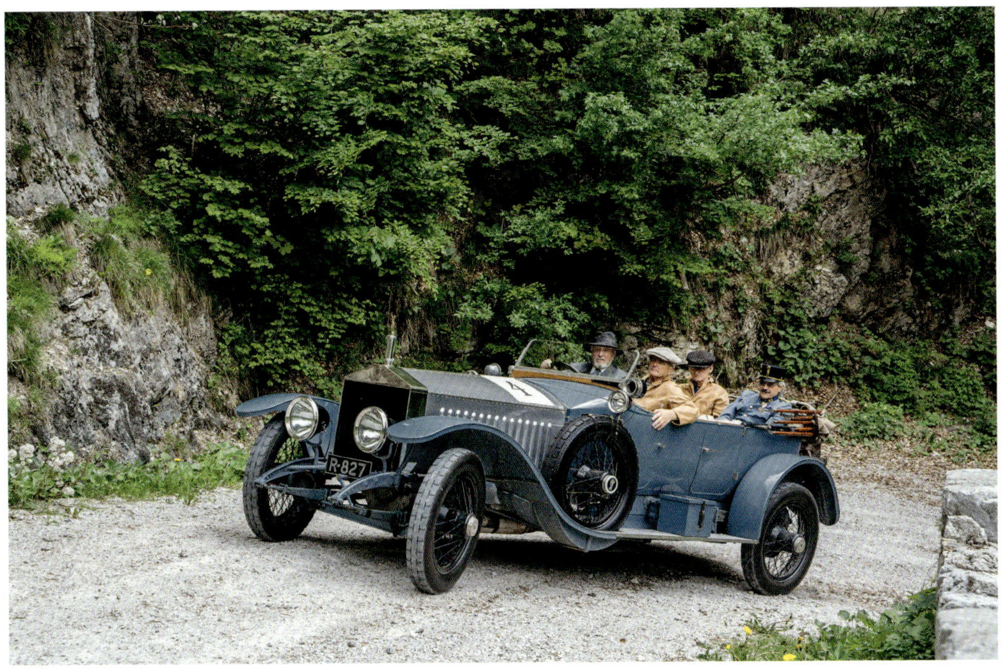
R·827

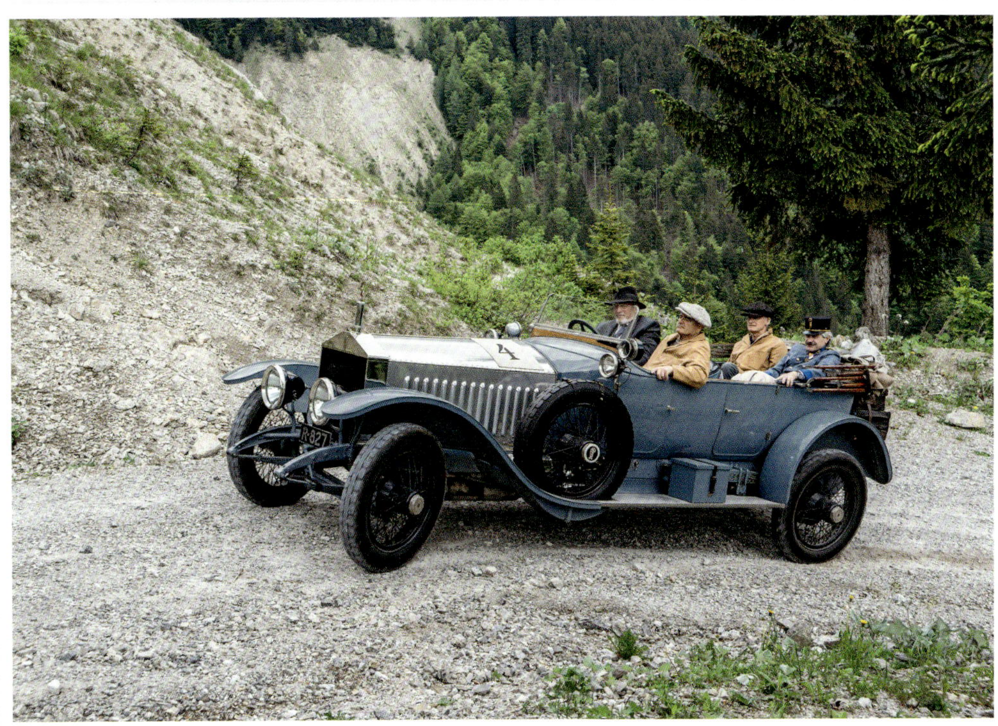

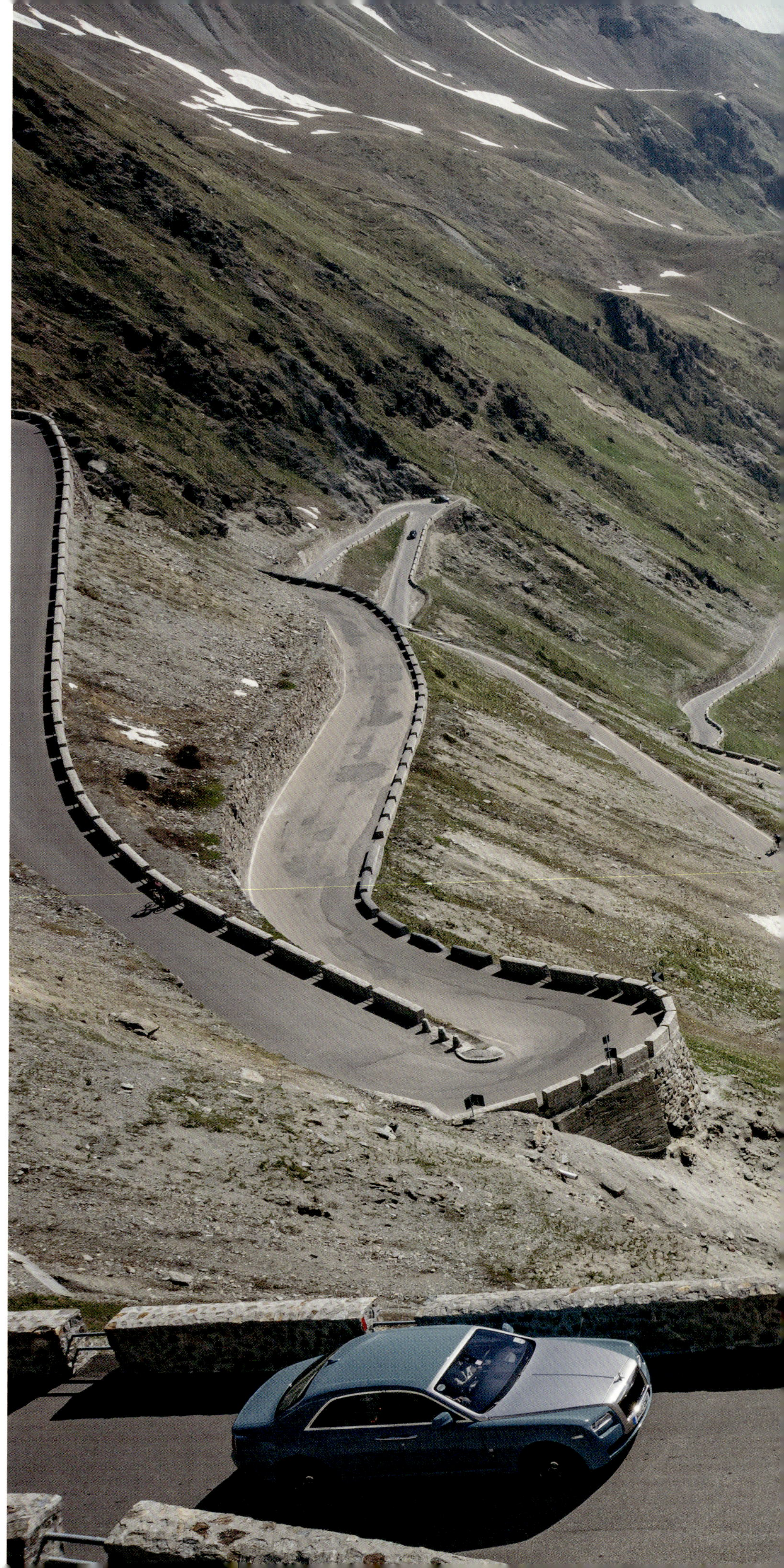

2013

Accompanied by a new Rolls-Royce inspired by the Radley car.

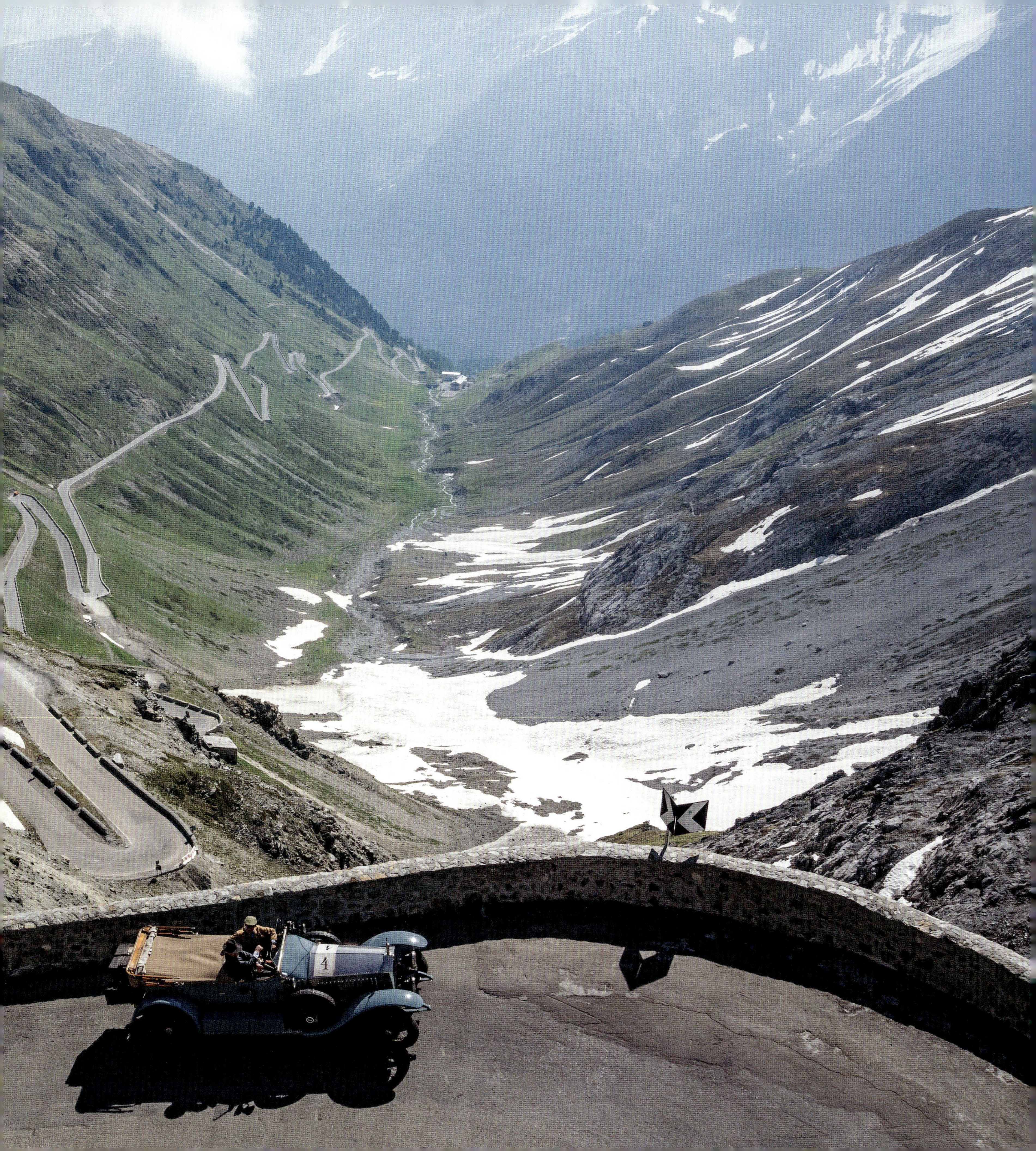
4

THE HISTORY OF THE AUSTRIAN ALPENFAHRT

The ÖAC (Österreichscher Automobil Club) began organising alpine trials for light cars in 1898, which is one of the oldest events in the world. In 1910 the already well established Semmering hill climb was cancelled due to problems with the authorities, which most probably laid the foundations for an event which then survived until 1973 as part of the Rally World Championship. The genesis of the Austrian Alpenfahrt goes back to the year 1907 when the ÖAC organised its first 'International Test Drive for Small Cars'. Similar trials were held in 1908 and 1909 but they were all fairly minor events where the cars traversed only a small number of mountain passes.

In 1910 the ÖAC (about to acquire royal patronage and soon to become the KKÖAC [Royal Austrian Automobile Club], the forerunner of the present ÖAMTC) organised the first contest officially called 'The Austrian Alpenfahrt'. A small but exclusive event of 870 km in four driving days with 16 cars participating, it was no longer restricted to light cars. Among the contestants were Baron Franz Meyr Melnhof of Frohnleiten in his 48 hp Mercedes and Count Paul Draskovich in a Laurin & Klement, one of three such cars which also won the team prize.

The next year, 1911, the event grew significantly in size, now over a distance of 1421 km, again taking four days and attracting 51 entrants. Extra mountain passes including the Loibl and Wurzen were added to the Katschberg to increase the difficulty. Altogether 41 cars arrived back in Vienna, only 12 with a clean sheet. Austro-Daimler had entered ten cars of which eight finished, five without any loss of points and they won the team prize.

In 1912 the event grew substantially again - in size, in number of participants and, most significantly, in international importance, as the other major sporting contests for cars, such as the Prince Henry trials, were discontinued. This year saw an event stretching over seven days and 2400 km and incorporating many famous mountain passes of the Dolomites including the Pordoi and Falzarego. The event was under the direct patronage of Archduke (Erzherzog) Leopold Salvator and the actual competitors included the Archduke Karl Franz Joseph and the Archduke Joseph Ferdinand. Other competitors were Prince Elias of Parma, Prince Alexander Croy, the Princess Charlotte of Saxe Meiningen, Count Alexander Kolowrat, Count Paul Draskovich, Count Heinrich Schönfeld, Count Siegfried Wimpffen, Count George Orssich, Count Eugen Lamberg, Baron Walter Franz and Baron Alexander Styrcea from an incredible total of 85 entrants representing 28 different marques.

One of the cars was a Rolls-Royce entered by the legendary James Radley of England. Although he was a highly experienced motorist he had not familiarised himself with the route as many other entrants had and was unprepared for the rigours of some of the passes. On the first day out from Vienna, Radley, in car number 2, stopped on the Katschberg, a six kilometre mountain climb of around 25 % gradient, but with a maximum gradient, for the last 20 metres, of 27.9 %. This stop did not bother Radley, but caused consternation to Rolls-Royce who were about to open a new Vienna depot. The results sheets showed that while 72 of the other entrants finished the course, 25 without loss of marks, the Rolls-Royce had been withdrawn on the very first day. Fiat and Opel shared the team prize.

The 1913 contest was even longer and more arduous - the most severe that had ever been held, with a total distance of 2650 km and 19 major alpine passes plus many minor passes. There were fewer entries, because many of the works teams threatened to boycott the event as they wished it to be held every two years, not annually. After some last minute team entries from Hansa, Fiat and Fischer, a total of 47 cars participated, which was still well down on the previous year. Four Rolls-Royce cars were entered, a three car works team plus James Radley, back again in car number 4 after his misadventure the previous year, intending to prove that both he and Rolls-Royce were a formidable combination. They all made non-stop runs, with Radley leading throughout the contest, starting and finishing first on each day. Each of the cars won one or more prizes and showed a cooling efficiency such that no water was added to the radiators on any day. In spite of this remarkable performance, two of the team cars lost marks on minor technicalities, leaving Audi to win the team prize. Rolls-Royce were more than exonerated for the 1912 fiasco, but the company never again entered competition motoring.

The 1914 contest was even more severe than the previous year, with the number of entrants nevertheless increased to 75, and with 31 marques represented. James Radley was back again in a further improved Rolls-Royce Silver Ghost, supported in the background by Rolls-Royce, even though they did not enter a works team.

The total distance this year had been increased to 2932 km and more additional mountain passes had also been included. Radley was once again the leader on all days except one, when he had travelled so fast that the marshals were not on hand to direct him to make a turning. He travelled about 60 km before discovering that he was on the wrong road. His performance was flawless and he won a major prize once again. The team prize was shared between Audi and Hansa.

Alas, that was the last such contest. Turmoil in the Balkans and the assassination in Sarajevo of Archduke Franz Ferdinand and his wife Sophie von Hohenberg plunged Europe into a long and costly war which ended with a re-drawn map of Europe and the end of the old Austro-Hungarian Empire.

Cars of at least 53 different marques took part in the original Austrian Alpine Trials between 1910 & 1914. Most European marques competed, as well as some British and even a few American marques, including Adler, ALFA, Apollo, Armstrong-Whitworth, Audi, Austin, Austro Daimler, Benz, Berliet, Bugatti, Cadillac, Chevrolet, Daimler (English), Darracq, de Dion Bouton, Delaunay-Belleville, Dixi, EBM, Ehrhardt, FIAT, Fischer-Ventillos, Ford, Gräf und Stift, Gregoire, Hansa, Horch, Hotchkiss, Laurin & Klement, Mathis, Mercedes, Minerva-Knight, Mors, NAG, Neckarsulm (NSU), Nesselsdorf, NW, Opel, Oryx, Overland, Peugeot, Praga, Protos, Puch, Raba, RAF-Knight, Renault, Rolls-Royce, Scat, Singer, Vauxhall, WAF, Wanderer, Wolseley. Other marques, including Isotta Fraschini and Siddeley-Deasley, were also involved as official or support vehicles.

Drivers in the early years were often the owners of the companies or the engineers of the cars: Porsche (Austro Daimler), Opel, Hieronimus (Laurin & Klement) and Horch (Audi) were among them as well as the Belgian de Jong, owner of Minerva, and Herbert Austin jnr. Most of the drivers were under 30 years of age.

Mr Radley Drives To Vienna

The circumstances which conspired

to make this unique project possible

OLD CAR INTEREST

As a small boy, living on a dairy farm in New Zealand, a cinema outing was an occasional treat. One of the films which stayed in my memory was the film 'Genevieve', a charming tale based on the London-Brighton veteran car run. The hero of the film was not a handsome man or lovely lady, but the car itself – 'Genevieve'.

Soon after seeing the film, we went on another day trip – always close enough to return home to milk the cows in the afternoon – to a town holding an Agricultural & Pastoral (A&P) Show. It always had plenty of farm animals, tractors, fairground attractions and various other items to keep all the family amused. This time, the show also had some old cars.

Now this was the 1950s, so old cars dated from the really early years – certainly no newer than the 1920s and sometimes earlier, maybe much earlier. And this time, one of the old cars was actually the star of the film – 'Genevieve' herself.

Soon after the film was made, 'Genevieve' had been sold to a New Zealander and here she was – and what a star! I was hooked! From then on I had a love of old cars, even though it would be many years before I was in a position to indulge the passion.

Not until the mid 1980s did I become the owner of my first old car, a Silver Ghost from 1922, which was then used for family holidays, not just minor day trips.

HOW THE ALPENFAHRT RE-ENACTMENT CAME ABOUT

The whole story started by winning the Alpine Trophy in 1986. This historic trophy is one of a pair of cut glass decanters originally presented by the Archduke Leopold Salvator of Austria as one of the prizes in the Austrian Alpine Trials in 1913. It was won by C. C. Friese (not James Radley as is popularly supposed) and subsequently presented to the 20-Ghost Club by Rolls-Royce. The sight of this trophy on the mantlepiece (or the dining table) was the catalyst for finding out more about the Austrian Alpine Trials.

Many people were aware that the Alpine Trials were held each year from 1910 to 1914 (and were to have been held again in 1915), that James Radley entered a Silver Ghost in 1912 and on the first day, on the Katschberg Pass, his car stopped on a very stiff gradient owing to its being geared too highly. The car restarted after unloading its passengers, but because Radley had spoiled his chances of winning, he withdrew from the event.

In 1913, of course, the Rolls-Royce team of three Silver Ghosts, plus Radley in a fourth Ghost performed superbly, and in 1914 Radley alone was again magnificent. In spite of this, there was little detailed information of the event itself and I set out to research 'The Alpine' to discover as much as I possibly could. Over the following months I gradually obtained information, much of it from the British Library and the National Motor Museum and built up enough data to more than fill a book.

Much interesting information had thus come to light, but after the research had reached a certain stage, it seemed that the best thing to do to really understand the event was to travel over the route to see what it was like 75 years after the first Silver Ghost came to the Alps. And what better way than in a Silver Ghost?

Much time was then spent researching a route, both to the Alps and within the Alps, as there were some differences in each of the years. After detailing the 1912, 1913 and 1914 routes we chose a route which most closely approximated the 1914 route but also included other portions unique to either 1912 or 1913.

With my wife, Rae, and children Jane and Robert, we set off in mid July 1987 in our 1922 Silver Ghost (100HG), travelling via France, Luxembourg and Germany and joining the Alpine Trials route near Innsbruck 5 days later. Our first trip was over the Brenner Pass (old road) down to Sterzing (Vipiteno) in Italy and return. Then off for our first really long Alpine journey of 228 miles to Villach. The three passes we crossed included the Radstadter Tauern, where the road was being rebuilt and the surface was very muddy – a little like some of the original roads - then on to the famous Katschberg Pass, rebuilt since the trials but still steep at about 18%. From a Villach base we headed on a round trip southwards into Yugoslavia up the very steep Wurzen Pass, which we immediately descended and then crossed into Italy where the Predil Pass was ascended, then back into Yugoslavia again. (These regions were all part of the Austrian Empire until 1919.)

We were now in quiet roads, little villages with flowers in profusion from window boxes, and cheering people as we glided by. We knew how it must have felt to the Times Correspondent from a report published on Saturday June 28th 1913. '"Schnell, Schnell!" the children cried to the cars as they flew past today, and flung flowers at us all. Flowers, sunshine, glorious scenery, and happy faces – that is what the runners in this great race see.'

Continuing southwards down a very scenic valley following the 1912 and 1913 routes, at Most na Soči (formerly St Lucia), we headed eastwards along quiet mountain roads to Kranj (formerly Krainburg) then on to the Loibl Pass road. This was a busy main road at the time with a steep climb leading to the tunnel which bypassed the old high pass route which in its day was more difficult and more feared than the Katschberg. The tunnel, now the boundary between Yugoslavia and Austria, was thus something of an anti-climax, but we continued on back to Villach without finding the Loibl Pass summit.

FINDING THE LOIBL

So much has been written about the Loibl Pass that it seemed essential to return and find the old road. So a day or two later I headed back from Villach, early on a drizzly, cloudy morning in search of the Loibl. An old gravel road seemed a likely choice and it turned out to be the old main road, now used only as a logging road. I drove up this steep gravel road round many hairpins, over countless canniveaux (drainage gulleys across the road) and up into the mist. It was an eerie sensation to find myself in solitude at the top of the pass, with its two high obelisks which still mark the border, and the barriers and derelict customs posts on either side. All this in a swirling mist certainly evoked the ghosts of the past and made this one of the most memorable locations on our whole trip.

While the Austrian side which I had ascended had gradients of up to 23 %, the Yugoslavian (formerly Carniola province of Austria) side which was always used for the ascent in the Alpine trials, with 13 hairpin bends and gradients from 17 % to 29 %.

As C. L. Freeston wrote in the 'Autocar' in 1914,

> 'The hairpins are all banked the wrong way and are acute enough in radius to compel the driver to take the inside edge if he does not want to stop and reverse. As a driving feat the Loibl is supreme.The corners are just wide enough to get round, and for this reason motorists who are proud of their cars and their driving skill alike must always be fascinated by the Loibl, and tackle it in preference to easier ascents.'

My impressions of this part of the Alpine Trials route, still in its original state, are best summed up in the log which I wrote on the day of my visit.

> 'Top of the Loibl Pass road on Austrian side.
>
> Obelisks; abandoned border posts; barriers across road; rain and mist.
>
> Road on Yugoslavian side unused and growing weeds on surface in many places.
>
> Walk down Loibl Pass road – steep, some minor land slips with small rocks on road; basic formation intact. Navigable.
>
> Down road past numerous hairpin corners; large rock about two metres wide blocks road. Further down some rain gullies also make road unnavigable.
>
> Could be easily repaired and weeds scraped away to make road usable.
>
> Road ends in locked gated fence within 100 metres of tunnel entrance on modern road.

Walk back up pass. Steep – hot work.

Road in very original state but many old side barriers broken or missing.

Stone barricades almost intact.

Return to summit – open barriers.

Reverse car down to second hairpin (from summit). Various photos. Evocative.

Restart (just) on slippery wet weed covered road for "mini-ascent" of old Loibl Pass.

Drive back to summit – close border barriers.

Descend on Austrian side. Over the canniveaux (about 30 in the descent of around two miles). Much more awkward to cross when descending. Braking very tricky on surface of fine gravel. Canniveaux bumpy if traversed at any speed over 10–15 mph.

End of Old Loibl Pass road. Back to busy main road.'

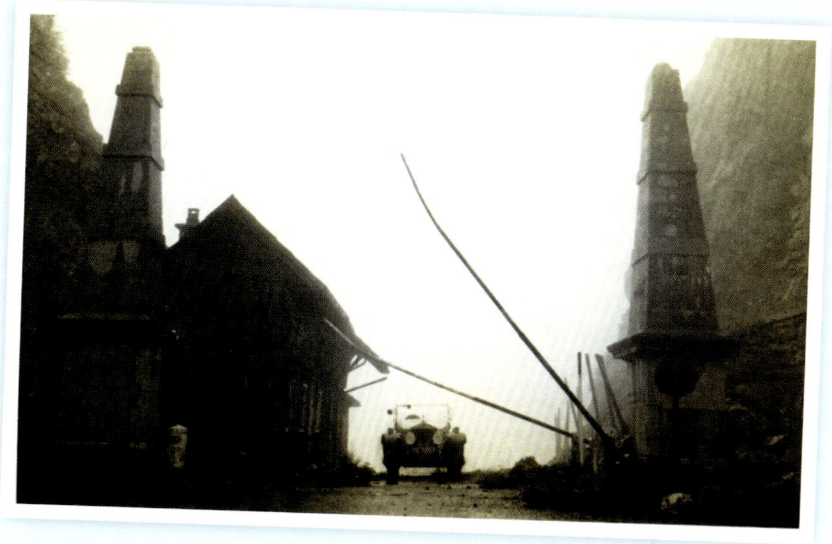

That was the Eureka moment!

Before leaving the top of the Loibl Pass to drive back down into Austria, I had decided to organise a re-enactment of the 1913 Alpenfahrt, on the 80th anniversary in June 1993. The route would once again include the fantastic old Loibl Pass road.

THE RADLEY SILVER GHOST

On the tour of Northern Spain in September 1985, the elderly Fred Watson accompanied me for an entire day's vintage motoring in my 1922 Silver Ghost. This was quiet rural Spain and we travelled up river gorges and through quiet villages, driving over 150 miles on a variety of roads, and with the conversation very much on a subject dear to Fred's heart – vintage motoring. This was the first time for many years that Fred had done a full days motoring in a Silver Ghost and he thoroughly enjoyed himself.

The subject moved in due course onto the subject of the 1913 Radley Alpine Eagle Silver Ghost, which had been in Fred's possession since 1951. It was assumed that the car would pass down through the family. But as a throwaway line at the end of the day, I did say – 'if you ever thought of selling the car, give me a call', not thinking much more about it.

At that time the Radley car, having been restored more than 30 years previously, was not in a fit condition for real touring, but was subsequently sent for restoration to its proper state of fitness. But while it was in this condition, I got the call to say that the car was to be sold – and was I interested? After recovering from the initial shock, I had to agree that I still was. And so it came to pass that I purchased an old car, sight unseen, which was now in a completely dismantled condition, as the restoration showed that the chassis was twisted and had to be straightened.

Being fortunate enough to acquire the car and continue the restoration process, it seemed logical to return the car to its identical original state of 1913, when Radley set out for Vienna and the Austrian Alpenfahrt. Now it was known that there were many unique features on the car when it was new. The problem was that many of them had been removed, the car was in pieces anyway and nobody knew precisely what all the special items looked like. So a lot more research was needed in order to complete this task as well.

RESEARCH & RESTORATION

In the beginning of 1988 I devised two cunning plans which most other people thought were crazy!

The first: a complete re-enactment of the 1913 Alpine Contest, in time for the 80th anniversary in 1993. Too long, too difficult, too expensive, too demanding and so it went on – and no-one would come, so it would not happen. We said that we had already done the journey and would do it again on our own anyway, so it would definitely happen. If that was not enough, the second plan was to completely restore the Radley Alpine 1913 Rolls-Royce, to a precise original condition which was as yet unknown.

Research for both projects continued apace, with much time spent in the British Library newspaper office, as well as periodic trips to Austria, to research in the 'Nationalbibliothek' (National Library), to find information on the original Alpenfahrt events and about the Rolls-Royce cars, particularly Radley's car from 1913. On every trip to Austria, further route research was undertaken as well, to discover every aspect of the route.

Information came to light from a wide variety of sources. The Bibliothek had detailed accounts of these early events in the local car magazine, 'Allgemeine Automobil-Zeitung', complete with many photographs and original entry forms as well as the precise route details with every village including intermediate distances and elapsed times. This was vital information to understand the tempo of the original events and was extremely useful to set timings now, particularly in the mountain regions. Additionally, the magazines had details what they referred to as 'Technical Jokes' on the Alpine Cars. Included in these categories was the radiator extension tube, not a Rolls-Royce invention but a device used by Fiat in 1912 which many car makers thought that they had better copy, in case it gave some advantage. The carburettor flooding device was also described in the article.

By a stroke of luck and quite unrelated to my other researches, I acquired the last known address of James Radley who had died more than 30 years earlier. It provided me with enough information to do some detective work and track down his stepson in law, David Scott, who had various artefacts, including the Radley scrap book. This contained a lot of information from his flying days and some original photographs, taken in Vienna by the professional photographer Heinrich Schumann. These pictures showed Radley and the Rolls-Royce team in Vienna in 1913. They provided an even greater incentive to continue my efforts.

Meanwhile the car restoration progressed and further important discoveries were made at the Royce Foundation, which had acquired some early Rolls-Royce blueprints, including those for the components of the flooding device described in the Austrian magazine. Discussion with other Rolls-Royce owners yielded the fact that one Silver Ghost in America even had a flooding device still working on the car! Original paint and leather colours proved difficult to establish with certainty, but after three years of experimenting with possible colours, the coach builders eventually found the original colour underneath the mudguards which were still original. 'Nobody ever takes off all the paint from there', they said. Amazingly, the colour we had decided to use was exactly the same as the original – but we would never have known!

Route investigations were never more complex than the Loibl Pass discussed elsewhere, but nonetheless every town through which we passed was investigated, as were all the small sections now bypassed, as well as sometimes large sections which could easily be overlooked. Where a small town to the right of the route could be entered at one end and exited at the other, we were able to include it in the route book, giving two particular advantages. Firstly, a chance to drive through a charming village with original buildings from the time of the original; secondly a chance to prevent modern traffic from being held up behind slower vehicles. Villages requiring a left turn to reach the centre were more difficult, as we discovered for our selves when on occasion it took up to five minutes to return to a busy road when necessary to cross back to the right hand side. We quickly realised that these villages would be excluded from the 1993 route!

While all this was happening, we were compiling a comprehensive route book with every historical aspect, particularly the mountain passes, described in detail and every turn documented with signs and distances, for this was to be a journey to match the original 1913 route as closely as possible. When the book was collated and a draft copy printed, each segment was then 'driven' on a map, to ensure that no left or right turns were incorrect and no distances between instructions were wildly inaccurate.

As time went on, more people realised that both plans were going to happen and now wanted to take part in the event. Some sponsorship was also organised, particularly from within Austria, which meant that we had contacts in most of the towns and villages so that the event could have the historic routes used as much as possible, so it all gradually came together. Other sponsorship made it possible to have some competitive elements and combined with the research, a decision was made to produce cut glass decanters identical to the original Leopold Salvator Trophy which inspired all this in the first place.

Europe, on the cusp of momentous change in 1913, was again experiencing significant change during the five years when the research was progressing. Many of these changes were particularly beneficial to the Alpine event. Whereas in 1913, the entire route was part of the Austro-Hungarian Empire and thus no borders to cross, the 1993 event crossed international borders no less than 12 times, with two more if taking the Stelvio option, plus two further borders with the separation of the Yugoslav states of Slovenia and Croatia. Fortunately during this period, the Schengen agreement came into force and many of the crossings with the most serious delays ceased to exist as a problem. Other difficult borders, which created enormous delays and major traffic problems, were the Wurzen Pass and Pordoi Pass borders. Then in 1991, when the Karawanken tunnel was opened as an alternative, the two problems were removed at a stroke, even though within a month of the opening, there was a fierce ten day battle, with the Yugoslav Army trying (unsuccessfully) to seize this new border crossing.

Car restoration was proceeding all the while and in April 1993 it was complete and the car ready for its road trials after a five year restoration period. At the same time, the detailed Route Book was being finalised and 50 cars were being readied for a June start in Vienna. By this time the BBC had become aware of the project and agreed to send their 'Top Gear' team to film the event.

THE LOIBL

After investigating the old Loibl Pass summit in 1987 and deciding to organise an Alpine tour, including the restoration of the pass, the problem we faced then was how to go about it. The original Alpenfahrt events from 1910 to 1914 were organised by the Royal Austrian Automobile Club, whose successor was the ÖAMTC in Vienna and so a meeting was arranged with them. Along with explaining the re-enactment tour we were planning, we asked if they could make contact with the Italian and Yugoslav organisations to explain our plans. This was particularly with regard to the Loibl Pass in Yugoslavia and an unused section of the Predil Pass, now in Italy.

We had followed the required protocol and can only imagine what must have happened next. A letter was duly despatched from Vienna to the required Italian motoring organisation in Rome. Nothing further was ever heard. The letter probably arrived in Rome, where it was immediately placed in the 'too hard' bin. Similarly a letter was despatched to Belgrade, where the command system would have decided that this belonged to Slovenia, so it was sent to Ljubljana. They decided that it sounded like rallying and there were two European champion rally drivers nearby. The rally drivers received the letter and wondered how someone from New Zealand could be asking about a Slovenian mountain pass which they had 'lost'. So off they went, in the summer of 1990, to locate the pass and get permission to investigate it.

At the end of that summer I received a letter from rally drivers Aleš Črnivec & Stojan Kastelic, who had climbed the pass and taken numerous photographs, inviting me to come out to Ljubljana and discuss my plans with them. I went out in the autumn, checked into a hotel on a gloomy, rainy Ljubljana evening, prior to a meeting the following morning. A sharp earthquake during the night made me wonder whether the meeting would actually take place! As so often happens in Slovenia, the morning dawned bright if cold and I duly met the two men, who told me that they had arranged for us all to go to the Loibl Pass and walk up the old road, closed to traffic after having been superseded by the road tunnel which opened in 1964. As the border area was under the control of the Yugoslav army, and civilians in the area under control of the Slovenian milicija (police), it was difficult for locals to visit such sensitive areas and there was currently no precedent for foreigners at all. They had arranged a special permission for me to visit this 'sensitive' border.

That was how I found myself, one day in November 1990, trudging up the old road in the company of the two local rally drivers, with a member of the milicija released from border passport control to accompany us, and for good measure having to first go back down the road to the army barracks to confirm our plans and obtain their approval before we set off again.

Unbeknownst to us, a patrol was already out in the hills and unaware of our plans, so when they came upon us on the route they were rather surprised. Fortunately the sight of a uniformed milicija man led them to presume that we were on some sort of official mission. When they caught up with us, all was explained – in Serbo-Croat, because the three army personnel, youthful conscripts of but 18 years of age who were armed with Kalashnikovs, came from Bosnia, Macedonia and Kosovo in the south of Yugoslavia. Our unlikely group thus ended up at the top of the Loibl Pass in thick snow, drinking Scotch whisky and all becoming rather enthusiastic about the prospect of proper cars once again being able to travel up this dramatic road. For my part I think it must have been one of the most unique and unusual days of my life! I only hoped it would turn out to have been time well spent.

There were still more than two years before the pass would be needed by us, however and the road, although in fair condition, would need some work done on it, not to mention getting approval from Austria to drive down the pass after crossing the border. At that time, Slovenia were about to hold a plebiscite to decide whether to become independent from Yugoslavia.

In the evening after my climb to the summit, I was back in Ljubljana, hosted by my new found rally drivers with whom I had climbed the Loibl a few hours earlier, together with their families. Over dinner that evening, I was asked what I would do if I was faced with such a plebiscite. How would I vote? I had never been confronted with such a question before. I thought about it, then answered as follows. 'The Slovene language dates back to before the year 1000 – even older than English. Slovenia has always been a part of another country. For the first time in 1000 years, there is a chance for Slovenia to control its own destiny. What would you say to your grandchildren if you did not take this chance?' I like to think that my comments swayed the result – only 94.8 % voted for independence in the December 1990 plebiscite!

In the more enlightened times since free elections in Slovenia people were now willing to make their own decisions and find their own solutions. But 1991 was a problem year, even as far as visiting the country was concerned, as it was threatened with war if it declared independence from Yugoslavia. Rental car companies either banned their cars from going into Slovenia or would not insure them at all, so a visit there had to be done with care. As far as the Loibl Pass situation was concerned, all the Slovenians said that until they actually had their independence it was better to wait before making firm plans. The Slovenian Declaration of Independence in June 1991 saw the subsequent ten day war, then an uneasy freedom until the Yugoslav army withdrew entirely, and finally, a recognition by European and other countries in January 1992. During this time in limbo it was still possible to visit and discuss the Loibl plans, even though at some risk. On a subsequent visit to Slovenia in the summer of 1992, when they were finally a free land, I met a man from the valley leading up to the Loibl Pass. Dušan Koren was his name. Known locally as grandpa Koren, he had lived there all his life and his dream was to see the old road restored and reused.

Discussions in Slovenia are very amicable affairs. A large bottle of local Slivovitz is produced and discussion proceeds, even though some translation is needed. The understanding was that we would be in Slovenia at the beginning of July 1993 with up to 50 vintage Rolls-Royce motor cars. The pass would be ready, but the work would not be done until just beforehand, in case heavy rains caused damage requiring a second restoration. Finally the Slivovitz was finished, so the meeting ended. And so it came to pass that the Loibl Pass (Ljubelj to the Slovenians) reverberated to the sound of Rolls-Royce Silver Ghosts once again.

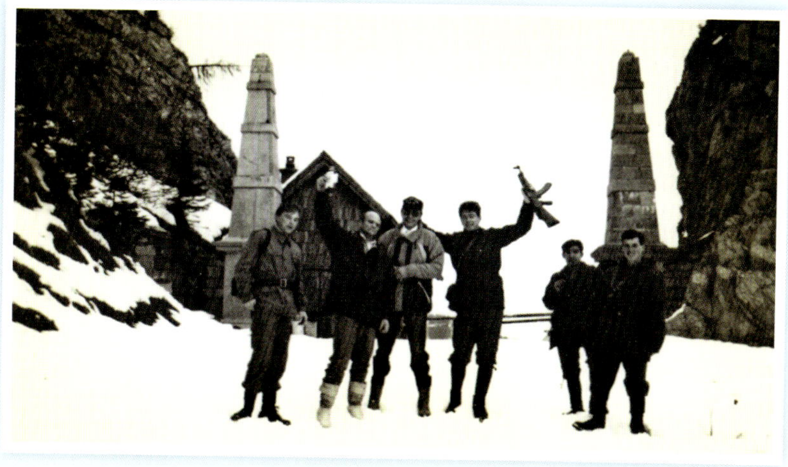

And was I acting the part of Mr Radley again? No, I was in a Ljubljana hospital with a broken arm from starting the car the previous afternoon. After seven years of endeavour – six since the Loibl discovery, my first drive up 'Ljubelj' would have to wait just a little bit longer.

Mr Radley Drives To Vienna

The Photo Album

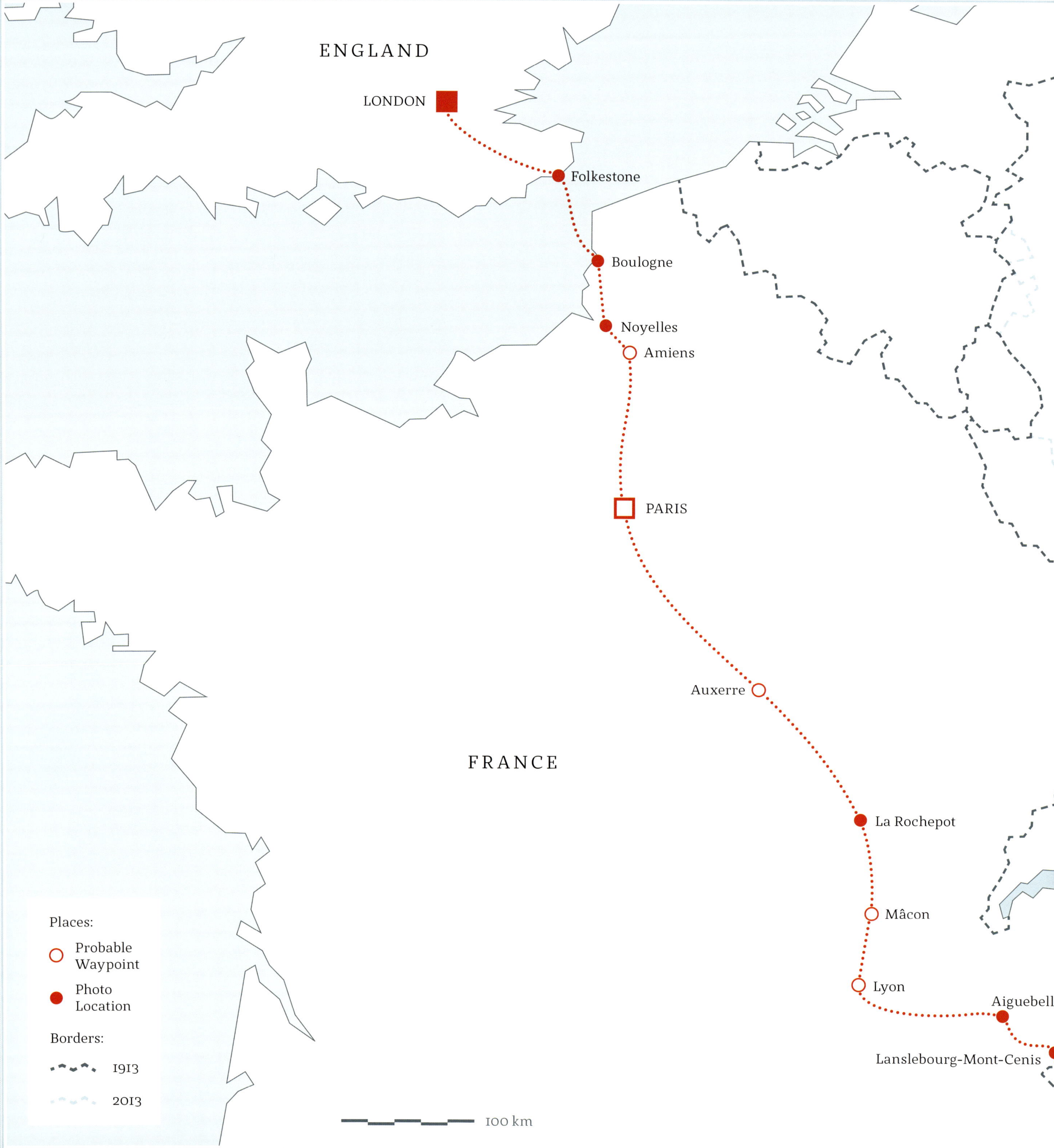
ENGLAND
LONDON
Folkestone
Boulogne
Noyelles
Amiens
PARIS
Auxerre
FRANCE
La Rochepot
Mâcon
Lyon
Aiguebelle
Lanslebourg-Mont-Cenis
Places:
Probable Waypoint
Photo Location
Borders:
1913
2013
100 km

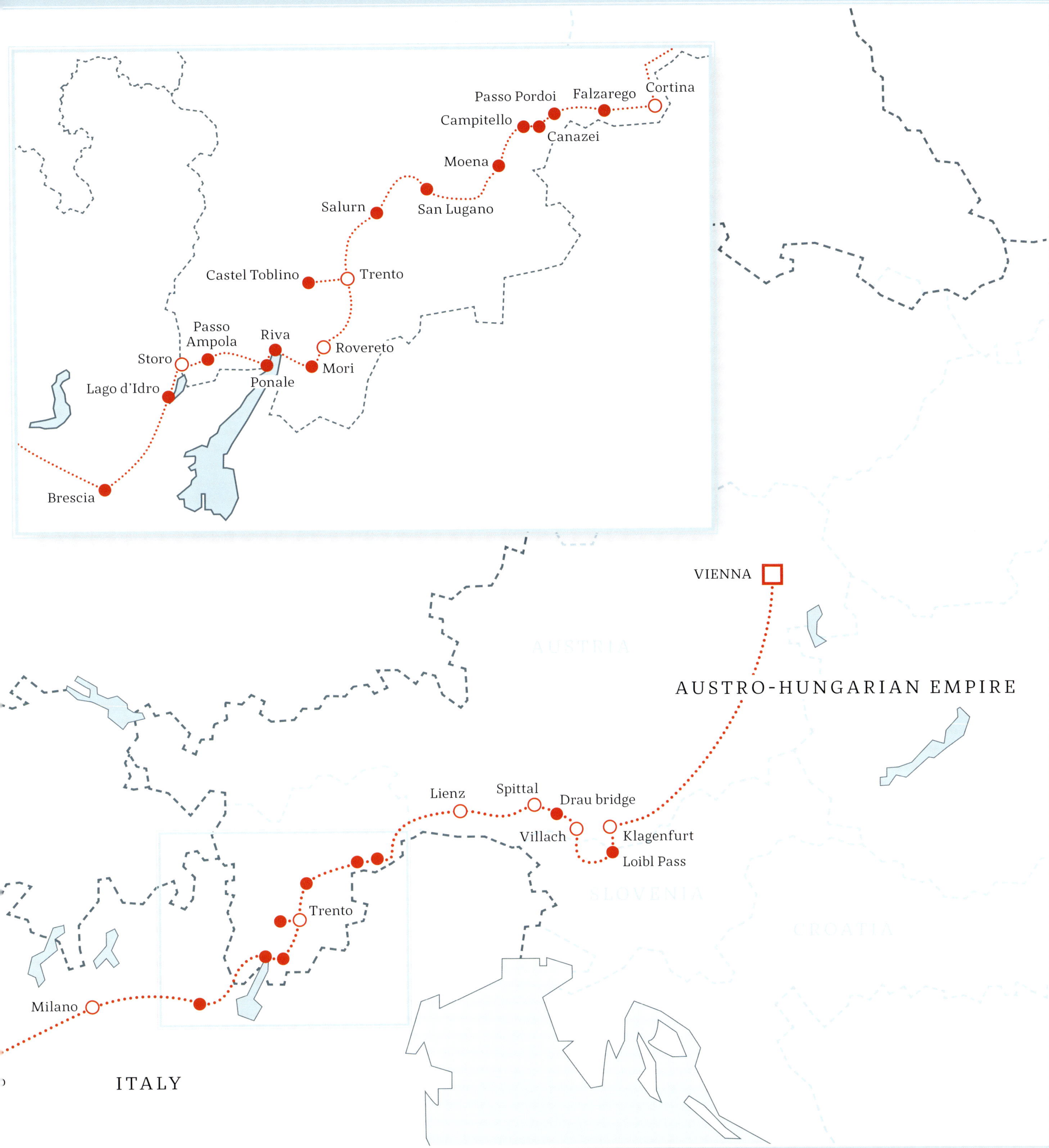
Passo Pordoi
Falzarego
Cortina
Campitello
Canazei
Moena
Salurn
San Lugano
Castel Toblino
Trento
Passo
Ampola
Riva
Storo
Rovereto
Mori
Ponale
Lago d'Idro
Brescia
VIENNA
AUSTRIA
AUSTRO-HUNGARIAN EMPIRE
Lienz
Spittal
Drau bridge
Villach
Klagenfurt
Loibl Pass
Trento
SLOVENIA
CROATIA
Milano
ITALY

FINDING THE ALBUM

The broadcasting of the BBC film of the Alpine 93 tour attracted a large viewing audience. Among those who watched the 50 minute screening were some of the descendants of Reggie Hope, who had been ground manager for Radley during 1910 and 1911, when he was one of the early flight pioneers. Awarded pilot's licence number 12, Radley set the World Air Speed Record at Lanark race course in Scotland just four months after buying his first aeroplane, assembling it himself, teaching himself to fly and taking part in the regular weekend Flying Circuses which were a feature of the summer of 1910.

One can imagine that whilst watching the broadcast at the end of 1993, it suddenly dawned on them that their father had not only known James Radley, but had also travelled to Vienna with him, and, armed with a camera, had recorded the journey out from England. They realised that the pictures probably still survived and a search of the attic or the recesses of seldom used cupboards yielded the treasure – the pictures of the journey, stored in an album and thus kept literally and metaphorically in the dark for all of their 80 year existence.

The album belonged to the late Reginald John Hooton Hope who died on 8 August 1956. It was donated to the Royce Foundation in February 1994 by Mrs Audrey Darke of Porthcothan Bay, Cornwall and Mrs Peta Jacobi, daughter and granddaughter respectively of Reggie Hope, and Denis Allen of Stevington, Bedfordshire, half brother of Mrs Darke and stepson of Reggie Hope. A great friend of Jimmy Radley (who died in March 1959), Reggie Hope was with Radley for all his early flying activities. In company with Tubby Ward and another, Hope travelled out to Vienna with Radley in the Rolls-Royce Silver Ghost for the 1913 Austrian Alpenfahrt.

Later in 1994 I was invited to examine the album. Almost too good to be true, the Radley/Hope album has 51 photographs in all; nearly half of them have a photograph of the 1913 Radley car.

CAPTIONING THE RADLEY/HOPE ALBUM

The album had no captions of any kind and few clues as to the locations. However, after seven years of researching and travelling over the route of the 1913 Alpenfahrt, a number of the pictures were directly identifiable. For other pictures the region where they were taken could be deduced. So, testing my knowledge, I decided to try to caption all of the pictures. I did not realise at the time that this would take the next 19 years to achieve completely!

It was soon apparent that all the photos were taken prior to reaching Vienna where the actual Alpine contest started. The early pictures appeared to be in London and there were photographs showing the car on a sling being loaded onto a steamer bound for France where more photos had also been taken. There was only one picture with anything written on it – a caption which read 'Mont Cenis May 22nd 1913'. This provided us with a big clue as to the route taken to Vienna. The only other known picture en route, showing the car in Italy in a town centre originally thought to be Riva, had been discovered to be Brescia. Now this part of the route was certain. It also meant that the route through France was primarily down the old N1 towards Paris, then on the old N6, which actually started in Paris and finished at the summit of the Col du Mont Cenis!

The first attempt at captioning was to list each picture and caption them with known information, producing a list with many assumptions such as 'Probably London' or 'On the Dolomitenstrasse' or 'Probably between two locations in France, or Italy'. An early objective was to establish where the two London pictures were taken. They were shown to be at the same place. Did it still exist? Was it damaged or destroyed during the war?

In the pre-internet age, solving such problems was much more difficult and for a long time I got nowhere. Then one day when checking some of the files I had on the Radley car, I realised that the delivery address given by Radley for his cars was Browns Hotel, London. I travelled to London the next day and sure enough, there was the location for the first two pictures. And it was exactly the same as in the photographs, unchanged since 1913!

A number of the pictures, such as those at Lake Garda, could be identified from knowledge of the route. Other pictures at the Channel could be captioned, even if they depicted a long gone method of crossing – cars no longer loaded onto ferries on a sling and there was no longer a boat train to Paris, which was visible in the picture which was then identified as Boulogne.

The French Château seemed very familiar, but the one we knew had a superb Burgundian tiled roof, whereas this one was in ruins. So for a year or more, we looked elsewhere, until it occurred to us that châteaux can be restored, not just cars. We had in fact found our château all along. Finding post cards at flea markets in France confirmed this and helped identify other locations as well, particularly Lanslebourg at the foot of the Mont Cenis Pass, which was on the route but had suffered much war damage. Only the churches remained; the rest of the town was rebuilt after the war. Now having achieved much better captioning it was time to look more closely for the missing parts of the puzzle by organising a tour through Austria, following what we knew of the route.

Armed with copies of the photographs we set off in May 1995 on a discovery journey, in the original Radley car. The plan was to try to repeat the photographs where the car was featured and the location still existed, beginning with the Browns Hotel pictures in London. As the channel crossing was now quite different, the next on the agenda was the Château la Rochepot. The precise location was easily found and although on the N6, this portion of the route had been bypassed, so that fast traffic no longer used it, allowing us to stop in the most suitable location to repeat a picture taken 82 years earlier! The problem encountered here and in other locations was that the actual spot was overgrown with trees. But there was a gap in the trees about 100 metres past the precise place, from which the château was clearly visible and the photograph was duly taken.

The search for locations continued as we travelled to Lanslebourg and the Mont Cenis Pass. A town en route, which the French Tourist Office in London thought might be St Jean de Maurienne proved not to be, even though the background mountains looked similar. Yet another photo to be identified at a later date.

Some locations were easy to find; others, although difficult, were still discovered. A few were found by sheer luck, especially those where the view was photographed from the rear of the moving car by Reggie Hope (it became apparent that Radley did not make many stops, apart from the mountain passes). In one instance when we were en route to Riva and had stopped at a bar on a very hot afternoon, we asked the locals if they knew one particular view which from research we believed to be in the vicinity. They looked at the photo, laughed, then said it was taken from less than a kilometre further down the road!

Many of the photos around Riva were confirmed. These included the Ponale Strasse, with its tunnels on the old road, as well as those from the town and Castel Toblino a few kilometres north. Some remained to be confirmed at a later time. Similarly the famous route over the Dolomites from Trento to Cortina confirmed many of the locations, including the mountain passes, but still leaving other pictures yet to be confirmed in the area where exact locations were not known. In the following years the captions were gradually improved as minor corrections continued to be made but by 2013 the precise location of some of the early pictures was still not established.

Author's Note:

When writing the captions, we were confronted with the issue of the use of correct place names in the two different time periods.

When the boundary changes were made in 1919, many places on the Alpine route were no longer in Austria but were then in Italy or Yugoslavia (later Slovenia or Croatia). There were some further changes after 1945 as well.

For the most part, we have chosen to use the Austrian names for the 1913 pictures, unless, as in parts of the Dolomites and areas which are now Trentino, the Austrians also used the Italian names for the 1913 Alpenfahrt, even when there was sometimes a German alternative.

For the 2013 photos the commonly used name of the modern country has been used.

We could only travel part way down unfortunately, because, in the conversion back to a cycling route, the road had been narrowed and traditional style log fences had been erected, which made the centre section just too tight to drive a Silver Ghost down and we did not want to get stuck fast on the track! But the man with the keys had a Citröen 2CV, to which, incongruously, he had fitted extremely wide tyres, so that this amazing machine could go anywhere – and did. So he drove us to the precise location of the two original photographs. Tree growth on the vertical cliffs to the lake below made the precise position impossible to repeat, but standing very close by was almost the same. As the location was close to the lower end of the old road, we were later able to drive up to the location and include the Radley car in one of the pictures.

p. 53 The Riva pictures were well known – getting identical versions was more difficult, mainly because the taller trees tended to block part of the view from the Lido Palace Hotel. However the view across the Lake towards the old Ponale corniche looks almost the same from anywhere on the lakeshore at Riva.

p. 57 Castel Toblino is another gem actually on the Alpine route, so already a known location. Getting the exact picture was a matter of avoiding the heavy traffic on this busy route into Riva from the north.

p. 59 On the road from Riva to Rovereto, the Mori picture remained an enigma for many years. With few identifiable landmarks, it was not until an early copy of the Austrian magazine showed captioned photos from the same location with a level crossing barrier in the foreground, that the potential location for the picture was narrowed down considerably. The precise spot had still not been found in 2013 when we were staying a few days in Riva to try to complete all the photos. Our friends there took us over to Mori to show us the precise location. Nothing is easy, however. The road is now an extremely busy route and the old level crossing had become an underpass. Behind the road is the main autostrada from the Brenner Pass to Verona, causing the long straight road to be realigned. When first at the location, a large lorry was parked in the only safe spot, its driver having his compulsory rest break. Fortunately for us, the following day when we drove there to try for the photo, the parking location was clear, but the road carried so much traffic that it took many minutes before a gap in the traffic allowed time to cross the road and take the photo. Reggie Hope, looking out the rear of the car while Radley stopped for a train, would have had no such problem in 1913.

p. 60 The Trento Road picture shows a deserted road in 1913. Not so now! Even with an autostrada nearby, this road has a constant traffic flow as well as tall trees on both sides, making it difficult to take a photograph which still shows the background hills. The original picture would once again have been taken looking out the back of the car.

p. 61 The road to San Lugano, which is the direct route from Trento into the Val di Fassa instead of taking the Alpenfahrt route over the Rolle Pass. The pass is a busy road and the realignment leaves the old road as a log storage area, making it possible to remake the photo from a quieter location.

p. 63 The Moena picture was another enigma. A seemingly nondescript photo of a stream tumbling down a hillside. From the mountains in the background, it seemed likely to be in the Val di Fassa, between Predazzo and Canazei, the village at the foot of the Pordoi. But why the picture at all? At the end of May 2013 we were in the Val di Fassa and because of the cold and unsettled weather we were waiting until we were certain that the Pordoi Pass route would not be blocked by snow. During this time, we investigated the pictures from the unknown locations. This picture seemed to be from a side stream so we drove up the valley and at Moena, the location was discovered. When we found it, we could understand why the picture was taken. The main road here passes a narrow gap between two old buildings, as it would have done 100 years before. Now there were traffic lights for control; in 1913 it would have depended on who arrived first. So while Radley stopped to allow another vehicle to pass down the hill, Hope would have taken the chance for another picture.

p. 65 At Campitello di Fassa, the Langkofel Sasolunga peaks in the Dolomites are so distinctive that they are easily recognised, and the precise location of the picture had been identified many years beforehand to be from the stream in the centre of Campitello. Now we had to try to find the most suitable location from which to take the picture. The problem was that although the mountains are unchanging and many of the old buildings from the earlier picture are still in existence, the original location now had an ugly modern brutalist concrete building from the 1970s in place of the charming Hotel Mulino which had been demolished to build it. Even the local minority Ladin speakers who we met in the ancient pub nearby, wished that the eyesore would be removed. In the meantime, we had to do the best we could from a position close to the original pictures, without the modern building completely overpowering it.

p. 67 Val di Fassa, in 1913 still an isolated region, has changed considerably with new roads, more trees and new developments in the valley. Now a popular ski region, it is difficult to do more than take another general view looking down the valley.

p. 69 The two Canazei pictures were easy to identify from the dramatic mountain backdrops. At the foot of the Pordoi Pass climb, Canazei is now a ski centre, with long chairlifts leading up to the ski runs. Although there are still many charming ancient buildings, there is also much new development which blocks some of the early views. Time spent walking in the old streets finally yielded the locations from where the two pictures were taken, even though one now contained many new buildings, requiring a slightly different view point for the mountains to be visible.

p. 73 The Pordoi Pass is easily recognised from the obelisk marking the opening of the pass in 1904. It is no longer a remote mountain road. Early in the season there are fewer tourists and still a good amount of snow, even though regular snow machines in 2013 have eliminated the need for a man with a shovel.

p. 75 The two Falzarego photos were front and rear of the same car in the same location just east of the pass. Quieter than the Pordoi and still freezing early in the season with light snow falling, the location is almost identical to that of a hundred years before.

p. 79 The Loibl, where the idea started. The view from the top of the Loibl, changed by the significant number of extra trees growing now, compared with one hundred years ago.

p. 81 The final picture from the album seemed easy to identify but was actually the most difficult of all, involving numerous people and organisations in southern Carinthia, including hoteliers, historic societies and government departments. Everyone readily knew it to be a crossing of the Drau, but the wholesale changes to the river in the period from the 1950s have obliterated many locations, including this one. After many false leads, all of which were followed up, it finally was discovered to be the old toll bridge over the Drau at the aptly named Mauthbrücken, a tiny hamlet all but obliterated by the building of a dam across the Drau. The old bridge has gone; the Gasthof Steiner in the background has also gone, both demolished or under the waters of the Drau. The alternative was to take the modern picture on the Hollenburg bridge, on the route to Klagenfurt from the Loibl Pass, as it is the only curved bridge remaining over the Drau.

The lack of additional pictures, either closer to Vienna or on the actual Alpenfahrt itself, suggest that Reggie Hope may have left the car in Carinthia and returned by train to England.

Mr Radley fährt nach Wien

Deutsche Übersetzung

VORWORT

Als Liebhaber von Automobilen und schönen Fahrerlebnissen – natürlich mit Rolls-Royce im Mittelpunkt meines Interesses – bin ich mit hohen Erwartungen nach Norditalien gefahren, um anlässlich der Feier zum hundertsten Jubiläum an der Oldtimer-Alpenfahrt teilzunehmen. John Kennedy zu treffen und zu wissen, dass der Wagen, den er fuhr – der berühmte Radley Car – die einzige im Originalzustand überlebende alpine Spezialanfertigung des Modells darstellte, war an sich schon außergewöhnlich. Als John mich einlud, ihn für die Tagesetappe zum Stelvio-Pass zu begleiten, sagte ich begeistert zu.

Die Fahrt am 20. Juni 2013, einem Donnerstag, stellte sich als die außergewöhnlichste Tagestour heraus, die ich je erlebt habe. Den dramatischen Stelvio-Pass zu erklimmen, von einem plötzlich hereinbrechenden mächtigen Gewittersturm überrascht zu werden, sich in ein kleines Dorf zu retten, um dort in einer einheimischen Kneipe die Sintflut auszusitzen, um dann schließlich bei Sonnenuntergang an den Gestaden des schönen Gardasees anzulangen, waren Erlebnisse, die ich nie vergessen werde. Und als Krönung des Ganzen schlossen sich uns gegen Abend fast hundert Rolls-Royce Silver Ghosts an, die größte Anzahl, die sich je an einem Ort versammelt hat. Das Ereignis markierte fast auf den Tag genau das Datum vor hundert Jahren, an dem die Teilnehmer der ursprünglichen Alpenfahrt-Rallye von 1913 von Wien aus aufbrachen.

Unter den vielen durch dieses Abenteuer ausgelösten Empfindungen haben sich mir zwei Dinge unvergesslich eingeprägt: Das Erlebnis des Fahrens in einem bewundernswert originalen und bei aller Kraft geschmeidig-weichen, hundert Jahre alten Rolls-Royce und die außergewöhnliche Gesellschaft, die ich an diesem Tag genoss – war ich eigentlich mit John Kennedy oder doch mit Mr. Radley unterwegs? Nachdem John seinen Platz hinter dem Steuerrad des Wagens eingenommen hatte, schienen mir beide fast ununterscheidbar.

Ich habe es genossen, jenen besonderen Tag beim Blick in das vorliegende Buch noch einmal zu erleben, und kann John Kennedy und dem Radley Car nur noch viele weitere gemeinsame Meilen wünschen.

Bon voyage, liebe Freunde.

Richard Carter

Richard Carter
Director of Global Communications
Rolls-Royce Motor Cars
Goodwood
März 2015

DASSELBE FAHRZEUG, DIESELBEN SCHAUPLÄTZE – HUNDERT JAHRE SPÄTER

Wien 1913 – das Herz Europas, Hauptstadt der Österreich-Ungarischen Monarchie, Zentrum der Kunstwelt, Heimat von Hitler und Tito, Refugium von Stalin und Trotzki, Geburtsort von Sigmund Freud und Gustav Klimt. Es sollte, was weder Einwohner noch Besucher ahnen konnten, das letzte goldene Jahr des Österreich-Ungarischen Reiches sein.

Franz Josef, der alternde, seit 1848 regierende Kaiser, sollte kurz darauf sterben, Franz Ferdinand, der designierte Thronerbe, im Juni 1914 ermordet werden. Die Umstände dieses Attentats hatten tiefgreifende und nachhaltige Veränderungen nicht nur im Kaiserreich und dem restlichen Europa, sondern in der ganzen Welt zur Folge.

Doch noch lebte man im Jahr 1913 – und lebte unbekümmert, obwohl die Vorzeichen des Untergangs für die, die sehen wollten, deutlich zu erkennen waren.

Das Automobil trat in jener Epoche seinen Siegeszug an und entwickelte sich in weniger als einem Jahrzehnt aus einem störungsanfälligen und gefährlichen Spielzeug zu einem modernen und verlässlichen Transportmittel. Oft war der technologische Fortschritt das Ergebnis von Wettbewerben, die ursprünglich als gesellschaftliche Ereignisse veranstaltet wurden, da die Autos seinerzeit fast ausschließlich Vertretern des europäischen Adels gehörten.

Für die Automobilhersteller waren diese Veranstaltungen meist von geringem Wert, weswegen eine Reihe aufwendigerer Wettbewerbe organisiert wurde. Ab 1911 war die bedeutendste und anspruchsvollste Veranstaltung die Österreichische Alpenfahrt oder der Alpenwettbewerb.

Meistens nahmen europäische Hersteller daran teil, wobei ihre Wagen häufig von den Ingenieuren oder Unternehmern selbst gesteuert wurden. Doch auch Privatleute, die Autos besaßen, stellten sich aus Sportbegeisterung ebenfalls der Herausforderung.

Ein solcher Mann war James Radley, ein Flugpionier, begeisterter Automobilist und Abenteurer, der sich mit einem neuen Rolls-Royce zu der wohl härtesten Materialprüfung dieser Zeit anmeldete: der Österreichischen Alpenfahrt 1912.

Der Wagen war wahrscheinlich das beste Fahrzeug am Start. In Unkenntnis der höchsten Straßen und steilen Bergpässe hatte man seinen Wagen mit einer dreigängigen Getriebeübersetzung ausgerüstet, das die Steigung am Katschbergpass am ersten Tag nicht ohne anzuhalten bewältigen konnte.

Radley verließ das Rennen, was beim Unternehmen Rolls-Royce für Bestürzung sorgte, da gerade eine größere Niederlassung in Wien eröffnet wurde, um den wachsenden Markt für ihre Autos zu versorgen.

Als Reaktion entwickelte Rolls-Royce ein besser auf die Gebirgsstrecken abgestimmtes Modell mit viergängiger Getriebeübersetzung und meldete offiziell ein aus drei Fahrzeugen bestehendes Team für den Wettbewerb im Juni 1913 an. Auch James Radley nahm wieder in einem verbesserten Rolls-Royce teil, war aber nicht offiziell Mitglied des Werksteams. Alle vier Wagen waren neu und wiesen gründlich geprüfte Verbesserungen auf, die aus intensiven Alpentestfahrten im Herbst 1912 resultierten.

Die Wagen des Rolls-Royce-Teams machten sich Ende April auf die Reise nach Österreich und erprobten die Fahrzeuge nach der Schneeschmelze auf den meisten der Bergpässen.

Der neue Wagen für James Radley wurde im März 1913 an seine Huntingdon-Werke geliefert, wo er die Karosserie baute. Im Mai 1913 machte er sich mit dem Rolls-Royce-Mechaniker Tubby Ward und zwei anderen Begleitern auf den Weg nach Österreich. Einer der Mitfahrer war der Freund Reginald Hooton Hope, ein Amateurfotograf, der die Reise nach Wien aufnahm.

Bemerkenswert ist, dass sowohl das Fahrzeug wie das Fotoalbum erhalten geblieben sind, wodurch die Wiederholung der Reise mit demselben Auto von 1913 und die Wiederholung der Fotografien an denselben Schauplätzen exakt hundert Jahre später, im Mai und Juni 2013, möglich wurden.

Resultat dieses einzigartigen Zusammentreffens von Voraussetzungen ist das vorliegende Buch.

DIE FOTOGRAFIEN AUS DEN JAHREN 1913 UND 2013

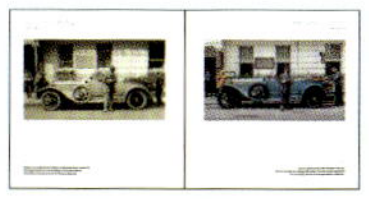

S. 12/13

BROWN'S HOTEL London, England
1913 Radleys Fahrzeug vor Brown's Hotel in der Albemarle Street 1 in London W1. Dieses elegante Hotel nutzte Radley als Londoner Adresse. Das Foto wurde beim Aufbruch der Gruppe nach Wien im Mai 1913 aufgenommen.

BROWN'S HOTEL London, England
2013 Brown's Hotel ist bis heute fast unverändert geblieben, auch der schmiedeeiserne Gitterzaun steht noch an derselben Stelle. Sogar das Mosaikschild hinter dem Wagen mit der Aufschrift »Browns & St Georges Hotel« ist noch da.

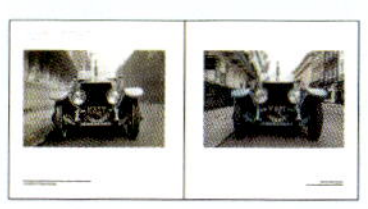

S. 14/15

ALBEMARLE STREET London, England
1913 Hier parkt der Radley-Wagen am selben Platz vor dem Brown's Hotel in London wie auf dem Foto der vorausgehenden Seite.

ALBEMARLE STREET London, England
2013 Die Ansicht ist dieselbe geblieben. Sogar die Gullydeckel existieren noch.

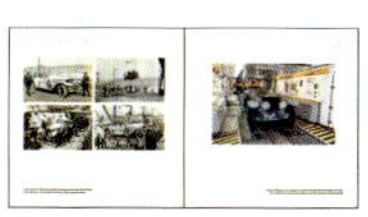

S. 16/17

KANALÜBERQUERUNG Folkestone, England
1913 Werft in Folkestone beim Warten auf die Autoverladung auf die Fähre nach Boulogne am späten Nachmittag, wahrscheinlich noch am Tag der Abfahrt aus London.

KANALÜBERQUERUNG Eurotunnel
2013 Folkestone und Boulogne werden heute nicht mehr für den Fährverkehr genutzt. Die Kapazität des Eurotunnels reicht aus, um den größten Teil des Verkehrs über den Kanal zu bewältigen.

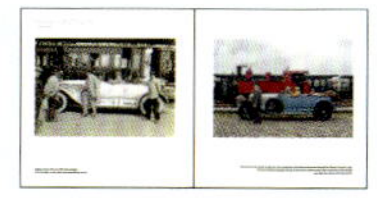

S. 18/19

DER PENDELZUG VON DER FÄHRE NACH PARIS
Boulogne, Frankreich
1913 Radley vor seinem Wagen, unmittelbar im Hintergrund die Waggons des Zuges von Boulogne nach Paris

SOMME-TOURISTENBAHN Noyelles, Frankreich
2013 Den Zug von der und zur Fähre gibt es seit der Einführung des direkten Zugverkehrs durch den Eurotunnel im Jahr 1993 nicht mehr. Doch die Museumsbahn entlang der landschaftlich reizvollen Baie de Somme besitzt alte Dampflokomotiven und Waggons, die sogar noch älter sind als die auf dem Foto von 1913.

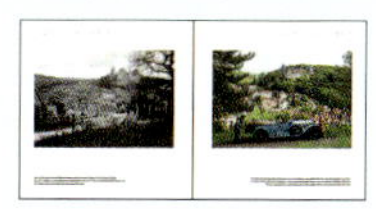

S. 20/21

CHÂTEAU LA ROCHEPOT Frankreich
1913 Der Wagen auf der alten N6 in der Nähe von Beaune, im Hintergrund das kleine Dorf La Rochepot.
Das auf einem Kalkfelsen errichtete Schloss aus dem 13. Jahrhundert wurde im 15. Jahrhundert von einem Kreuzritter namens Régnier Pot wieder aufgebaut. Das Château erhebt sich auf dem Höhenrücken, der heute seinen Namen trägt.

CHÂTEAU LA ROCHEPOT Frankreich
2013 Das schimmernde burgundische Dach aus farbigen glasierten Ziegeln erhielt das Schloss erst nach der Fotoaufnahme von 1913. Es war nach der Revolution völlig verfallen und wurde von einem Sohn des französischen Staatspräsidenten Marie François Sadi Carnot restauriert. Der Wagen ist auf einer ruhigen Landstraße geparkt, da die moderne N6 nun als neue Straße nach Westen führt.

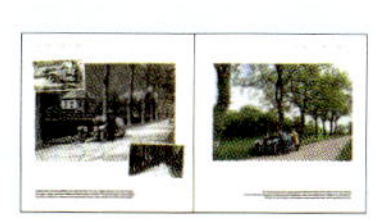

S. 22/23

KONTROLLEN AM STRASSENRAND Frankreich
1913 Ein Stop am Straßenrand in Frankreich, wahrscheinlich auf der N6 im Département Côte-d'Or. Radley wirft einen prüfenden Blick unter die Motorhaube.

[Insert oben:] Reparatur einer Reifenpanne. Radley und Ward am Werkzeugkasten. Derselbe Standort wie auf dem nächsten Foto.
[Insert unten:] Der Radley-Wagen ist auf einer baumbestandenen Straße in Frankreich in der Entfernung zu sehen. Alle drei Fotos an ein und demselben Ort aufgenommen.

KONTROLLEN AM STRASSENRAND Frankreich
2013 Die Alleebäume an den Straßen vor hundert Jahren sind häufig aus Sicherheitsgründen oder wegen Straßenerweiterungen gefällt worden, doch auf Teilstrecken der alten Routes Nationales, wo die Straße – wie in diesem Bild – einen neuen Verlauf hat, gibt es sie noch. Dass sich 2013 keine Reifenpannen ereigneten, ist vielleicht dem Umstand zuzuschreiben, dass kaum mehr Pferde genutzt werden und insofern auch keine Hufeisennägel auf der Straße liegen.

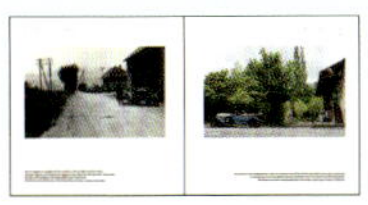

S. 24/25

HALT AN DER STRASSE Frankreich
1913 Der Wagen hält hier auf gerader Strecke, links der Straße verlaufen Eisenbahnschienen, im Hintergrund sieht man hoch aufragende Berge. Ein Passagier scheint das Gepäck oder das Hinterrad zu überprüfen: Das Straßenschild trägt die Aufschrift »Chapareillan«. Das Schild auf dem Gebäude an der Straßenkreuzung besagt: »Hotel Tissot«. Es ist die alte Kreuzung der N6 mit der N90 kurz vor Montmélian.

HALT AN DER STRASSE Frankreich
2013 Die Kreuzung ist heute völlig umgestaltet; eine neue Autobahn schneidet die alte Seitenstraße ab, die nun nur noch als Zufahrtsstraße zu einigen Häusern dient. Sie ist durch einen neuen Kreisverkehr etwa 200 Meter westlich der alten Kreuzung ersetzt worden. Die N6 ist seither zu D1006 umbenannt worden und eine verkehrsreiche Straße geblieben; die N90 ist nun die D1090.

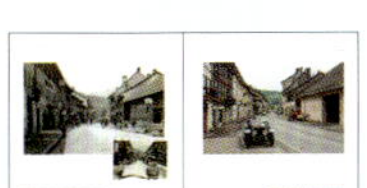

S. 26/27

AIGUEBELLE Frankreich
1913 Straßenszene in Aiguebelle auf der Route N6, 60 Kilometer vor Beginn der Passstraße zum Col du Mont Cenis.
Rechts: Blick auf den Straßenmarkt; diese Aufnahme wurde 100 Meter vor dem großen Foto von dem Beifahrer auf dem Vordersitz gemacht und zeigt die beiden Passagiere auf dem Rücksitz mit Autobrillen und Schutzkappen.

AIGUEBELLE Frankreich
2013 Die Bauernkarren wurden durch einen Traktor ersetzt, die Schuppentore zur Aufnahme moderner landwirtschaftlicher Maschinen nach oben erweitert. Ein Gebäude auf der rechten Seite ist aufgestockt worden; die Gebäude zur Linken sind seit 1913 unverändert geblieben.

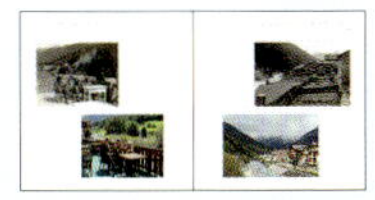

S. 28/29

LANSLEBOURG-MONT-CENIS Frankreich

DER FLUSS ARC, LANSLEBOURG-MONT-CENIS Frankreich

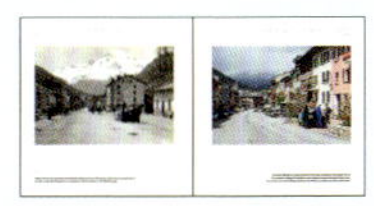

S. 30/31

LANSLEBOURG-MONT-CENIS Frankreich
1913 Dorfszene in den Bergen, Grenzbeamte betrachten den Wagen. Diese Aufnahme zeigt das Auto beinahe von vorn: Der Mann links im Bild bereitet sich darauf vor, das auf der folgenden Seite abgebildete Foto aufzunehmen.

LANSLEBOURG-MONT-CENIS Frankreich
2013 Keine Grenzbeamten, sondern einheimische Mechaniker verlassen ihre Werkstatt, um sich den Wagen anzuschauen. Das Bergdorf Lanslebourg wurde während des Zweiten Weltkrieges 1944 vollkommen zerstört. Von den 1913 fotografierten Gebäuden ist die Kirche das einzige, das im Jahr 2013 noch zu sehen ist.

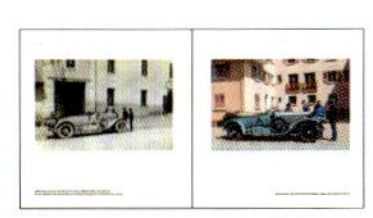

S. 32/33

LANSLEBOURG-MONT-CENIS Frankreich
1913 Radley, an seinen Wagen gelehnt, spricht mit zwei Zollbeamten, während ein Einheimischer interessiert zuhört. Der Wagen ist in derselben Position wie auf der vorhergehenden Seite geparkt, jedoch von der rechten Seite gesehen.

LANSLEBOURG-MONT-CENIS Frankreich
2013 Derselbe Standort, diesmal mit einheimischen Mechanikern, die sich sehr für das Autor interessieren.

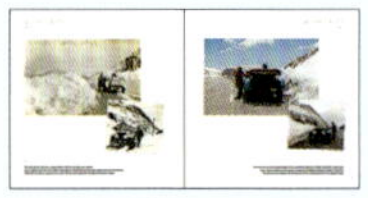

S. 34/35

MONT CENIS Frankreich
1913 Das einzige Bild aus dem originalen Album mit Datum und Überschrift.
[Insert:] Ein nicht aus dem Radley-Hope-Album stammendes Bild, das versehentlich mit Pordoipass beschriftet wurde. Erst nach der Aufnahme des gegenüberstehenden Bildes wurde deutlich, wo das Foto gemacht worden war.

MONT CENIS Frankreich
2013 Hundert Jahre danach – auf dem Gipfel (2084 Meter) haben sich nach dem seit vielen Jahren kältesten Winter Schneeverwehungen gebildet.
[Insert:] Ein Bild, genau am hundertsten Jahrestag von Radleys Ankunft am Pass Mont Cenis aufgenommen. Es belegt, wo das Foto auf der gegenüberliegenden Seite gemacht worden war.

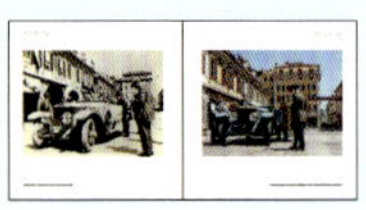

S. 36/37

BRESCIA Italien
1913 Radley macht Mittagspause am Corso Zanardelli.

BRESCIA Italien
2013 Hundert Jahre später sind die Gebäude am Corso Zanardelli unverändert geblieben.

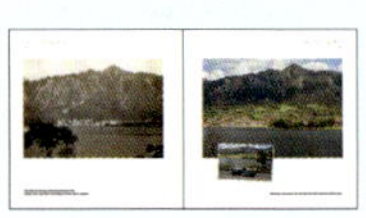

S. 38/39

LAGO D'IDRO Italien
1913 Blick von der alten Hauptverkehrsstraße zwischen Brescia und Riva über den Lago d'Idro auf die Orte Crone, Idro und Lemprato.

LAGO D'IDRO Italien
2013 Mehr Bäume, mehr Häuser, doch ansonsten ist der Blick von der Straße derselbe geblieben.

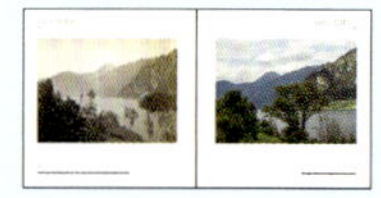

S. 40/41

LAGO D'IDRO Italien
1913 Ansicht des Lago d'Idro in Richtung Nordosten von einer Stelle nahe dem vorherigen Aufnahmeort.

LAGO D'IDRO Italien
2013 Auch hier gibt es kaum Veränderungen gegenüber dem Foto von 1913.

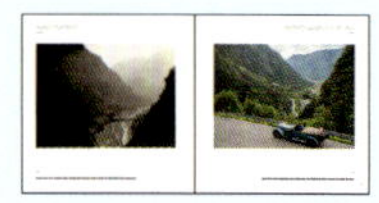

S. 42/43

AMPOLAPASS Österreich
1913 Malerische Ansicht des Ampolatals, mit Blick hinab auf die Straße, deren Steigung ab Storo beginnt.

AMPOLAPASS-STRASSE Italien
2013 Mit Ausnahme der üppigeren Vegetation und der verbreiterten Straße ist der Anstieg ab Storo gleich geblieben.

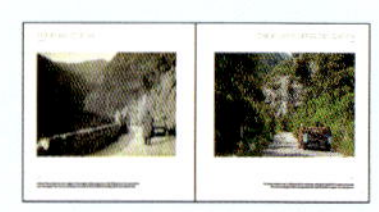

S. 44/45

DIE STRASSE NACH RIVA Österreich
1913 Eine Aufnahme des Wagens von hinten während eines Halts in der Schlucht des Ampolatals, einige Kilometer östlich von Storo nicht weit vom Ampolapass. Die Sonne scheint auf das Heck des Autos, das nach Nordosten gen Riva ausgerichtet ist.

DIE STRASSE NACH RIVA DEL GARDA Italien
2013 Die Straße zum Passo Ampola ist immer noch schmal, doch sehr befahren, sodass man unmöglich in der Schlucht halten kann. Der nunmehr gesperrte Teil der Route bietet den idealen Standpunkt zur Wiederholung des vor hundert Jahren aufgenommenen Fotos.

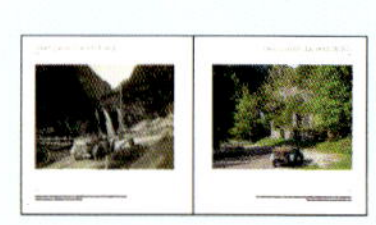

S. 46/47

WASSERFALL AM AMPOLAPASS Österreich
1913 Radley und sein Beifahrer pausieren im Wagen vor einem Wasserfall auf dem Ampolapass (749 Meter) in der Nähe des Gipfels, einen Kilometer östlich von Storo.

PASSO AMPOLA, WASSERFALL Italien
2013 Heute führt eine Straße anstelle der fragilen Holzkonstruktion im früheren Bild über die Schlucht. Das zerfallene Bauwerk vor dem Wagen wurde nach 1913 gebaut.

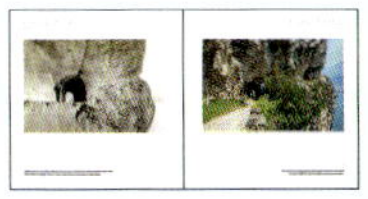

S. 48/49

PONALETUNNEL Österreich
1913 Radley posiert vor einem der zahllosen Felsentunnel auf der berühmten, nach Riva führenden Ponale-Corniche-Straße. Zu seinen Füßen fällt der Felsen 200 Meter steil zum Gardasee hin ab.

PONALETUNNEL Italien
2013 Der Tunnel wurde später erweitert und die Straße ist heute für den Autoverkehr gesperrt, wird aber von Wanderern und Mountainbikern genutzt.

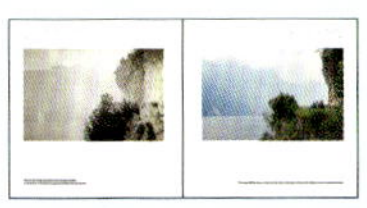

S. 50/51

DIE PONALESTRASSE Österreich
1913 Ansicht der Ponalestraße, vom selben Standort aufgenommen wie das Bild auf der vorherigen Seite, aber mit Blick zurück auf die Straße.

STRADA DEL PONALE (Ponalestraße) Italien
2013 Der Felsvorsprung existiert nicht mehr, doch die gesperrte Straße heißt den Radley-Wagen auf seiner hundertjährigen Jubiläumstour wieder willkommen.

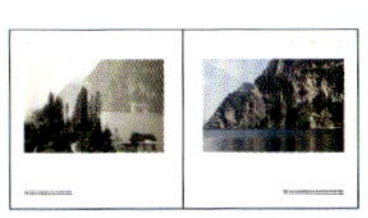

S. 52/53

RIVA Österreich
1913 Der Gardasee, vom Lido Palasthotel aus gesehen. Zwei weitere Varianten dieses Bildes wurden nicht gezeigt.

RIVA DEL GARDA Italien
2013 Höhere Bäume versperren heute teilweise die Aussicht vom Hotel Lido Palace. Doch die Sicht über den See zur Ponale-Corniche bleibt weiterhin offen.

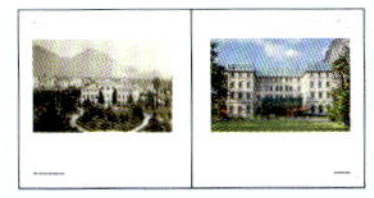

S. 54/55

RIVA Österreich
1913 Die Villa Lido vom Lido Palasthotel aus gesehen.

RIVA DEL GARDA Italien
2013 Das Hotel Lido Palace

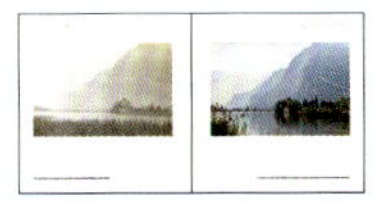

S. 56/57

CASTEL TOBLINO Österreich
1913 Die Alpenfahrtroute verläuft vorbei an Castel Toblino und seiner beschaulichen Umgebung im Norden von Riva.

CASTEL TOBLINO Italien
2013 Ein Jahrhundert später ist das Castel Toblino zu einem bekannten Restaurant geworden, doch der Blick bleibt derselbe.

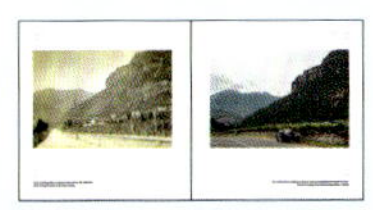

S. 58/59

MORI Österreich
1913 Auf der Straße von Riva nach Rovereto, dann gen Norden in die Dolomiten: Warten am beschrankten Bahnübergang.

MORI Italien
2013 Die Straße wurde neu trassiert, da jetzt eine Autobahn direkt hinter den Weinstöcken verläuft.
Der einst hier befindliche beschrankte Bahnübergang ist durch eine Unterführung ersetzt worden.

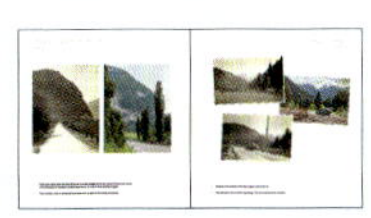

S. 60/61

TRIENT / TRENTO-STRASSE Österreich / Italien
1913 Straßenansicht, aufgenommen aus dem Heckfenster des Autos auf einer langen geraden Strecke auf der S12 nördlich von Trient in der Nähe von Salurn, an der Grenze der Provinzen Südtirol und Trentino, auf dem Weg nach Auer und San Lugano.
2013 Dieselbe Stelle, ungeachtet der nahen Autobahn heute eine überaus belebte Hauptstraße.

SAN LUGANO Österreich / Italien

1913 Eine Pause auf dem Scheitelpunkt der San Lugano-Straße (1097 Meter).

2013 Die alte Straße wird heute als Holzlagerplatz genutzt. Die Abzweigung zur neuen Straße liegt in der Nähe.

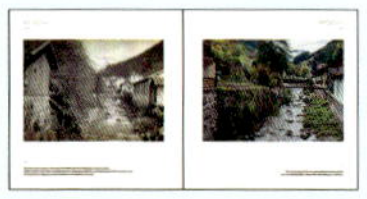

S. 62/63

MOENA Österreich

1913 Bergszene in Moena. Die aus der Stadt führende Straße steigt über eine Engstelle nach oben. Radley muss hier seine Fahrt verlangsamt oder kurz angehalten haben, was ein schnelles Foto der Szenerie ermöglicht hat, die den Rio San Pellegrino und die Dolomiten im östlichen Hintergrund zeigt.

MOENA Italien

2013 Die Engstelle und die Einbahnstraße entlang des Flüsschens werden nun durch Verkehrsampeln kontrolliert. Viele von den alten Gebäuden sind erhalten geblieben.

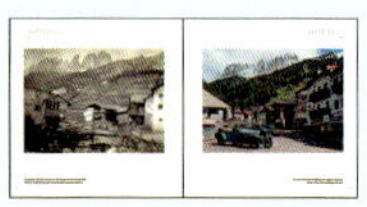

S. 64/65

CAMPITELLO Österreich

1913 Campitello mit dem Hotel Mulino im Vordergrund links und steil zur Langkofelgruppe in den Dolomiten im Hintergrund ansteigenden Feldern.

CAMPITELLO Italien

2013 Ein nicht gefälliges modernes Gebäude ersetzt heute das Hotel. Viele der anderen Gebäude existieren noch.

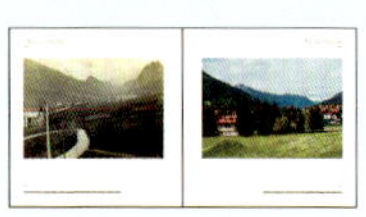

S. 66/67

VAL DI FASSA Österreich

1913 Das Val di Fassa ist bis zur Eröffnung der Straße über den Pordoipass vor einem Jahrzehnt ein abgeschiedenes Tal gewesen.

VAL DI FASSA Italien

2013 Die moderne Entwicklung und eine größere Anzahl von Bäumen lassen die alten Ansichten erheblich verändert erscheinen.

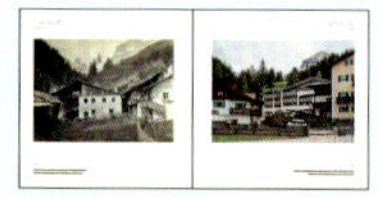

S. 68/69

CANAZEI Österreich

1913 Zwischen den rustikalen Bauernhäusern und den Gipfeln der Dolomiten ist die neue Straße zum Pordoipass zu sehen.

CANAZEI Italien

2013 Moderne Skiunterkünfte haben den Platz einiger alter Bauernhäuser eingenommen, und der im Vergleich zu früher vermehrte Baumbestand verdeckt fast die Pordoistraße.

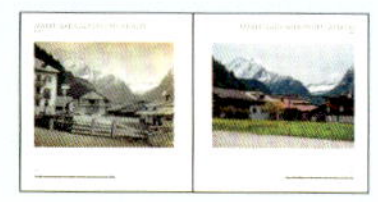

S. 70/71

MARMOLADA-ALPEN VON CANAZEI Österreich

1913 Die hohen Berge beherrschen die Aussicht nach Osten von diesem alten Bergdorf aus.

MARMOLADA-ALPEN VON CANAZEI Italien

2013 Auf dieser ein Jahrhundert später aufgenommenen Ansicht sind noch viele der alten Gebäude zu sehen.

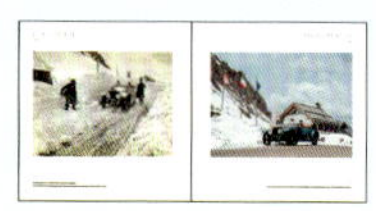

S. 72/73

PORDOIJOCH Österreich

1913 Radley legt auf der Passhöhe des Pordoijochs (2239 Meter) eine Pause ein. Der Obelisk im Hintergrund erinnert an die Eröffnung der Straße im Jahr 1904.

PASSO PORDOI Italien

2013 Auf dem Pordoijochs gibt es nun viele Gebäude, die den Gästen dieses Skigebiets zu Diensten stehen. Der Obelisk ist geblieben.

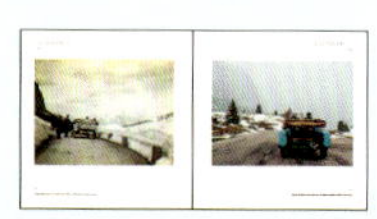

S. 74/75

FALZAREGO Österreich

1913 Auf dem Gipfel des Falzàrego (2117 Meter). Die Straße wurde im Jahr 1909 gebaut.

FALZAREGO Italien

2013 Dieselbe Stelle einhundert Jahre später. Eine breitere Straße, aber wieder schneebedeckt.

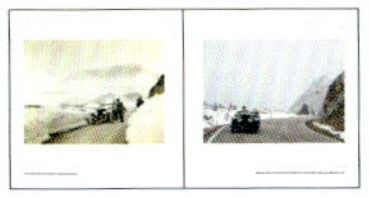

S. 76/77

FALZAREGO Österreich
1913 Aufnahme von vorn an derselben Stelle wie im vorhergehenden Bild.

FALZAREGO Italien
2013 Falzàrego mit dem Gipfelhotel im Hintergrund. Derselbe Standort, breitere Straße, leichter Schneefall, Kälte.

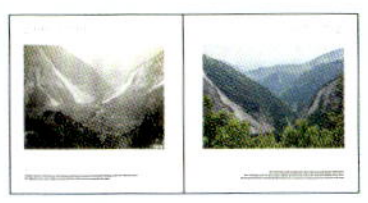

S. 78/79

DER LOIBLPASS / LJUBELJ Österreich
1913 Der Loiblpass (1370 Meter). Die berühmte Aussicht vom Gipfel Richtung Süden zeigt die gewundene Straße unten im Tal. Die Passhöhe war bis zur Eröffnung des Loibltunnels in den 1960er-Jahren ein wichtiger Alpenübergang.

DER LOIBLPASS / LJUBELJ Slowenien
2013 Heute befindet sich an dieser Stelle die Grenze zwischen Österreich und Slowenien, wohin sich der Blick nach Süden richtet. Pass und Straße zählen mittlerweile zum Kulturerbe und werden nur für spezielle Ereignisse wie zum Beispiel den Besuch des Radley Silver Ghost geöffnet. Die Sicht ist im Vordergrund teilweise durch Bäume verstellt, da die Bauern ihre Tiere nicht mehr auf dem Pass grasen lassen dürfen.

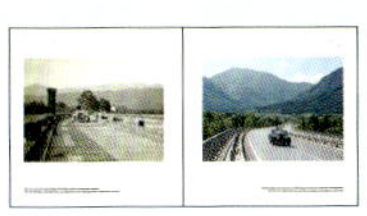

S. 80/81

DRAUBRÜCKE Österreich
1913 Der Wagen auf der kurvig geschwungenen Holzbrücke, Radley und sein Mitfahrer sind ausgestiegen. Diese alte Zollbrücke in Mauthbrücken in der Nähe von Spittal versank später, als ein Staudamm gebaut wurde, in den Fluten.

DRAUBRÜCKE Österreich
2013 Moderne Brücke über die Drau in Hollenburg, zwischen dem Loiblpass und Klagenfurt.
Hier gibt es jetzt einen Staudamm und so wurde diese neue höhergelegene Brücke gebaut.

ROLLS-ROYCE UND DIE ALPENFAHRT VON 1913

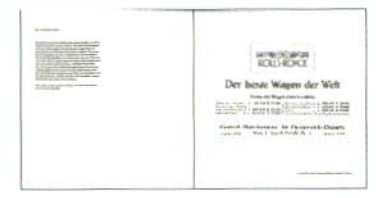

S. 84/85

HINTERGRUND
Mit dem letzten Bild aus dem Radley-Hope-Album bricht die Geschichte der Reise nach Wien plötzlich ab. Die leeren Seiten am Ende des Albums lassen vermuten, dass der Fotograf Reggie Hope in Kärnten den Wagen verlassen hat und nach England zurückgekehrt sein könnte. Die Reise vom Passo Ampola, in der Nähe von Riva, nach Klagenfurt stimmt nahezu ganz mit der Alpenfahrtroute überein, wir wissen also, dass wichtige Etappen der Strecke überprüft wurden. Es gibt eigenständige Bildbelege, dass die Rolls-Royce-Fahrzeuge an unterschiedlichen Orten getestet wurden, darunter am Katschbergpass, wo Radley während des Rennens im Jahr 1912 anhalten musste und erst im zweiten Anlauf die Steigung bewältigen konnte. Zwar sind keine Fotos gefunden worden, die Radley bei Probefahrten auf diesem Pass zeigen, doch ist es wahrscheinlich, dass Radley die Zeitspanne von einem Monat zwischen seiner Ankunft am Mont-Cenis-Pass bis zum Start der Alpenfahrt 1913 dazu genutzt hat, um am Katschberg Tests durchzuführen.
Der folgende Abschnitt enthält auf den Rolls-Royce bezogenes Material und seine Rolle bei der Alpenfahrt 1913.

[Faksimile] Der beste Wagen der Welt

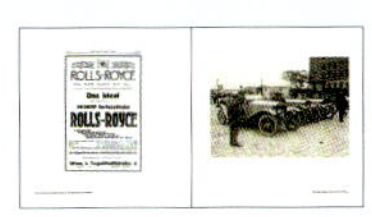

S. 86/87

[Faksimile] Das Ideal: Rolls-Royce
1913 Der Silver Ghost wurde als »Der beste Wagen der Welt« vermarktet.

1913 Das Rolls-Royce-Team bei seiner Ankunft in Wien.

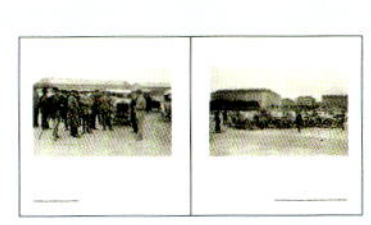

S. 88/89

1913 Mr. Radley schließt sich in Wien dem Rolls-Royce-Team an.

1913 Alle Rolls-Royce-Fahrzeuge stehen zur Abfahrt aus Wien bereit, um sich auf den Weg zur Alpenfahrt von 1913 zu machen.

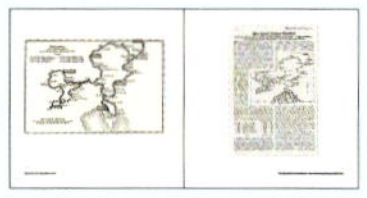

S. 90/91

1913 Skizzierte Karte der Alpenfahrtroute von 1913.

[Faksimile Zeitungsartikel]
1913 Die Alpenfahrt wird als »eines der Großereignisse des Jahres« beschrieben.

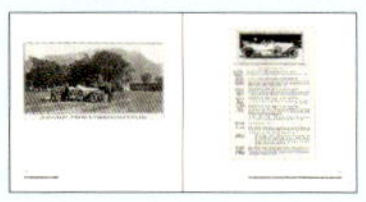

S. 92/93

[Zeitungsausschnitt – Bildlegende:] »Der erste Zwischenstopp in Riva. Der Rolls-Royce Nr. 4, der Mr. James Radley gehört und von ihm gefahren wird.«
1913 Mr. Radley zeigt eine souveräne Leistung.

[Faksimile Zeitungsartikel:] »Mr. Radley und sein Rolls-Royce, in dem er als Erster Wien erreichte.«
1913 Mr. Radley liegt an jedem Tag des Wettbewerbs auf dem ersten Platz. Das gesamte Rolls-Royce-Team kann sich bei allen Etappen der Alpenfahrt auf den ersten vier Plätzen positionieren.

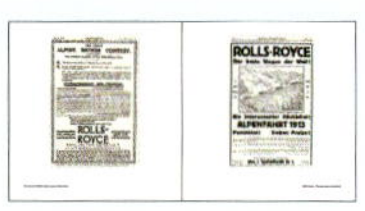

S. 94/95

[Faksimile]
1913 Das siegreiche Abschneiden der Rolls-Royce-Autos festigt ihren Status.

[Faksimile]
1913 Rolls-Royce – der beste Wagen der Welt!

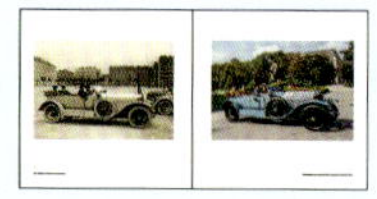

S. 96/97

1913 Mr. Radley im Juni 1913 in Wien.

2013 Der Radley-Wagen wiederholte ein Jahrhundert später die Alpenfahrt.

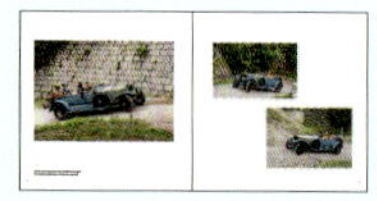

S. 98/99

2013 Alle Bergpässe wurden noch einmal erklommen, die historische Leistung von 1913 wiederholt.

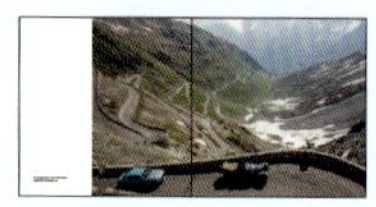

S. 100/101

2013 Begleitet von einem neuen, vom Radley-Wagen inspirierten Rolls-Royce.

DIE GESCHICHTE DER ÖSTERREICHISCHEN ALPENFAHRT

Schon 1898 begann der Österreichische Automobilclub (ÖAC) Prüfungen für leichte Fahrzeuge in den Bergen zu organisieren. 1910 wurde das bekannte Semmeringrennen behördlich untersagt, das möglicherweise den Grundstein für eine andere Veranstaltung legte, die erst 1973 als Lauf zur Rallye-Weltmeisterschaft endete.

Der Anfang der Alpenfahrt geht auf das Jahr 1907 zurück, in dem der ÖAC die »Erste internationale Prüfungsfahrt für Kleinwagen« ausschrieb. 1908 und 1909 folgten ähnliche Fahrten in kleinem Rahmen über wenige Pässe. 1910 organisierte der ÖAC, der bald zum k. k. ÖAC (kaiserlich königlicher Österreichischer Automobil Club) werden sollte, ein Vorläufer des jetzigen ÖAMTC, den ersten Wettbewerb unter dem offiziellen Namen »Die Österreichische Alpenfahrt«.

Eine kleine, aber exklusive Fahrt, nicht mehr nur auf Kleinwagen beschränkt, über vier Tage und 870 Kilometer mit sechzehn Teilnehmern. Darunter Baron Fritz Mayr-Melnhof mit seinem 48 HP Mercedes, Graf Paul Draskovich auf einem der drei teilnehmenden Laurin & Klement, die auch den Teampreis errangen. Im Jahr 1911 erhöhte sich die Zahl der Teilnehmer auf 51 und der Kilometer auf 1421 bei wiederum vier Tagen Dauer signifikant.

Um die Schwierigkeit weiter zu erhöhen, wurde neben dem bisherigen Katschberg noch der Wurzen- und Loiblpass befahren. Von den 41 Fahrzeugen, die Wien wieder erreichten, blieben nur zwölf ohne Strafpunkte. Austro Daimler trat mit zehn Fahrzeugen an, acht kamen ins Ziel, fünf ohne Punkte, das war der Teampreis. 1912 wuchs die Veranstaltung weiter, mehr Teilnehmer, größere Strecke, wachsende internationale Bedeutung, da andere große Veranstaltungen wie die deutschen Prinz-Heinrich-Fahrten nicht weitergeführt wurden. Man erweiterte auf sieben Fahrtage und 2400 Kilometer einschließlich der Dolomiten mit Pordoi- und Falzàregopass.

Die Fahrt stand unter der Schirmherrschaft von Erzherzog Leopold Salvator. Unter den unglaublichen 85 Teilnehmern mit 28 verschiedenen Marken befanden sich die Erzherzöge Karl Franz Joseph (später Kaiser Karl I. von Österreich-Ungarn) sowie Joseph Ferdinand von Österreich-Toskana. Die Prinzen Elias von Bourbon-Parma und Alexander Croÿ, die Prinzessin Charlotte von Sachsen-Meiningen, die Grafen Alexander Kolowrat, Paul Draskovich, Heinrich Schönfeld, Siegfried Wimpffen, Georg Orssich, Eugen Lamberg und die Barone Walter Franz und Alexander Styrcea waren auf der Teilnehmerliste zu finden. Auch der legendäre James Radley, ein sehr erfahrener Automobilist, war mit einem Rolls-Royce gemeldet.

Im Gegensatz zu anderen Teilnehmern hatte er sich mit der Strecke nicht genug vertraut gemacht und war auf die Unerbittlichkeit der Alpenpässe ungenügend vorbereitet. Am ersten Fahrtag von Wien kam er mit seinem Rolls-Royce, Startnummer Zwei, am Katschberg, einem 6 Kilometer langen Anstieg mit 25 Prozent Steigung, die sich aber auf den letzten 200 Metern noch auf 27,5 Prozent erhöhte, zu einem Halt. Radley beunruhigte dieses kleine Missgeschick nicht, doch die Firma, die in Wien eine Niederlassung eröffnen wollte, hingegen sehr. 72 Teilnehmer erreichten das Ziel, 25 davon ohne Strafpunkte, der Rolls-Royce wurde als am ersten Tag zurückgezogen ausgewiesen. Der Teampreis ging an Fiat und Opel.

1913 war die Fahrt noch länger und anstrengender. Sie war mit einer Distanz von 2650 Kilometern und neben einigen kleineren sowie neunzehn großen Pässen die bisher schwierigste. Doch gab es weniger Anmeldungen, weil die Werke mit einem Boykott eine Durchführung alle zwei Jahre durchsetzen wollten. Nachdem noch kurzfristig Anmeldungen von Hansa, Fiat und Fischer eingegangen waren, starteten 47 Fahrzeuge, deutlich weniger als im Vorjahr.

Vier Rolls-Royce waren am Start, ein Werksteam mit drei Fahrzeugen und James Radley, um seine Schmach vom Vorjahr auszugleichen und um zu zeigen, dass er und Rolls-Royce eine vorzügliche Kombination sind. Alle legten eine Fahrt ohne außerplanmäßige Aufenthalte zurück. Radley führte die ganze Veranstaltung, er startete jeden Tag als Erster und war auch der Erste im Ziel. Jedes Fahrzeug gewann einen oder mehrere Preise. Bei keinem Fahrzeug musste auf der gesamten Strecke Kühlwasser nachgefüllt werden. Trotz dieser besonderen Leistung erhielten zwei Teamfahrzeuge Strafpunkte wegen kleinerer technischer Mängel, sodass der Teampreis an Audi ging. Die Firma Rolls-Royce war vom Fiasko von 1912 mehr als eindrucksvoll entlastet und hat seit damals an keinem motorsportlichen Wettbewerb mehr teilgenommen.

1914 wurde die Veranstaltung nochmals verschärft, trotzdem stieg die Zahl der Teilnehmer auf 75 mit 32 Marken. James Radley war mit einem weiter verbesserten Rolls-Royce Silver Ghost mit

Werksunterstützung im Hintergrund wieder dabei. Diesmal wurden 2932 Kilometer und zusätzliche Bergpässe gefahren. Radley führte wiederum an allen Tagen bis auf einen, an dem er so weit vor der Zeit lag, dass er wegen eines noch nicht besetzten Kontrollposten 60 Kilometer auf einer falschen Strecke fuhr. Trotzdem lieferte er eine tadellose Leistung und erhielt einen Hauptpreis. Hansa und Audi erhielten den Teampreis. Das war der letzte dieser Wettbewerbe. Der unruhige Balkan, der Mordanschlag am österreichischen Thronfolger Franz Ferdinand und seiner Gemahlin Sophie von Hohenberg in Sarajevo stürzten Europa in einen langen und teuren Krieg, der mit dem Untergang der Monarchie und einer neuen europäischen Landkarte endete.

Fahrzeuge 53 verschiedener Marken nahmen an den Österreichischen Alpenfahrten von 1910 bis 1914 teil. Die meisten europäischen, einige englische und wenige amerikanische Marken darunter Adler, Alfa, Apollo, Armstrong-Whitworth, Audi, Austin, Austro Daimler, Benz, Berliet, Bugatti, Cadillac, Chevrolet, Daimler (englisch), Darracq, De Dion-Bouton, Delaunay-Belleville, Dixi, EBM, Erhardt, Fiat, Fischer-Ventillos, Ford, Gräf und Stift, Gregoire, Hansa, Horch, Hotchkiss, Laurin & Klement, Mathis, Mercedes, Minerva-Knight, Mors, NAG, Neckarsulm (NSU), Nesselsdorf, NW, Opel, Oryx, Overland, Peugeot, Praga, Protos, Puch, Raba, RAF-Knight, Renault, Rolls-Royce, Scat, Singer, Vauxhall, WAF, Wanderer und Wolseley. Andere Firmen wie Isotta-Fraschini oder Siddeley-Deasley stellten offizielle oder Begleitfahrzeuge zur Verfügung. Die Fahrer der frühen Jahre waren meistens unter dreißig Jahre alt und auch oft Besitzer oder Ingenieure ihrer Marke wie Ferdinand Porsche (Austro-Daimler), Adam Opel, Otto Hieronimus (Laurin & Klement), August Horch (Audi), Sylvain de Jong (Besitzer der belgischen Marke Minerva) oder Herbert Austin Junior.

VORAUSSETZUNGEN EINES EINZIGARTIGEN PROJEKTS

INTERESSE AN ALTEN AUTOS

Ich bin als kleiner Junge auf einem Milchbauernhof in Neuseeland aufgewachsen. Damals zählte ein gelegentlicher Kinobesuch für mich zu den seltenen Genüssen. Unter den Filmen, die mir im Gedächtnis geblieben sind, war der Streifen »Geneviève«, eine entzückende Geschichte auf der Grundlage des Oldtimerrennens von London nach Brighton. Held des Films war kein gut aussehender Mann, keine reizende Dame, sondern das Auto »Geneviève«.

Bald danach unternahmen wir wieder einen Tagesausflug – wie immer nicht zu weit von zu Hause entfernt, um am Nachmittag rechtzeitig zum Melken der Kühe zurück zu sein – und zwar in eine Stadt, in der gerade eine Landwirtschafts- und Schafzuchtausstellung stattfand. Auf dieser Messe waren immer eine Fülle von Nutztieren, Traktoren, Jahrmarktsattraktionen und verschiedenen anderen Dingen zu sehen, genug, um die ganze Familie zu unterhalten. Diesmal zeigte die Schau auch einige alte Autos.

Wir befanden uns damals in den 1950er-Jahren, und die alten Autos stammten aus der wirklich frühen Zeit des Automobils – nicht jünger als aus den 1920er-Jahren, in einigen Fällen sogar älter, vielleicht erheblich älter. Und diesmal war einer der alten Wagen sogar der Star des Films – »Geneviève« selbst.

Kurz nach Fertigstellung des Films war »Geneviève« nämlich an einen Neuseeländer verkauft worden, und hier war sie also – welch ein Star! Ich war Feuer und Flamme! Ab diesem Zeitpunkt liebte ich Oldtimer, obwohl es viele Jahre dauern sollte, bis ich in der Lage war, dieser Leidenschaft zu frönen.

Erst Mitte der 1980er-Jahre wurde ich Besitzer meines ersten Oldtimers, eines Silver Ghost aus dem Jahr 1922, der damals für die Ferien der Familie genutzt wurde, nicht nur für kleine Tagesausflüge.

WIE ES ZUR NEUAUFLAGE DER ALPENFAHRT KAM

Angefangen hat die ganze Geschichte mit dem Gewinn der Alpentrophäe im Jahr 1986. Diese historische Trophäe ist eine von zwei Karaffen aus geschliffenem Glas, die ursprünglich von Erzherzog Leopold Salvator von Österreich als Preise anlässlich der Österreichischen Alpenprüfungsfahrt im Jahr 1913 gestiftet wurden. Die Trophäe gewann 1913 Curt Cornelius Friese, Leiter der Wiener Rolls-Royce-Niederlassung, nicht James Radley, wie allgemein angenommen wird. Rolls-Royce schenkte sie danach dem 20-Ghost-Club. Der Anblick dieser Trophäe auf dem Kaminsims oder dem Esstisch war für mich der Auslöser, um mehr über die österreichischen Prüfungsfahrten in den Alpen herauszufinden.

Viele Menschen bekamen damals mit, dass die Alpen-Prüfungsfahrten von 1910 bis 1914 alljährlich abgehalten wurden und auch 1915 wieder stattfinden sollten, dass James Radley 1912 in einen Silver Ghost stieg und dass sein Wagen am ersten Tag auf dem Katschbergpass an einer sehr steilen Steigung zum Stehen kam, weil er einen zu hohen Gang eingelegt hatte. Der Wagen ließ sich erneut starten, nachdem die Fahrzeuginsassen ausgestiegen waren. Doch da Radley seine Gewinnchancen verspielt hatte, zog er sich aus dem Rennen zurück.

1913 lieferte das aus drei Silver Ghosts bestehende Rolls-Royce-Team zusammen mit Radley in einem vierten Ghost eine wie zu erwarten hervorragende Leistung ab; auch 1914 war Radley allein ebenfalls großartig. Ungeachtet dessen gab es wenig genaue Informationen über das Ereignis selbst und ich machte mich an die Recherchen über »die Alpenfahrt«, um so viel herauszufinden, wie ich konnte. Allmählich gelangte ich im Lauf der folgenden Monate an die gewünschten Informationen, viele davon erhielt ich aus der British Library und dem National Motor Museum. Ich trug genügend Daten zusammen, um mehr als ein Buch zu füllen.

Auf diese Weise waren viele interessante Details ans Licht gekommen. An einem bestimmten Punkt der Recherchen schien es aber das Beste zu sein, um das Ereignis 75 Jahre nach Ankunft des ersten Silver Ghost in den Alpen wirklich zu verstehen, die Route abzufahren und nachzuempfinden. Und wie konnte das besser geschehen als in einem Silver Ghost?

Wir verbrachten viel Zeit mit der Erkundung der Routen zu und in den Alpen, denn die Strecken waren in jedem Jahr ein wenig anders verlaufen. Nachdem wir die von 1912, 1913 und 1914 genauestens recherchiert hatten, legten wir uns auf eine fest, die der von 1914 am nächsten kam, aber auch Abschnitte sowohl aus der Route von 1912 wie aus der von 1913 enthielt.

Zusammen mit meiner Frau Rae und den Kindern Jane und Robert machte ich mich Mitte Juli 1987 in unserem Silver Ghost (100 HG) von 1922 auf die Reise über Frankreich, Luxemburg und Deutschland und erreichte nach fünf Tagen die Route der Alpen-Prüfungsfahrt bei Innsbruck. Unser erster Weg führte uns über den Brennerpass – die alte Passstraße – hinunter nach Sterzing (Vipiteno) in Italien und zurück. Dann wagten wir uns auf unsere erste wirklich lange Alpenfahrt von 367 Kilometern nach Villach. Zu den drei Pässen, die wir überwanden, gehörte der Radstädter Tauern, wo gerade die Straße erneuert wurde und es sehr matschig war – ein wenig wie einige der älteren, unbefestigten Straßen – dann ging es weiter zu dem berühmten Katschbergpass, der seit den Prüfungsfahrten umgebaut, aber immer noch mit etwa 18 Prozent Steigung sehr steil war. Von unserem Stützpunkt in Villach aus unternahmen wir eine Rundreise gen Süden nach Jugoslawien, fuhren dann nach Überwindung des sehr steilen Wurzenpasses nach Italien, wo der Predilpass erklommen wurde, dann wieder zurück nach Jugoslawien (all diese Regionen waren bis 1919 Teil der Österreich-Ungarischen Monarchie).

Auf stillen Straßen fuhren wir nun durch kleine Dörfer, an deren Häusern in üppiger Flut Blumen aus den Fensterkästen quollen und deren Einwohner uns beim Vorüberfahren zuwinkten. Aus einem Zeitungsartikel vom 28. Juni 1913, einem Samstag, wissen wir, wie sich das Abenteuer seinerzeit für den Korrespondenten der »Times« angefühlt haben muss. »›Schnell! Schnell!‹, riefen die Kinder den Wagen zu, als diese heute an ihnen vorbeiflogen und bewarfen uns alle mit Blumen. Blumen, Sonnenschein, eine herrliche Landschaft und glückliche Gesichter – das ist es, was die Teilnehmer dieses großen Rennens sehen.«

Den Routen von 1912 und 1913 folgend, setzten wir unsere Fahrt südwärts durch ein sehr malerisches Tal hinunter nach Most na Soči (vormals St. Lucia) fort, wandten uns auf stillen Bergstraßen ostwärts nach Kranj (vormals Krainburg), dann weiter zur Loiblpassstraße. Damals eine belebte Hauptstraße, die mit einer steilen Steigung zum Tunnel führte, der zur Umgehung des Loiblpasses gebaut worden war. Sie galt seinerzeit als schwieriger und gefürchteter als der Katschberg. Heute liegt der Tunnel an der Grenze zwischen Österreich und Jugoslawien. Wir kehrten nach Villach zurück, ohne den Gipfel des Loiblpasses zu finden.

AUF DER SUCHE NACH DEM LOIBLPASS

Über den Loiblpass ist so viel geschrieben worden, dass es mir unerlässlich erschien, zurückzukehren und die alte Straße zu finden. Daher fuhr ich einen oder zwei Tage später von Villach noch einmal los und machte mich an einem wolkenverhangenen Morgen bei Nieselregen auf die Suche nach dem Loibl. Eine alte Schotterstraße erschien mir erfolgversprechend, und tatsächlich stellte sich heraus, dass es sich hier um die alte Hauptstraße handelte, die nunmehr lediglich als Forststraße genutzt wurde. Ich fuhr diese steile Schotterstraße, durch viele Haarnadelkurven und über zahllose quer über die Straße geführte Drainage-Abflussrinnen hinauf in den Nebel. Mich beschlich ein gespenstisches Gefühl, als ich mich so einsam und allein auf der Höhe des Passes mit seinen beiden hohen Obelisken befand, die immer noch die Grenze markieren, Schlagbäume und verlassene Zollhäuschen zu beiden Seiten. All dies war in einen wabernden Nebel getaucht und zweifellos geeignet, die Geister der Vergangenheit heraufzubeschwören, was dieses Szenario zu einem der denkwürdigsten Orte auf unserer ganzen Reise machte.

Die österreichische Seite, die ich hinaufgefahren war, wies Steigungen bis zu 23 Prozent auf. Die jugoslawische Seite – das ehemals österreichische Kronland Krain, nach 1919 in Slowenien aufgegangen –, die stets für den Aufstieg bei den Alpenprüfungsfahrten benutzt wurde, hatte hingegen 13 Haarnadelkurven und Steigungen von 17 bis 29 Prozent.

Charles L. Freeston schrieb 1914 in der Zeitschrift »Autocar«:

> »Die Haarnadelkurven neigen sich alle zur falschen Seite und die Kehren haben einen so spitzen Winkel, dass der Fahrer gezwungen ist, den inneren Fahrbahnrand zu schneiden, wenn er nicht anhalten und zurücksetzen will. Als Fahrerlebnis ist der Loibl großartig. Die Kurven sind gerade breit genug, um das zügige Passieren auch von Spitzkehren zu erlauben und aus diesem Grund werden Autofahrer, die gleichermaßen stolz auf ihre Wagen und ihre Fahrkünste sind, stets vom Loibl fasziniert sein und ihn gegenüber anderen leichteren Aufstiegen bevorzugen.«

Meine Eindrücke von diesem Teil der Alpenprüfungsroute, der noch im ursprünglichen Zustand verblieben ist, sind am besten in den Tagebucheintrag zusammengefasst, den ich am Tag meines Besuches niedergeschrieben habe.

> »Gipfel der Loiblpassstraße auf der österreichischen Seite.
>
> Obelisken; verlassene Grenzposten; Schlagbäume quer über die Straße; Regen und Nebel.
>
> Straße auf der jugoslawischen Seite unbenutzt, an vielen Stellen ist die Oberfläche von Unkraut überwuchert.
>
> Erkundete zu Fuß die Loiblpassstraße nach unten – steil, einige kleinere Erdrutsche mit kleinen Felsstücken auf der Straße; der Unterbau intakt. Befahrbar.
>
> Der Weg bergab führt über zahlreiche Haarnadelkurven; ein großer Felsen, etwa zwei Meter breit, blockiert die Straße. Weiter unten machen einige Abflussrinnen die Straße ebenfalls unbefahrbar.
>
> Um befahren zu werden, könnte die Straße leicht repariert und vom Unkraut befreit werden.
>
> Die Straße endet an einem Zaun, mit Gatter verschlossen, weniger als 100 Meter vom Tunneleingang zur modernen Straße entfernt.
>
> Fußmarsch zurück zum Pass. Starkes Gefälle – schweißtreibend.
>
> Straße noch ganz im ursprünglichen Zustand, viele alte Leitplanken jedoch zerbrochen oder verschwunden.
>
> Die steinernen Barrieren fast intakt.
>
> Rückkehr zum Gipfel – öffne die Schlagbäume.
>
> Setze den Wagen zurück bis zur zweiten Haarnadelkurve (vom Gipfel aus). Verschiedene Fotos. Beschwörung der Vergangenheit.

Neustart (knapp gelungen) auf dem schlüpfrigen nassen Unkraut, das die Straße bedeckte, für einen ›Miniaufstieg‹ zum alten Loiblpass.

Fahre zurück zum Gipfel – schließe die Schlagbäume.

Rückkehr auf die österreichische Seite. Über die Drainage-Abflussrinnen (etwa dreißig auf der Fahrt bergab im Umkreis von ungefähr 3 Kilometern). Auf dem Weg nach unten viel schwieriger zu passieren. Bremsen auf dem Straßenbelag aus feinem Schotter sehr schwierig. Abflussrinnen holprig, versetzen dem Wagen bei allem, was über 20 bis 25 Stundenkilometer Geschwindigkeit liegt, einen Stoß.

Ende der alten Straße über den Loiblpass. Zurück zur belebten Hauptstraße.«

Das war der Moment der Erkenntnis!

Bevor ich den Gipfel des Loiblpasses verließ, um weiter hinunter nach Österreich zu fahren, hatte ich beschlossen, eine Neuauflage der Alpenfahrt von 1913 an ihrem 80. Jahrestag im Juni 1993 zu organisieren. Und die Route sollte wieder die alte, fantastische Loiblpassstraße einschließen.

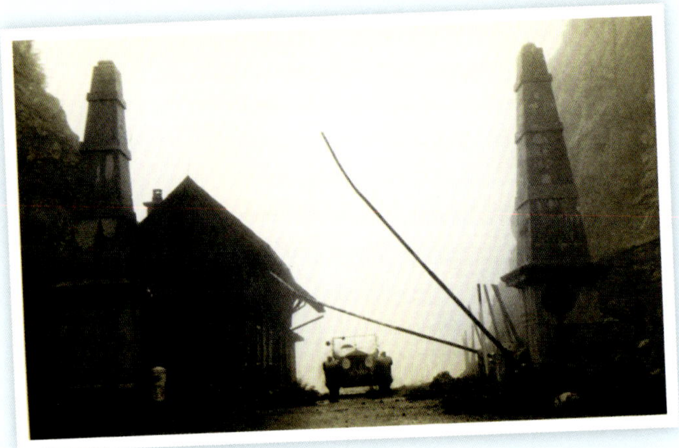

RADLEYS SILVER GHOST

Auf der Nordspanientour im September 1985 begleitete mich der alte Fred Watson bei einer eintägigen Oldtimerfahrt in meinem Silver Ghost von 1922. Wir waren im stillen ländlichen Teil Spaniens und fuhren über 241 Kilometer auf vielen unterschiedlichen Straßen durch Flussschluchten und ruhige Dörfer, während unsere Unterhaltung sich um das Thema drehte, das Fred am Herzen lag – Oldtimerrallys. Das war das erste Mal seit vielen Jahren, dass Fred einen vollen Tag in einem Silver Ghost gefahren war, was er vollauf genoss.

Zu gegebener Zeit sprachen wir über den Radley Alpine Eagle Silver Ghost, der seit 1951 in Freds Besitz war. Im Allgemeinen war davon auszugehen, dass der Wagen innerhalb der Familie vererbt werden würde. Gleichwohl sagte ich zum Abschied beiläufig: »Wenn Sie jemals daran denken, das Auto zu verkaufen, rufen Sie mich an«, ohne jedoch meinen Worten größere Bedeutung beizumessen und weiter daran zu denken.

Zu dieser Zeit war der Radley-Wagen, der mehr als dreißig Jahre zuvor restauriert worden war, nicht fit für eine echte Tour, wurde jedoch anschließend zum Überholen gegeben, um wieder in seinen eigentlichen Tauglichkeitszustand versetzt zu werden. Doch erhielt ich in dieser Zeit den Anruf mit der Nachricht, dass der Wagen verkauft werden sollte – und ob ich interessiert sei. Nachdem ich mich von dem ersten Schreck erholt hatte, versicherte ich, dass dies immer noch zutraf. Und so geschah es, dass ich unbesehen einen alten Wagen kaufte, der sich zu jener Zeit in einem vollkommen zerlegten Zustand befand, da die Restaurierung gezeigt hatte, dass das Fahrgestell verbogen war und auf die richtigen vorgegebenen Maße gebracht werden musste.

Da ich das Glück hatte, den Wagen zu erwerben und den Restaurierungsprozess fortzuführen, erschien es folgerichtig, das Auto in seinen ursprünglichen Zustand von 1913, in dem es war, als Radley sich auf den Weg nach Wien und zur Österreichischen Alpenfahrt machte, zurückzuversetzen. Nun war bekannt, dass der Wagen im Neuzustand viele einzigartige Besonderheiten besessen hatte und das Problem war, dass viele von ihnen entfernt worden waren. Der Wagen war sowieso in Teile zerlegt und niemand wusste genau, wie all diese speziellen Elemente aussahen. Insofern war noch viel mehr Recherche erforderlich, um auch diese Aufgabe zu meistern.

RECHERCHEN UND RESTAURIERUNG

Anfang 1988 entwarf ich zwei wohldurchdachte Pläne, die von den meisten Menschen für völlig verrückt gehalten wurden.

Der erste: Eine komplette Wiederaufnahme der Alpenwettfahrt von 1913, rechtzeitig zum 80. Jahrestag 1993. Zu lang, zu schwierig, zu teuer, zu anspruchsvoll hieß es – und überhaupt würde niemand kommen, sodass der Plan zum Scheitern verurteilt sei. Wir sagten, dass wir die Fahrt bereits erprobt hätten und wir sie sowieso auf eigene Faust wiederholen würden, der Plan also definitiv durchgeführt werden würde. Damit nicht genug, bestand der zweite Plan darin, den Radley Alpine Rolls-Royce von 1913 komplett zu restaurieren, nämlich in den Originalzustand zurückzuversetzen, der noch unbekannt war.

Die Recherchen für beide Projekte wurden zügig weitergeführt, wobei wir viel Zeit im Zeitungsleseraum der British Library verbrachten, aber auch mit regelmäßigen Reisen nach Österreich, um in der Nationalbibliothek nach Informationen über die ursprünglichen Alpenfahrten und die Rolls-Royce-Automobile zu suchen, insbesondere Radleys Wagen von 1913. Jede Reise nach Österreich nutzten wir für neue Erkundungen, um möglichst alles über die Route zu erfahren.

Die Informationen entsprangen einer Vielfalt von Quellen. Die Bibliothek verfügte über detaillierte Berichte dieser frühen Ereignisse im lokalen Automagazin »Allgemeine Automobil-Zeitung«, reich mit vielen Fotografien und originalen Teilnehmerformularen illustriert sowie mit präzisen Details über die Strecke einschließlich den Entfernungen und Fahrzeiten zwischen den entlang der Route liegenden Ortschaften. Das waren wichtige Informationen, die uns über das Tempo der ursprünglichen Rallye in Kenntnis setzten; auch erwiesen sie sich als überaus nützlich, um den zeitlichen Ablauf der heutigen Zeit anzupassen, besonders in den Gebirgsregionen. Darüber hinaus brachten die Magazine unter der Überschrift »Technisches« weitere Details zu den Teilnehmerfahrzeugen dieser Alpenfahrt. Dazu gehörte das Heizungsverlängerungsrohr – keine Erfindung von Rolls-Royce, aber eine von Fiat 1912 verwendete Vorrichtung, die viele Autohersteller in der Annahme, dass dies irgendeinen Vorteil bringen würde, zu kopieren suchten. Die Schwimmernadel im Vergaser wurde ebenfalls in der Zeitschrift beschrieben.

Durch einen glücklichen Zufall und unabhängig von meinen anderen Recherchen gelangte die letzte bekannte Adresse von James Radley, der vor mehr als dreißig Jahren gestorben war, in meine Hände. Das setzte mich auf die richtige Spur, sodass ich mit ein wenig Detektivarbeit seinen Stiefschwiegersohn David Scott finden konnte, der verschiedene Dinge aus dem Nachlass besaß, darunter das »Radley scrap book«, das Sammelalbum mit eingeklebten Zeitungsausschnitten. Es enthielt eine Menge Informationen aus Radleys Zeit als Flieger und einige in Wien von dem Berufsfotografen Heinrich Schumann aufgenommene Originalfotos. Diese Bilder zeigten Radley und das Rolls-Royce-Team im Jahr 1913 in Wien. Sie waren ein weiterer großer Ansporn für mich, meine Bemühungen fortzusetzen.

Währenddessen schritt die Restaurierung fort und der Royce Foundation gelang, da sie einige frühe Rolls-Royce-Blaupausen erworben hatte, weitere wichtige Entdeckungen, denn darunter befanden sich auch jene für die Komponenten der in der österreichischen Zeitschrift beschriebenen Schwimmernadel. Durch Gespräche mit anderen Rolls-Royce-Besitzern erfuhren wir von einem Silver Ghost in Amerika mit einer noch funktionstüchtigen Schwimmernadel am Wagen! Die ursprünglichen Farben der Lackierung und des Leders mit Sicherheit zu bestimmen, erwies sich als schwierig. Doch nach drei Jahren des Experimentierens fanden die Autobauer sie schließlich unterhalb der Kotflügel, mutmaßlich noch im Originalzustand, denn sie meinten: »An dieser Stelle entfernt niemand alle Farbe«. Erstaunlicherweise entsprach die Lackierung, zu der wir uns entschlossen hatten, genau jener Originalfarbe – was wir aber nie erfahren hätten!

Die Erkundungen zur Route waren nicht mehr so komplex wie beim erwähnten Loiblpass, dennoch wurde jeder Ort, durch den wir fuhren, die kleinen, mitunter größeren, heute abseits liegenden Abschnitte, die leicht zu übersehen waren, ausfindig gemacht. Wo sich die Gelegenheit bot, in eine rechts an der Route gelegene Kleinstadt hinein- und am anderen Ende hinauszufahren, konnten wir sie in unser Streckenbuch eintragen, was speziell zwei Vorteile hatte: Zum einen bot sich die Möglichkeit, durch einen reizvollen Ort mit Originalgebäuden aus der Zeit der ursprünglichen Tour zu fahren; zweitens ließ sich so verhindern, dass der moderne Verkehr durch die langsameren Fahrzeuge behindert wurde. Links an der Straße liegende Orte, deren Zentrum nur durch ein Abzweigen von der Route zu erreichen war, stellten eine größere Schwierigkeit dar.

Das mussten wir selbst erfahren, als es einmal bis zu fünf Minuten dauerte, um auf die befahrene Hauptstraße und zurück zu unserer Route zu kommen. Uns war sofort klar, dass diese Ortschaften von der Alpen-Route 1993 auszuschließen waren.

Derweil stellten wir ein umfassendes Routenbuch zusammen, in dem alle historischen Details, insbesondere die Gebirgspässe, berücksichtigt und beschrieben, dabei jede Etappe mit Hinweistafeln und Entfernungen dokumentiert wurden, denn diese Fahrt sollte der ursprünglichen Route von 1913 so genau wie möglich entsprechen. Nachdem das Buch in einem Probeexemplar vorlag, wurde jeder Abschnitt auf einer Landkarte nachvollzogen, um sicherzugehen, dass die Links- oder Rechtsabbiegungen nicht falsch angegeben waren und unsere Entfernungsangaben nicht zu sehr abwichen.

Währenddessen wurde für immer mehr Menschen deutlich, dass beide Pläne umgesetzt werden würden. Viele wollten nun auch an dem Ereignis teilhaben. Auch ließ sich die Mitwirkung von Sponsoren organisieren, insbesondere von österreichischer Seite aus, was bedeutete, dass wir Berührungspunkte in den meisten Städten und Dörfern hatten. Die Veranstaltung konnte also die historischen Strecken weitmöglich nutzen und beteiligen. Auf diese Weise fügte sich alles Schritt für Schritt zusammen. Die Teilnahme anderer Sponsoren ermöglichte die Einbindung neuer Wettbewerbe und so wurde auf Grundlage unserer Recherche die Herstellung von Glaskaraffen nach dem Vorbild der ursprünglichen, von Erzherzog Leopold Salvator gestifteten Trophäen beschlossen. Sie waren ja an erster Stelle die Inspiration zu alledem gewesen.

Europa hatte sich 1913 an der Schwelle umwälzender Ereignisse befunden. Während der fünf Jahre, in denen die Recherchen voranschritten, erlebte es erneut tiefgreifende Veränderungen, die sich vielfach als besonders vorteilhaft für die Alpenfahrt erwiesen. War noch 1913 die gesamte Route Teil der Österreich-Ungarischen Monarchie gewesen und waren daher keine Grenzen zu überwinden, hatte die Alpenfahrt von 1993 nicht weniger als zwölfmal Grenzen zu passieren; wählte man die Stelvio-Option, so kamen zwei weitere hinzu ebenso wie durch die Trennung der beiden jugoslawischen Staaten Slowenien und Kroatien. Glücklicherweise trat in dieser Phase das Schengen-Abkommen in Kraft und viele Grenzüberschreitungen mit den entsprechenden starken Verzögerungen stellten kein Problem mehr dar. Andere schwierige Grenzen, die enorme Zeitverluste und große Verkehrsprobleme mit sich brachten, waren die Übergänge am Wurzenpass und am Pordoipass. Doch mit der Eröffnung des Karawankentunnel 1991 als Alternative fielen diese beiden Erschwernisse mit einem Schlag fort, obwohl es innerhalb eines Monats danach einen heftigen Zehntagekrieg mit der jugoslawischen Armee gab, die (erfolglos) versuchte, den neuen Grenzübergang einzunehmen.

In dieser Zeit ging die Fahrzeugrestaurierung weiter und war im April 1993 abgeschlossen. Nach einer Restaurierungsphase von fünf Jahren war er bereit für die Prüfung der Straßentauglichkeit. Zugleich wurde das detaillierte Routenbuch abgeschlossen und fünfzig Fahrzeuge wurden für den Start im Juni in Wien bereitgemacht. Inzwischen hatte die BBC Notiz von dem Projekt genommen und erklärte sich bereit, ein »hochkarätiges Team« nach Wien zu entsenden, um das Ereignis zu filmen.

DER LOIBL

Nach meiner Erkundung des alten Loiblpassgipfels im Jahr 1987 und meinem Entschluss, eine Alpenfahrt zu organisieren inklusive der Instandsetzung des Passes, standen wir nun vor der Frage, wie wir dies bewältigen sollten. Die mit der ursprünglichen Alpenfahrt von 1910 bis 1914 zusammenhängenden Ereignisse waren vom Kaiserlich-Königlichen Österreichischen Automobilklub organisiert worden, dessen Nachfolger der ÖAMTC in Wien war. Also vereinbarten wir ein gemeinsames Treffen. Wir erklärten ihnen die von uns geplante Neuinszenierung der Tour und fragten an, ob sie den Kontakt zu den italienischen und jugoslawischen Organisationen herstellen könnten, um diesen unsere Pläne nahezubringen. Dies geschah besonders mit Blick auf den Loiblpass nach Jugoslawien und einen ungenutzten Abschnitt des heute von Slowenien nach Italien führenden Predilpasses.

Wir hatten das erforderliche Protokoll verfolgt und konnten uns nur vorstellen, was als nächstes geschehen musste. Ein Brief wurde ordnungsgemäß von Wien an die gewünschte italienische Motorsportorganisation in Rom gerichtet. Seither hörte man nichts mehr von dort. Der Brief hatte mutmaßlich Rom erreicht, wo er sofort in das »Zu schwierig«-Fach abgelegt worden war. Auch nach Belgrad wurde ein solcher Brief geschickt, wo wahrscheinlich entschieden wurde, dass die Anfrage Slowenien betraf, und so ging das Schreiben weiter nach Ljubljana. Dort meinte man, dass dieser Plan nach einer Rallye klang und da zwei europäische Rallyefahrer in der Nähe waren, beschloss man, den Brief dorthin weiterzugeben. Die beiden Männer wunderten sich, wie jemand aus Neuseeland um die Freigabe eines slowenischen Gebirgspasses bitten konnte, den sie »verloren« hatten. So machten sie sich im Sommer 1990 daran, den Pass zu lokalisieren und beantragten die Erlaubnis, ihn zu erkunden.

Zum Ende des Sommers erhielt ich einen Brief von Aleš Črnivec und Stojan Kasteliç, den beiden Rallyefahrern, die den Pass erklommen und zahlreiche Fotos gemacht hatten; sie luden mich ein, nach Ljubljana zu kommen und mein Vorhaben mit ihnen zu besprechen. Im Herbst machte ich mich auf den Weg und checkte am düsteren und regnerischen Vorabend unserer für den nächsten Morgen vorgesehenen Besprechung in einem Hotel in Ljubljana ein. Ein heftiges Erdbeben während der Nacht ließ mich zweifeln, ob das Treffen stattfinden würde. Doch wie so oft in Slowenien brach ein strahlender, wenn auch kalter Morgen an, und ich traf die beiden Männer verabredungsgemäß. Sie erklärten mir, dass sie einen gemeinsamen Ausflug zum Loiblpass für uns alle arrangiert hätten: Zu Fuß wollten wir den Pass erklimmen, und zwar auf der alten, für den öffentlichen Verkehr seit Eröffnung des Entlastungstunnels im Jahr 1964 gesperrten Straße. Da das Grenzgebiet unter Kontrolle der jugoslawischen Armee stand und die Zivilisten der Gegend unter der Kontrolle der slowenischen Polizei (»milicija«), war es für Ortsansässige schwierig, derlei prekäre Gebiete zu besuchen, und für Ausländer war dies sowieso beispiellos. Die beiden hatten eine Sondererlaubnis für mich erwirkt, um diese »sensible« Grenze zu besuchen.

So fand ich mich eines Tages im November 1990 auf der alten Passstraße in Gesellschaft zweier lokaler Rallyefahrer wieder, wie wir gemeinsam zu Fuß nach oben stapften, Seite an Seite mit einem Mitglied der »milicija«, der von seinen Pflichten der Passkontrolle freigestellt worden war, um uns zu begleiten. Dazu musste er auch noch zuerst die Straße wieder hinunter zur Kaserne gehen, um unsere Pläne zu bestätigen und genehmigen zu lassen, bevor wir uns wieder auf den Weg machten.

Ohne unser Wissen war bereits eine Militärpatrouille in den Bergen unterwegs, die nichts von unseren Plänen wusste, daher waren die Soldaten ziemlich erstaunt, als sie uns auf der Route trafen. Glücklicherweise ließ sie der Anblick eines uniformierten Polizisten annehmen, dass wir uns auf irgendeiner offiziellen Mission befanden. Als sie uns einholten, wurde alles erklärt – auf Serbokroatisch, weil die drei Rekruten, jugendliche Wehrpflichtige von nicht mehr als 18 Jahren, die mit Kalaschnikows bewaffnet waren, aus Bosnien, Mazedonien und dem Kosovo im Süden von Jugoslawien kamen. Unsere seltsame Gruppe endete daher am Gipfel des Loiblpasses in dichtem Schnee, schottischen Whisky trinkend und insgesamt von einer wachsenden Begeisterung über die Aussicht angesteckt, dass richtige Autos erneut diese dramatische Straße befahren könnten. Was mich betrifft, so halte ich diesen Tag für einen der einzigartigsten und ungewöhnlichsten meines Lebens!

Noch lagen mehr als zwei Jahre vor uns, bevor wir den Pass überqueren würden, und der Zustand der Straße, wenngleich nicht schlecht, erforderte noch einiges an Arbeit, ganz zu schweigen davon, dass wir auch von österreichischer Seite eine Genehmigung brauchen würden, um nach dem Überschreiten der Grenze den Pass hinunterzufahren. Zu dieser Zeit hielt Slowenien gerade eine Volksbefragung für oder gegen die Unabhängigkeit von Jugoslawien ab.

Am Abend nach meiner Bergtour zum Gipfel war ich zurück in Ljubljana, von meinen neuen Freunden, den Rallyefahrern, mit denen ich vor einigen Stunden den Loibl erklommen hatte, und ihren Familien herzlich aufgenommen und bewirtet. Beim Abendessen wurde ich gefragt, was ich angesichts einer solchen Volksabstimmung tun würde. Wie würde ich abstimmen?

Niemals zuvor war ich mit einer solchen Frage konfrontiert worden. Ich dachte darüber nach und antwortete: »Die Anfänge der slowenischen Sprache reichen zurück bis vor das Jahr 1000 – sie ist sogar älter als das Englische. Slowenien ist immer Teil eines anderen Landes gewesen. Zum ersten Mal seit tausend Jahren gibt es für Slowenien die Chance, das eigene Schicksal in die Hand zu nehmen. Was würden Sie Ihren Enkeln sagen, wenn Sie diese Chance nicht ergreifen würden?« Ich schmeichle mir, dass mein Kommentar das Resultat beeinflusst hat – 94,8 Prozent votierten für die Unabhängigkeit bei der Volksbefragung im Dezember 1990!

Nach den freien Wahlen in Slowenien, in den nun aufgeklärteren Zeiten, waren die Menschen bereit, eigene Entscheidungen zu treffen und eigene Lösungen zu finden. Doch 1991 war ein problematisches Jahr, was auch die Reisen in das Land betraf, da Krieg drohte, sobald es die Unabhängigkeit von Jugoslawien erklären würde. Man konnte nicht mit Leihwagen nach Slowenien einreisen oder die Autoverleihfirmen verweigerten die Versicherung – bei einem Besuch war also alle Vorsicht geboten. Hinsichtlich der Situation am Loiblpass erklärten alle Slowenen, es wäre besser, zu warten bis sie wirklich ihre Unabhängigkeit erlangt hätten, bevor feste Pläne gemacht würden. Auf die slowenische Unabhängigkeitserklärung im Juni 1991 folgte der Zehntagekrieg, darauf bis zum völligen Rückzug der jugoslawischen Armee eine noch unsichere Freiheit, schließlich im Januar 1992 die Anerkennung durch europäische Staaten und andere. Während dieser Phase, in denen sich alles in der Schwebe befand, war es jedoch immer noch möglich, das Land zu besuchen und die Loiblpläne zu diskutieren, wenngleich mit einem gewissen Risiko. Anlässlich einer weiteren, bald darauf nach Slowenien unternommenen Reise im Sommer 1992, als das Land endlich unabhängig war, traf ich einen Mann aus dem Tal, das zum Loiblpass führte. Sein Name war Dušan Koren. Allgemein als Großvater Koren bekannt, hatte er sein ganzes Leben hindurch in dieser Gegend gelebt und träumte von der Wiederherstellung und Nutzung der alten Straße.

Diskutiert wird in Slowenien auf sehr freundschaftliche Weise. Eine große Flasche des einheimischen Sliwowitz' kommt auf den Tisch und die Debatte nimmt ihren Lauf, selbst wenn hie und da übersetzt werden muss. Wir vereinbarten, dass wir uns Anfang Juli 1993 mit bis zu fünfzig Vintage-Rolls-Royce-Autos in Slowenien einfinden würden. Der Pass sollte dann zwar bereit sein, doch die Arbeit erst kurz zuvor abgeschlossen werden, falls heftiger Regen eine zweite Restaurierung erforderlich machen würde. Schließlich war der Sliwowitz ausgetrunken und das Meeting war zu Ende. Und so geschah es, dass auf dem Loiblpass (für die Slowenen der Ljubel) das Motorengeräusch von Rolls-Royce Silver Ghosts erneut zu hören war.

Übernahm ich wieder die Rolle von Mr. Radley? Nein. Ich lag in einem Krankenhaus in Ljubljana, weil ich mir beim Anlassen des Wagens am Abend zuvor den Arm gebrochen hatte. Nach sieben Jahren unablässiger Bemühungen – sechs seit meiner Loiblentdeckung – sollte meine erste Fahrt hinauf zum Ljubel noch ein bisschen länger auf sich warten lassen.

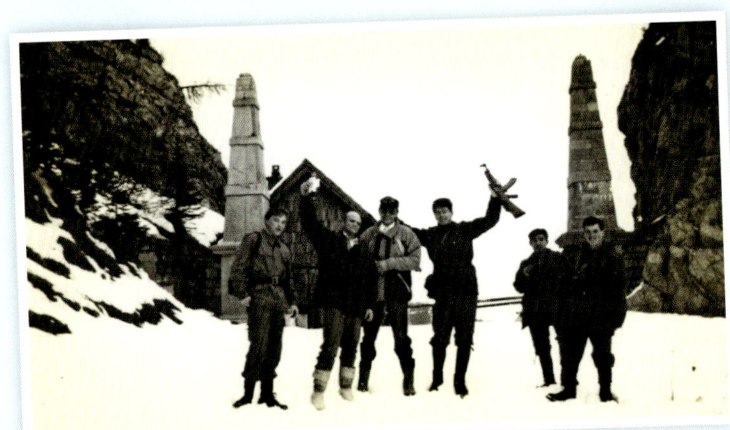

DAS FOTOALBUM

DIE ENTDECKUNG DES ALBUMS

Die Ausstrahlung des BBC-Films über die Alpenfahrt 1993 fand ein großes Publikum. Unter den Zuschauern des fünfzig Minuten währenden Films befanden sich auch Nachkommen von Reggie Hope, der 1910 und 1911 Radleys Bodenmanager gewesen war, als dieser zu den ersten Flugpionieren gehörte. Mit der Nummer 12 auf seinem Pilotenschein stellte Radley den Weltgeschwindigkeitsrekord beim Lanark-Rennen in Schottland auf, gerade mal vier Monate nach dem Kauf seines ersten Flugzeugs, das er selbst zusammensetzte und mit dem er sich das Fliegen beibrachte. Gleichzeitig nahm er an den regelmäßigen Wochenendvorführungen im Kunstflug teil, eine im Sommer 1910 sehr typische und beliebte Darbietung.

Als Reggie Hopes Söhne den Film Ende 1993 sahen, wurde ihnen plötzlich bewusst, dass ihr Vater nicht nur James Radley gekannt, sondern mit ihm auch zusammen nach Wien gefahren war und mit einer Kamera ausgerüstet die Reise ab England festgehalten hatte. Gut möglich war, wie sie erkannten, dass die Bilder noch existierten. Nach einer Durchsuchung des Dachbodens oder selten geöffneter Schubladen förderten sie den Schatz zutage – die in einem Album aufbewahrten Fotos von der Reise, die von daher sowohl im wörtlichen als auch im metaphorischen Sinn während ihrer achtzigjährigen Existenz im Dunkeln ausgeharrt hatten.

Das Album gehörte dem am 8. August 1956 verstorbenen Reginald John Hooton Hope. Es wurde der Royce Foundation im Februar 1994 gestiftet, und zwar von Mrs. Audrey Darke aus Porthcothan Bay, Cornwall, und Mrs. Peta Jacobi, der Tochter, beziehungsweise der Enkelin von Reggie Hope, sowie von Denis Allen aus Stevington, Bedfordshire, Halbbruder von Mrs. Darke und Stiefsohn von Reggie Hope. Als enger Freund des im März 1959 verstorbenen Jimmy Radley war Reggie Hope während der frühen Flugaktivitäten Radleys immer dabei. In Begleitung von Tubby Ward fuhr Hope zusammen mit Radley im Rolls-Royce Silver Ghost zur österreichischen Alpenfahrt 1913 nach Wien.

Im Lauf des Jahres 1994 wurde ich eingeladen, das Album anzuschauen. Es war fast zu schön, um wahr zu sein: Das Radley-Hope-Album weist insgesamt 51 Fotos auf, fast die Hälfte davon zeigt den historischen Radley-Wagen von 1913.

DIE BESCHRIFTUNG DER FOTOS IM RADLEY-HOPE-ALBUM

Das Album wies keinerlei Bildunterschriften auf und enthielt nur wenige Anhaltspunkte und Hinweise auf die Örtlichkeiten. Doch nach sieben Jahren Recherche und Reisen entlang der Alpenfahrtroute von 1913 war es doch möglich, eine Reihe der Bilder unmittelbar zu identifizieren. In anderen Fällen ließ sich die Gegend, in der die Fotos aufgenommen worden waren, erschließen. Auf der Grundlage meines Wissens und meiner Erfahrung beschloss ich, alle diese Bilder zu untertiteln oder es zumindest zu versuchen. Mir war zu diesem Zeitpunkt nicht klar, dass mich die Durchführung dieser Aufgabe die nächsten 19 Jahre beschäftigen würde!

Wie sich bald erwies, waren alle diese Fotos vor der Ankunft in Wien, wo die Alpenwettfahrt beginnen sollte, gemacht worden. Die frühen Bilder schienen in London aufgenommen zu sein, denn es gab Fotos mit dem auf einer hölzernen Plattform verankerten Wagen, die zeigten, wie er durch einen Hebekran mit Tragseilen direkt vom Boden empor- und über die Ladebordwand der Frankreich-Fähre an Bord gehoben wurde. Es gab nur ein einziges Bild, auf dem etwas vermerkt war – eine Überschrift mit den Worten »Mont Cenis, 22. Mai 1913«. Das lieferte uns einen beachtlichen Schlüssel zur Klärung der nach Wien eingeschlagenen Route. Das einzige andere Bild von unterwegs zeigt den Wagen in Italien inmitten einer Stadt. Anfangs hielten wir sie für Riva, konnten sie aber als Brescia erkennen. Nun stand uns dieser Teil der Strecke klar vor Augen: Der Weg durch Frankreich verlief hauptsächlich auf der alten N1 nach Paris, dann auf die alte N6, die tatsächlich in Paris begann und auf dem Col du Mont Cenis endete.

Für eine Bildtitelliste war es erforderlich, jedes Bild erst einmal aufzulisten und mit den uns bekannten Informationen zu versehen. Dies ergab eine Liste voller Vermutungen, wie etwa »wahrscheinlich London« oder »auf der Dolomitenstraße« oder »wahrscheinlich zwischen zwei Orten in Frankreich oder Italien«. Früh schon nahmen wir uns vor herauszufinden, wo die beiden Londoner Bilder aufgenommen worden waren. Sie zeigten offensichtlich ein und denselben Schauplatz. Existierte er noch? Oder war er im Krieg zerstört worden?

In der Zeit vor dem Internet war die Lösung derartiger Probleme viel schwieriger, und lange Zeit hindurch tappte ich im Dunkeln. Eines Tages prüfte ich Teile der Unterlagen, die ich über den Radley-Wagen besaß, und erkannte, dass Radley als Lieferadresse für sein Auto das Brown's Hotel in London angegeben hatte. Am nächsten Tag fuhr ich nach London und siehe da, es war die Umgebung der beiden ersten Bilder. Sie zeigte sich genauso wie in den Fotos, unverändert seit 1913!

Eine Reihe von Bildern, etwa die vom Gardasee, ließ sich aufgrund unserer Kenntnis der Route identifizieren. Andere am Kanal aufgenommene Fotos erhielten eine Bildunterschrift, auch wenn sie eine überholte Lademethode zeigten – Autos wurden längst nicht mehr an Tragseilen hängend per Hebekran auf Fähren gehievt, und es gab auch keine Pariser Züge mit Anschluss an die Fähre mehr, wie in dem Bild zu sehen, dessen Schauplatz später als Boulogne identifiziert wurde.

Das französische Château erschien uns sehr vertraut. Das Dach lag allerdings in Trümmern, während das Château, das wir kannten, ein wunderbares Ziegeldach im burgundischen Stil hatte. Es verging ein Jahr vergeblicher Suche, bis uns einfiel, dass nicht nur ein Auto, sondern auch ein Château reparaturbedürftig sein kann und das, das wir vor Augen hatten, tatsächlich das uns bekannte war. Postkarten, die wir auf Flohmärkten in Frankreich fanden, bestätigten dies und trugen auch dazu bei, andere Örtlichkeiten zu identifizieren, insbesondere Lanslebourg am Fuß der Passhöhe des Col du Mont Cenis. Eine auf der Route gelegene Stadt, die aber durch den Krieg stark zerstört worden war. Nur die Kirchen sind geblieben; der Rest wurde nach dem Krieg neu aufgebaut. Nachdem wir nun so viele passende Bildunterschriften gefunden hatten, war es an der Zeit, sich gründlich nach den noch fehlenden Teilen des Puzzles umzusehen; zu diesem Zweck organisierten wir eine Tour durch Österreich, bei der wir dem uns bekannten Verlauf der Strecke folgten.

Ausgestattet mit vielen Fotoabzügen brachen wir im Mai 1995 im originalen Radley-Car zu einer Entdeckungsreise auf. Unser Plan bestand darin, die Fotos dort zu wiederholen, wo das Auto seinerzeit aufgenommen worden war, falls der betreffende Schauplatz noch existierte. Der Anfang wurde mit den Londoner Bildern am Brown's Hotel gemacht. Da die Kanalüberquerung nun ganz anders ablief als damals, war der nächste Punkt auf der Agenda das Château la Rochepot. Die genaue Stelle war leicht zu finden. Obwohl an der N6 gelegen, war dieser Teil der Route einer Ortsumgehung zum Opfer gefallen und wurde vom Schnellverkehr nicht mehr benutzt. Das erlaubte uns, an der nächstgelegenen passenden Stelle anzuhalten, um ein Bild zu wiederholen, das vor 82 Jahren geschossen worden war! Es gab nur ein Problem, dem wir hier und an anderen Orten begegneten, nämlich dass die betreffende Stelle nunmehr mit Bäumen bewachsen war. Doch etwa hundert Meter hinter dem ehemaligen Schauplatz gab es eine Lücke zwischen den Bäumen, von der aus das Château deutlich zu sehen war, und so wurde das Foto ordnungsgemäß aufgenommen.

Die Suche nach früheren Routen-Stationen ging während unserer Fahrt nach Lanslebourg und der Passhöhe des Col du Mont Cenis weiter. Eine Stadt, die laut dem französischen Fremdenverkehrsamt in London St. Jean de Maurienne sein sollte, blieb trotz ähnlicher Berge im Hintergrund unerkannt. Ein weiteres Foto, das der Identifizierung zu einem späteren Zeitpunkt harrte.

Manche Schauplätze waren leicht zu finden, andere schwer, obwohl die Identifizierung dann doch gelang. Andere, besonders diejenigen, bei denen Reggie Hope die Ansicht vom Rücksitz des fahrenden Autos aus fotografiert hatte, fanden wir wiederum nur mit Glück. Wie sich herausstellte, hatte Radley mit Ausnahme der Gebirgspässe nur wenige Stops eingelegt. An einem sehr heißen Nachmittag auf der Fahrt nach Riva fragten wir bei einem Stopp Einheimische in einer Bar nach einem besonderen Aussichtspunkt, von dem wir wegen unseren Recherchen glaubten, er müsse in der Nähe sein. Sie schauten das Foto an, lachten und erklärten, es sei einen knappen Kilometer weiter unten auf der Straße aufgenommen worden!

Viele der um Riva aufgenommenen Fotos haben wir hinsichtlich der Schauplätze identifizieren können, darunter die Ponalestraße mit ihren Tunnels auf der alten Straße ebenso wie die von Stadt und Burg Castel Toblino ein paar Kilometer weiter nördlich. Bei einigen konnten wir die Stelle erst später identifizieren. Ähnlich ließen sich auf der berühmten Route über die Dolomiten von Trento (Trient) nach Cortina viele der Schauplätze finden, einschließlich der Gebirgspässe. Andere Bilder aus dieser Region sind, weil uns ihre exakte Lage nicht bekannt war, noch nicht zu lokalisieren. In den folgenden Jahren wurden die Bildunterschriften weiter korrigiert und verbessert. Bis 2013 stand noch bei einigen der frühen Bilder nicht fest, wo sie aufgenommen worden waren.

Anmerkung des Verfassers:

Als wir die Bildunterschriften für die Fotos verfassten, mussten wir die für die unterschiedlichen Epochen historisch korrekten Ortsnamen verwenden.

Als 1919 die Grenzen neu festgelegt wurden und sich verschoben, lagen viele Orte an der Alpenstraße nicht mehr in Österreich, sondern gehörten zu Italien oder Jugoslawien (später Slowenien oder Kroatien). Nach 1945 gab es auch noch weitere Veränderungen.

Zumeist haben wir die österreichischen Namen für die 1913 aufgenommenen Bilder verwendet, falls nicht ohnehin, wie in Teilen der Dolomiten oder in den heute zum Trentino gehörigen Gebieten, ebenfalls die italienischen Namen für die Alpenfahrt von 1913 verwendet wurden, selbst wenn es eine deutsche Alternative gab.

Für die Fotos aus dem Jahr 2013 ist der jeweils gebräuchliche Name der modernen Länder verwendet worden.

DIE FOTOGRAFIEN VON 2013

Für das hundertjährige Jubiläum der Österreichischen Alpenfahrt 1913 hatten wir stets geplant, das Radley-Auto zurück nach Wien zu bringen und mit ihm die gesamte Alpenfahrtroute noch einmal abzufahren. Unterschiedliche Optionen, die Hundertjahrfeier zu begehen, wurden seit der ersten über die gesamte Route führenden Tour, die wir 1993 organisiert hatten, in Erwägung gezogen. Das Event erfreute sich großer Beliebtheit, sodass für 2013 bis zu vier Veranstaltungen zur Debatte standen.

Dann kam ein Anruf von der Firma Rolls-Royce, die an der Jubiläumstour mit einem Firmenteam samt dem Radley-Wagen und einem modernen, vom Radley Ghost inspirierten Rolls-Royce in Spezialanfertigung teilnehmen wollte. Er war sogar alpenblau lackiert, mit einer silbernen Kühlerhaube, um Radleys Originalfahrzeug zu kopieren. Darüber hinaus sollten beide Autos im Mai 2013 bei einer Veranstaltung in der Villa d'Este am Comer See gezeigt werden, einen Monat vor der Neuinszenierung der Alpenfahrt. Obwohl es einen Plan gab, die Autos nach Como zu transportieren, erkannten wir anhand der Daten, dass es möglich sein würde, den gesamten Weg abzufahren – an denselben Tagen und über dieselbe Route, die Radley 1913 eingeschlagen hatte.

Schnell wurde ein Plan entworfen. Donnerstag, 23. Mai 2013, wurde der Wagen am Comer See benötigt. Das alte Foto von Radley auf dem Mont-Cenis-Pass war am 22. Mai 1913 geschossen worden. Der einzig mögliche Tag, um draußen vor dem Brown's Hotels eine Aufnahme zu machen, war der Sonntag, 19. Mai. Dies ließ grade genug Zeit, durch Frankreich zu fahren, um den Schnappschuss von Radley auf der Passhöhe des Mont Cenis zu wiederholen, genau hundert Jahre nach der Originalaufnahme.

Nun, da die Beschriftungen der Fotos für das Radley-Hope-Album fertiggestellt und die Schauplätze identifiziert waren, warum sollte man da nicht alle Fotografien wiederholen und zeigen, wie sich die Dinge im Lauf des Jahrhunderts verändert hatten? Es blieb uns keine Zeit, darüber nachzudenken, ob diese Idee, einen hundert Jahre alten Wagen quer durch Europa zu fahren und ein Album mit Fotos zu schaffen, die mit jenen verglichen werden sollten, die hundert Jahre zuvor von und mit demselben Wagen aufgenommen wurden, verrückt war. Es gab keine vorab getroffenen Regelungen oder Straßenabsperrungen. Alle Fotos wurden unter den vorherrschenden Bedingungen aufgenommen. Die folgenden Details beschreiben, wie sie zustande kamen.

[S. 3] Brown's Hotel und Albemarle Street. Wahrscheinlich das beste Beispiel dafür, dass sich im vergangenen Jahrhundert nichts verändert hat. Beide Bilder zeigen den Wagen in demselben Umfeld; mit Ausnahme der Hotelvorhänge als einzigem Unterschied konnten wir einen fast deckungsgleichen Schnappschuss einfangen. Ein derartiges Foto kann nur an einem Sonntag gelingen, da die Straße nun eine Einbahnstraße und der Wagen in Gegenrichtung geparkt ist.

[S. 17] Kanalüberquerung. Das reizvolle Bilderquartett von Folkestone veranschaulicht eine längst überholte Verlademethode. Im Eurotunnel bekundete das Personal des Autozuges großes Interesse an unserem modernen Transit. Freundlicherweise hat es – ohne pflichtgemäß Alarm auszulösen – Fotos von dem Wagen gemacht, als er in Frankreich von Bord rollte.

[S. 19] Boulogne und der Shuttlezug mit Anschluss an die Fähre. Heute ebenfalls eine längst vergangene Art der Kanalüberquerung. Doch gibt es hundert Kilometer südlich von Calais an der Somme-Mündung eine altmodische Dampfeisenbahn, die im Mai täglich verkehrt. Eine rasche Fahrt vom Tunnel dorthin machte es uns möglich, das Auto vor dem Hintergrund einer Dampflok zu fotografieren, die wahrscheinlich älter war als die Zugwaggons in Boulogne im Jahr 1913.

[S. 21] Château La Rochepot. Am folgenden Tag, nach einer Fahrt von nahezu fünfhundert Kilometern, fotografiert. Ursprünglich am Spätnachmittag bei niedrig hängenden Wolken und wiederholten Regenschauern mit Stativ und Funkfernsteuerung aufgenommen. Nach unserer Übernachtung in etwa zehn Kilometer Entfernung brach nach einer verregneten Nacht ein schöner Tag an. Es lohnte sich also, noch einmal zu dem Château zurückzukehren, um bessere Bilder zu machen, obwohl wir dann für den Rest des Tages die Verspätung aufholen mussten.

[S. 23] Baumbestandene Straßen sind noch vielerorts zu finden, doch stehen die Bäume oft an so dicht befahrenen Straßen, dass es zu gefährlich und an einen Halt zum Fotografieren nicht zu denken ist. Glücklicherweise gab es ein schönes Plätzchen auf einem alten Abschnitt der N6 bei La Rochepot. Es war zwar unmöglich, den ursprünglichen Standort zu finden, doch atmete diese Stelle die Atmosphäre des Originals und es ist auch davon auszugehen, dass wir uns hier in der Nähe des Aufnahmeorts des Fotos von 1913 befinden.

[S. 25] Der richtige Standpunkt, doch hier hat sich fast alles verändert. Immer noch die N6, jetzt überaus belebt, mit nur kleinen Unterbrechungen im fließenden Verkehr. Die Seitenstraße führt heute nirgendwohin, da die betreffende Abzweigung weiter nach unten verlegt wurde, während eine Autobahn parallel zur N6 gebaut worden ist. Ein nervenaufreibendes Umfeld für ein mittelmäßiges Bild!

[S. 27] Den Schauplatz dieses Fotos kannten wir zunächst nicht und vermuteten ihn in einer Stadt nahe dem Mont-Cenis-Pass, etwa in St. Michel de Maurienne, hatten sich doch Nachforschungen in anderen Städten der Region zuvor als fruchtlos erwiesen. Bei der Ankunft in Aiguebelle hielt ich jedoch in einer Parkbucht an der Hauptstraße und ging mit dem Originalfoto in der Hand durch die Stadt. Ich machte einen kurzen Spaziergang, wobei mir der Hintergrund bekannt vorkam, nur verlief die Kurve der Straße in die falsche Richtung. Bald jedoch gelangte ich an eine Stelle, wo die Straße eine andere Richtung nahm und alles dem Foto mehr ähnelte. Dann bemerkte ich die schmiedeeisernen Balkongitter an den Häusern zu meiner Rechten und kurz darauf den Schuppen gegenüber, ganz wie auf der originalen Vorlage. Nach langem Suchen hatte ich die Stadt gefunden, die sich im Lauf von hundert Jahren kaum verändert hatte. Dann musste ich nur noch den Wagen an einer passenden Stelle parken und für die Aufnahme, die ich benötigte, auf einen Betonblumenkübel auf der Straße steigen.

[S. 28] Lanslebourg. Da wir spät ankamen, reichte an diesem Tag die Zeit nicht, um die Bilderstrecke in der Stadt zu machen. Am Abend zeigten wir die Fotos dem Hotelier und seiner Frau, die schon von unserem Wagen fasziniert waren. Als sie die alten Bilder sahen, erklärten sie, sie könnten uns am nächsten Morgen an die genauen Standorte führen, obwohl sich durch die Zerstörungen des Krieges fast alles verändert habe. Damit nicht genug, sorgten sie auch für »Extras« in Gestalt der Protagonisten, die wir für die Fotografien benötigten.

[S. 35] Mont-Cenis-Pass. Ein Foto des Wagens auf dem Scheitelpunkt des Passes musste unbedingt am Tag unserer Ankunft in Lanslebourg gemacht werden, weil sich da genau die Aufnahme von 1913 zum hundertsten Mal jährte. Der Pass erforderte nur einen kurzen Anstieg auf leichtem Gefälle, daher fuhr ich für das Foto allein bei eisiger Kälte hinauf. Seit unserer Abfahrt von zu Hause waren erst drei Tage vergangen und wir konnten bereits auf über 1200 gefahrene Kilometer samt Fotopausen zurückblicken. Was hätte wohl Mr. Radley darüber gedacht?

[S. 37] Brescia war nach dem Umweg über den Comer See der nächste Aufenthalt. Es gab keinen Zeitdruck mehr, weil nun, wie damals bei Radley, drei Wochen zu unserer freien Verfügung vor uns lagen, bevor wir in Wien sein mussten. Zwar hatten wir die Möglichkeit, uns bereits am Sonntag auf den Weg zu machen, entschieden uns aber stattdessen für eine geruhsamere Fahrt am Montag. Das traf sich gut, denn am Sonntag fand das Ende des Giro d'Italia in Corso Zanardelli statt und die Gegend war voller Radfahrer. Selbst am Montag mussten wir den Wagen geschickt abstellen, um den Restbestand an Tischen und Stühlen im Bild zu verbergen.

[S. 39] Die beiden Bilder vom Lago d'Idro galten zunächst als Ansichten vom Gardasee, doch wir erkannten bald, dass die Straße auf der Westseite des Sees erst in den 1930er-Jahren gebaut worden war. Auf unserer letzten Fahrt an einem sehr heißen Nachmittag auf der Straße von Brescia nach Riva hatten wir an einer Bar haltgemacht, um uns zu erfrischen, und dabei den Einheimischen die Bilder gezeigt, die unserer Meinung nach den Blick auf den Lago d'Idro zeigten. Wir hatten großes Glück, da sie nicht nur die Bilder erkannten, sondern uns auch erklärten, dass diese kaum einen Kilometer entfernt von der Straße aus aufgenommen worden seien. Diesmal fanden wir den Ort, aber da es sich um eine stark befahrene Straße handelt, war es schwierig, ein entsprechendes Foto zu machen, denn wir wollten nicht nur die Originalaufnahmen wiederholen, sondern auch ein zusätzliches Bild mit dem Auto im Vordergrund zeigen.

[S. 43] Auf der Straße zum Passo Ampola, die von Storo über eine Reihe von Haarnadelkurven nach oben führt, konnten wir nahe an einer Spitzkehre parken und dann zur nächsthöheren Kurve gehen, um das Auto gut aufs Bild zu bekommen.

[S. 45] Die Straße nach Riva ist immer noch schmal und heute sehr belebt, sodass es schwierig war, die alten Fotos zu wiederholen. Die Stelle, an der das Originalfoto entstanden war, erwies sich als zu gefährlich, um dort zu fotografieren oder anzuhalten. Daher wählten wir stattdessen einen etwas weiter entfernten Platz, auf dem heute gesperrten Teil der Ponalestraße. An diesem stillen Weg mussten wir lediglich darauf warten, dass der dünne Strom von Spaziergängern und Radfahrern kurzzeitig verebbte, bevor wir das Bild machten.

[S. 47] Am Wasserfall des Passo Ampola, wo die Straße inzwischen neu ausgebaut ist, wachsen Bäume, die nun den Blick auf das Wasser verstellen. Daher mussten wir dort, wo es überhaupt nur möglich war, den Wagen an entsprechender Stelle auf das Foto zu bekommen, dicht neben der Straße parken.

[S. 49] Die alten Bilder von der Ponalestraße konnten schon bei der ersten Durchsicht des aufgefundenen Albums leicht identifiziert werden. Heutzutage aber die passende Stelle zu finden, hat noch niemand zuvor versucht, da das Bild nur einige Meter von den ursprünglichen Schauplätzen entfernt ganz anders aussah. Jetzt aber hatten wir genügend Zeit, die wir auf der alten Straße verbringen konnten, da unsere guten Freunde in Riva endlich das Rätsel gelöst hatten, wer die Schlüssel zu den Absperrungen an jedem Ende der Straße besaß! Ohne die Schlüssel konnten sie nur Radfahrer und Fußgänger überwinden. Nun aber durften auch wir die Straße entlangfahren, zur Freude der vielen Radfahrer und Fußgänger, für die unser hundert Jahre alter Wagen, der die Fahrt und die Fotos des Jahres 1913 nachvollzog, eine besondere Anziehungskraft ausstrahlte. Der Mann mit den Schlüsseln kannte jeden Teil der Straße im Detail und erlaubte uns, von ganz oben hinunterzufahren. Leider gelang dies nur für einen Teil der Strecke, weil die Straße beim Rückbau zu einem Radweg verengt worden war und traditionelle Holzzäune den Mittelteil flankierten, sodass sie zu schmal wurde, um mit einem Silver Ghost durchzufahren, und wir wollten schließlich nicht auf der Strecke stecken bleiben! Doch der Mann mit den Schlüsseln besaß einen Citroën 2CV, an den er unpassende extrem breite Reifen montiert hatte, sodass dieses erstaunliche Fahrzeug überallhin gelangen konnte – und das tat es auch. So fuhr er uns zur genauen Stelle der beiden Originalfotos. Baumbewuchs auf den senkrechten zum See abfallenden Felsen machte es unmöglich, die einstige Position zu wiederholen, doch ganz nahe daneben zu stehen, war fast dasselbe. Da die Stelle in der Nähe des unteren Abschnitts der alten Straße lag, konnten wir später von unten her hinauffahren und den Radley-Wagen in eines der Bilder integrieren.

[S. 53] Die Bilder von Riva waren leicht zu erkennen – schwieriger war es, identische Versionen von ihnen zu erhalten, vor allem da die heute in die Höhe geschossenen Bäume Teile der Aussicht vom Lido Palace Hotel aus versperrten. Doch der Blick über den See zur alten Ponale-Corniche sieht von jedem Punkt am Seeufer von Riva aus fast gleich aus.

[S. 57] Castel Toblino ist ein weiteres Juwel auf der Alpenroute und von daher bereits ein bekannter Anziehungspunkt. Bei der Wiederholung des alten Fotos mussten wir darauf achten, den starken Verkehr auf dieser belebten, von Norden nach Riva führenden Straße zu vermeiden.

[S. 59] Aufgenommen zwischen Riva und Rovereto, blieb das Bild von Mori lange Jahre ein Rätsel. Aufgrund seiner wenigen identifizierbaren Orientierungshilfen konnte die Suche nach dem potenziellen Schauplatz des Bildes erst dann merklich eingeengt werden, als ein frühes Exemplar der österreichischen »Allgemeine Automobil-Zeitung« mit Bildunterschriften versehene Fotos derselben Stelle mit einem beschrankten Bahnübergang im Vordergrund zeigte. Doch der genaue Standpunkt war auch im Jahr 2013 noch nicht gefunden, als wir uns einige Tage in Riva aufhielten, um die Fotos zu komplettieren. Freunde dort nahmen uns mit nach Mori, um uns die genaue Stelle zu zeigen, was nicht leicht war. Die Straße ist heute überaus verkehrsreich und der alte beschrankte Bahnübergang ist zu einer Unterführung geworden. Daneben verläuft die Autobahn vom Brennerpass nach Verona, weswegen die lange gerade Straße einen neuen Verlauf erhielt. Als wir das erste Mal an Ort und Stelle waren, parkte gerade ein großer Laster auf dem einzigen geeigneten Parkplatz, während der Fahrer seine vorgeschriebene Fahrpause absolvierte. Glücklicherweise war der Parkplatz am folgenden Tag für uns frei, doch herrschte so viel Verkehr, dass wir eine Weile benötigten, um durch eine Lücke die Straße zu überqueren und das Foto aufzunehmen. Als Reggie Hope 1913 aus dem Heckfenster des Wagens schaute und fotografierte, während Radley vor einem vorbeifahrenden Zug anhielt, hätte er wohl kaum ein solches Problem gehabt.

[S. 60] Das Bild der Straße nach Trento von 1913 zeigt eine verlassene Wegstrecke. Das ist heute ganz anders! Auch wenn die Autobahn in der Nähe verläuft, weist diese Straße einen konstanten Verkehrsfluss auf und ist von hohen Bäumen gesäumt, die es erschweren, ein Foto mitsamt der Berge im Hintergrund aufzunehmen. Das Originalfoto wurde sicherlich wieder vom Rücksitz des Autos aus dem Heckfenster gemacht.

[S. 61] Die Straße nach San Lugano, die direkte Route von Trento in das Val di Fassa, sofern man nicht die Alpenfahrtroute über den Rollepass wählt. Der Pass ist heute vielbefahren und wegen der neuen Straße dient die alte nun als ein Holzlagerplatz, was es uns ermöglichte, das Foto von einem ruhigeren Fleckchen aus aufzunehmen.

[S. 63] Das Bild von Moena bot ein weiteres Rätsel. Ein anscheinend nichtssagendes Foto von einem Bach, der einen Hügel hinabfließt. Aus den Bergen im Hintergrund zu schließen, schien es sich hier um einen Ort im Val di Fassa zu handeln, zwischen Predazzo und Canazei gelegen, dem Dorf am Fuss des Pordoi. Aber warum wurde das Bild überhaupt aufgenommen? Wir waren Ende Mai 2013 im Val di Fassa und warteten aufgrund des kalten und unbeständigen Wetters, bis wir sicher sein konnten, dass die Route über das Pordoipass nicht durch Schnee blockiert sein würde. Während dieser Zeit untersuchten wir die von unbekannten Standorten aufgenommenen Bilder. Das vorliegende Foto schien einen Seitenarm des Bachs zu zeigen, wir fuhren also das Tal flussaufwärts und entdeckten schließlich den Ort der Aufnahme in Moena. Als wir ihn gefunden hatten, konnten wir verstehen, warum das Bild entstanden war. Die Hauptstraße verläuft an einer engen Stelle zwischen zwei alten Gebäuden hindurch, wie es wohl auch vor hundert Jahren der Fall war. Inzwischen sind Verkehrsampeln installiert, 1913 aber hatte wohl derjenige freie Fahrt, der zuerst angekommen war. Als daher Radley damals anhielt, um einem anderen Fahrzeug die Vorfahrt zu gewähren, hat Hope wahrscheinlich die Gelegenheit für eine weitere Aufnahme genutzt.

[S. 65] In Campitello di Fassa sind die Gipfel der Langkofel-(Sassolungo)-Gruppe in den Dolomiten so unverwechselbar, dass sie leicht zu erkennen sind. Daher war die genaue Position des Fotografen schon viele Jahre zuvor identifiziert worden: Das Bild war von dem Bach im Zentrum von Campitello aus aufgenommen. Nun mussten wir die geeignetste Stelle für unser Foto finden. Obwohl die Berge natürlich unverändert geblieben sind und viele der alten Gebäude aus dem früheren Bild immer noch existieren, hatten wir damit zu kämpfen, dass sich in dem ursprünglichen Szenario nun ein hässlich-modernes brutalistisches Betongebäude aus den 1970er-Jahren anstelle des charmanten Hotels Mulino erhob, das abgerissen worden war, um Platz für das neue Gebäude zu schaffen. Selbst der einheimischen Minderheit der ladinisch sprechenden Einwohner, die sich in einer nahegelegenen alten Bar trafen, missfiel es. So mussten wir von einem in der Nähe der Originalfotos gelegenen Standort aus unser Möglichstes tun, das moderne Bauwerk nicht allzu dominant ins Bild zu rücken.

[S. 67] Val di Fassa, im Jahr 1913 noch eine abgelegene Region, hat sich durch die Anlage neuer Straßen, die Anpflanzung von Bäumen und Neuentwicklungen in den Tälern beträchtlich verändert. Heute ist es ein beliebtes Skigebiet und man kann kaum mehr tun als einen weiteren umfassenden Blick auf das Tal einzufangen.

[S. 69] Die beiden Bilder von Canazei waren anhand der dramatischen Gebirgsformationen im Hintergrund leicht zu identifizieren. Am Fuß des Aufstiegs zum Pordoipass gelegen, ist Canazei heute ein Skizentrum mit langen Sesselliftbahnen, die zu den Pisten führen. Obwohl immer noch viele reizvolle alte Häuser erhalten geblieben sind, gibt es auch viele neue Entwicklungen, die einige der frühen Ansichten blockieren. Nachdem wir einige Zeit damit verbracht hatten, in den alten Straßen herumzustreifen, fanden wir schließlich die Szenarien der beiden Aufnahmen, obwohl das eine von ihnen nunmehr viele neue Gebäude aufwies und dadurch einen leicht veränderten Blickwinkel erforderte, um die Berge ins Bild zu rücken.

[S.73] Der Pordoipass ist unschwer durch den Obelisken zu erkennen, der als markantes Zeichen bei der Eröffnung des Passes 1904 gesetzt wurde; es ist heute keine abgeschiedene Bergstraße mehr. In der Frühsaison gibt es weniger Touristen und immer noch eine ansehnliche Menge Schnee, obwohl 2013 regelmäßig eingesetzte Räummaschinen den Mann mit der Schaufel verdrängt haben.

[S. 75] Die beiden Fotos vom Falzàregopass zeigten jeweils das Fahrzeug von der Vorder- und Rückseite in gleicher Umgebung genau östlich des Passes. Stiller als der Pordoipass und in der Frühsaison noch mit frostigen Temperaturen bei leichtem Schneefall, ist das Szenario fast identisch mit dem vor fast hundert Jahren fotografierten.

[S. 79] Der Loibl, wo die Idee zur Wiederholung der Alpenfahrt entstand. Der Blick vom Gipfel des Loibl, verändert durch die beträchtliche Menge neu hinzugekommener und üppig wachsender Bäume, im Vergleich mit der Aussicht vor hundert Jahren.

[S. 81] Das letzte Bild aus dem Album schien leicht zu identifizieren, war aber tatsächlich das schwierigste von allen und beschäftigte zahlreiche Menschen und Organisationen in Südkärnten, einschließlich Hoteliers, historische Vereine und staatliche Stellen. Jedermann erkannte sofort, dass es sich hier um einen Übergang über die Drau handelte, aber die zahlreichen Veränderungen, die dem Fluss in der Zeit ab den 1950er-Jahren zugefügt wurden, haben viele Schauplätze getilgt, einschließlich des hier gezeigten. Nach vielen akribisch verfolgten falschen Fährten fand man schließlich heraus, dass es sich hier um die alte Zollbrücke über die Drau in einem Ort mit dem passenden Namen Mauthbrücken handelte, ein winziges Dorf, das durch den Bau eines Staudamms über die Drau sozusagen ausgelöscht worden ist. Die alte Brücke ist verschwunden; der alte Gasthof Steiner im Hintergrund ebenfalls, beide abgerissen oder im Wasser der Drau versunken. Eine Alternative für uns bestand darin, das moderne Foto auf der Route vom Loiblpass nach Klagenfurt auf der Hollenburgbrücke aufzunehmen, da sie als einzige kurvig geschwungene Brücke über die Drau übrig geblieben ist.

Weitere Bilder von der Strecke in Richtung Wien wie auch von der Alpenfahrt an sich fehlen. Dies legt nahe, dass Reggie Hope möglicherweise in Kärnten nicht mehr weiter mitfuhr und per Bahn nach England zurückkehrte.

Front Cover:
Top: Mr Radley with his Rolls-Royce Silver Ghost at Brown's Hotel, London.
Bottom: Same car, same location 100 years later, possibly to the day.
Endpapers: Blueprints of special features designed for the 1913 trials cars.

Text, Photographs & Research by John Kennedy.
Additional Photographs by Rae Kennedy.
Photographs from 2013 taken on Nikon D800 digital camera.
Early black & white photos by Reginald Hooton Hope.
Mr Radley & the 1913 Rolls-Royce Silver Ghost photos at Vienna.
(Photos by Heinrich Schumann from James Radley's own scrapbook.)

Acknowledgement to The Sir Henry Royce Memorial Foundation, Paulerspury, England for the endpaper blueprints and the insert picture on page 32 and Brescia picture on page 34, believed to originate from the album of H A (Tubby) Ward, the Rolls-Royce Test Driver/Mechanic. Acknowledgements also for the use of the Radley-Hope picture album, donated to the foundation by the family of Reggie Hope.

Bibliographic information published by the Deutsche Nationalbibliothek.
The Deutsche Nationalbibliothek lists this publication in the Deutsche Nationalbibliografie; detailed bibliographic data are available on the Internet at http://dnb.dnb.de.

Project Management: Jutta Allekotte, Rainer Arnold
English copyediting: Vanessa Magson-Mann, So to Speak English Language Services, Icking
Translation English / German: Ingrid Hacker-Klier and Thomas Billicsich, Austria, 2010
German copyediting: Katrin Boskamp-Priever
Design: Gunnar Musan, Munich
Fonts: St Marie, Arnold Boecklin
Prepress: Reproline Mediateam, Munich
Paper: GardaMatt Art, 130 g/m²
Printing and Binding: Printer Trento, Trento
Printed in Italy

ISBN 978-3-7774-2346-3

www.hirmerpublishers.co.uk
www.hirmerverlag.de

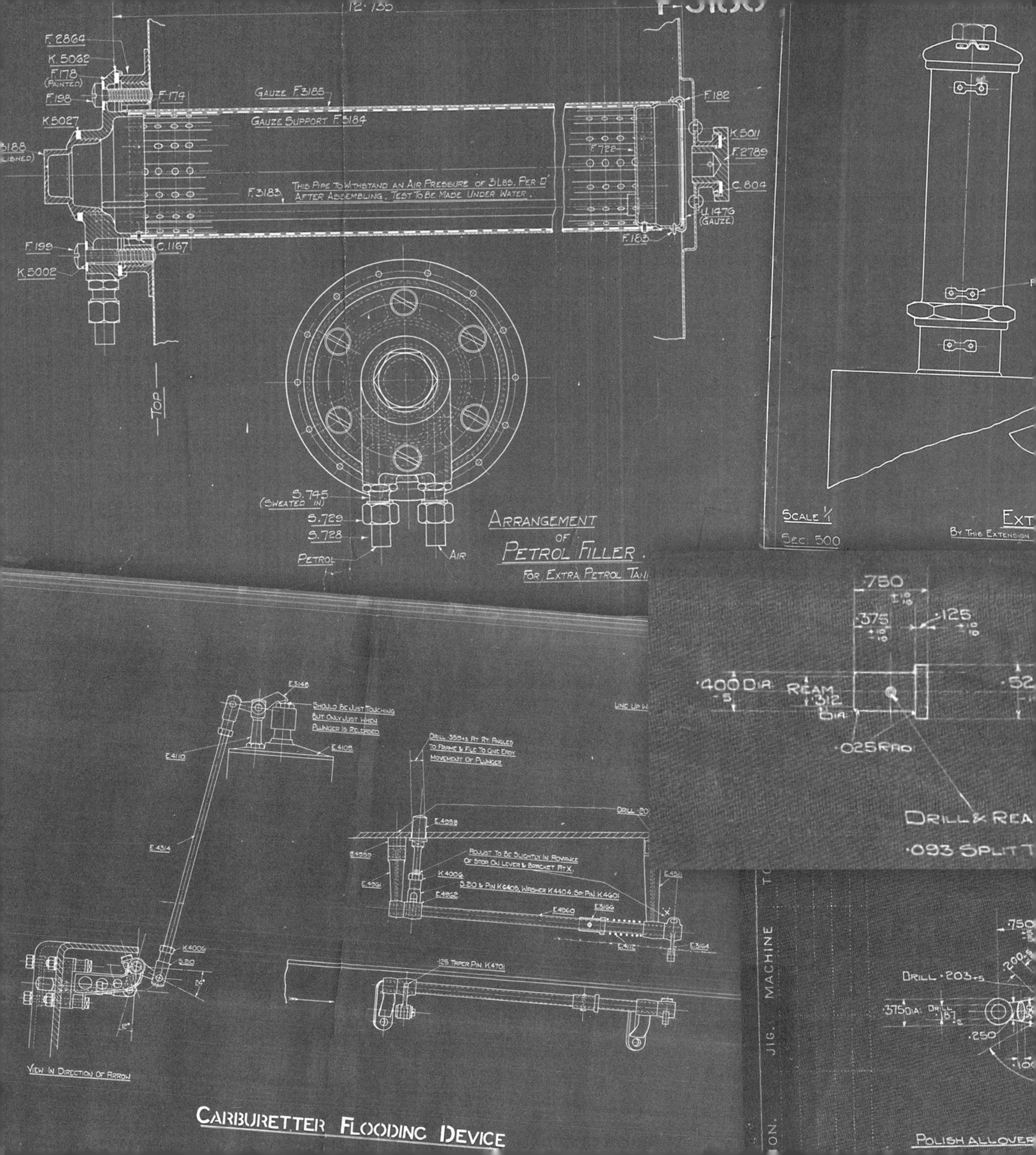
12·755
F.2864
K.5062
F.178
(PAINTED)
F.198
F.174
GAUZE F.3185
GAUZE SUPPORT F.3184
K.5027
F.182
K.5011
F.2789
F.722
F.3183
THIS PIPE TO WITHSTAND AN AIR PRESSURE OF 3LBS. PER ☐" AFTER ASSEMBLING. TEST TO BE MADE UNDER WATER.
C.804
U.1476
(GAUZE)
F.183
F.199
C.1167
K.5002
TOP
S.745
(SWEATED IN)
S.729
S.728
PETROL
AIR
ARRANGEMENT OF PETROL FILLER
FOR EXTRA PETROL TAN
SCALE ¼
SEC. 500
EXT
BY THIS EXTENSION
·750
·375
·125
·400 DIA.
REAM ·312 DIA.
·025 RAD.
DRILL & REA
·093 SPLIT T
E.3148
SHOULD BE JUST TOUCHING BUT ONLY JUST WHEN PLUNGER IS RELEASED
E.4110
E.4108
DRILL ·359+3 AT RT. ANGLES TO FRAME & FILE TO GIVE EASY MOVEMENT OF PLUNGER
LINE UP W
E.4314
E.4958
E.4559
ADJUST TO BE SLIGHTLY IN ADVANCE OF STOP ON LEVER & BRACKET AT X.
K.4006
E.4561
E.4862
S.20 & PIN K.6408, WASHER K.4404, SP. PIN K.4601
E.4960
E.3166
E.4112
E.3164
K.4006
S.210
·125 TAPER PIN K.4701
VIEW IN DIRECTION OF ARROW
CARBURETTER FLOODING DEVICE
JIG. MACHINE
DRILL ·203-5
·3750 DIA.
·250
POLISH ALL OVER